D0192702

ON THE ROAD BIKE

NED BOULTING

ON THE ROAD BIKE

BIKE

THE SEARCH FOR A NATION'S CYCLING SOUL

Or

SNIFFING THE YAK-SKIN SHOE

Or

THE GREAT ECCENTRICS OF BRITISH CYCLING

YELLOW JERSEY PRESS
LONDON

Published by Yellow Jersey Press 2013

2 4 6 8 10 9 7 5 3 1

Copyright © Ned Boulting 2013

Ned Boulting has asserted his right under the Copyright, Designs
and Patents Act 1988 to be identified as the author of this work

First published in Great Britain in 2013 by
Yellow Jersey Press
Random House, 20 Vauxhall Bridge Road,
London SW1V 2SA

www.vintage-books.co.uk

Addresses for companies within The Random House Group Limited can be found at:
www.randomhouse.co.uk/offices.htm

The Random House Group Limited Reg. No. 954009

A CIP catalogue record for this book
is available from the British Library

ISBN 9780224092081

The Random House Group Limited supports the Forest Stewardship Council® (FSC®), the
leading international forest-certification organisation. Our books carrying the FSC label are
printed on FSC®-certified paper. FSC is the only forest-certification scheme supported by the
leading environmental organisations, including Greenpeace. Our paper procurement policy
can be found at www.randomhouse.co.uk/environment

Set in Fairfield LH Light 11/15 pt
Typeset by Palimpsest Book Production Limited, Falkirk, Stirlingshire
Printed and bound in Great Britain by
Clays Ltd, St Ives plc

To Everyone at Number 100

I just explained to the police what I was doing and told them that things like that were normal on the Continent, and they said they were happy and that they'd try to help.

Percy Stallard

CONTENTS

AFTERTHOUGHT

The heat had blown in from the south, sweeping the race along with it. It had been cooked up over the Pyrenees, piling isobars high into the air, over the heads of the circling eagles keeping watch on the riders toiling up the mountains.

The hot air rushed on, spreading out across France, further north, through the Tarn valley, skirting the Haute-Vienne, swallowing Châteauroux and Chartres whole before its assault on Paris.

Here it slowed its pace and held steady. Warmth engulfed the city, turning the stone of the old capital white. The golden tip of the towering obelisk in the Place de la Concorde burnt so keenly you could hardly look at it without squinting. Far below, in the oily fetid dark of the subterranean car park, a thousand official Tour de France vehicles stood in long rows, their engines ticking as they cooled. The race had roared into Paris. It was done.

At street level, the dust and grime baked, despite the shade of a hundred mathematically manicured plane trees whose precise rows marked the edges of the road. *Gendarmes* on overtime, freighted in from outlying provinces, stood cheerlessly guarding every side street. The people who had come to see the spectacle fanned themselves with whatever merchandising tat had been flung their way by the passing publicity caravan. They were held back from the road by not one, but two sets of barriers.

Over their heads huge French tricolour flags had been unfurled to catch an absent breeze, but were adrift in the doldrums. The Tour was going nowhere today. Paris, its painterly sky alive with the criss-crossing of helicopters, was falling deeply in love with itself. Just as its residents, bored by the annual invasion of this astonishing race, profess a world-weary indifference, so the rest of us non-Parisians are subject to our own Pavlovian responses to its beauty. What a city!

This was the place: the Champs-Elysées on 22 July 2012. The Tour de France in its ninety-ninth incarnation.

And in the middle of it, on a huge podium, stood a gangly bloke from Kilburn with an unlikely name: Bradley Wiggins.

His hair had grown over the month he had been away, and brightened at the fringes in the sun. His sideburns, uncared for during three weeks on a bike, had thickened and spread. This was quaint enough, but he was also spectacularly thin. As a result, he looked like a character from a Victorian children's cautionary story. There he stood, saluting the crowd, a half-smile decorating his cautious face.

From this point, facing east, he would have seen, at the end of the avenue the wrought-iron gates of the Jardin des Tuileries and behind that the Louvre. He would have gazed back at the temporary stands filled with the great and good of the corporate world, sitting in cushioned rows in the Tribune Présidentielle, the Tribune Marigny and Tribune Concorde. And in front of him, held back by a rope that spread across the whole width of the boulevard, hundreds of lenses, catching the late-afternoon sun and winking at him.

I was familiar with this pageant. Ten times, each year since 2003 when I first started to follow the Tour, I had stood to the side of the podium watching on as Armstrong, Landis, Sastre, Contador and Evans had all thrown their arms aloft in victory. Wiggins would have watched it, too, sometimes in the flesh a little further down that cobbled road, half dismounted from his bike, ignored by everyone: a finisher, not a winner.

I had seen the moment repeated, when from nowhere a microphone appears, thrust at the champion by one of the Tour's army of green-shirted roadies. I had seen each different winner right himself, pause, and level some carefully scripted words in the general direction of the Tour de France, France Itself, The World and History.

'*Mesdames et Messieurs* . . .' or 'Ladies and Gentlemen. It is a great honour . . .' or 'I am highly honoured to be standing here . . .'

'*Merci au Tour de France* . . .' Applause.

Except on this day that's not what happened. Firstly, there was some confusion over the order of events. Instead of going straight to the speech, the French nation were first treated to a surprisingly unpleasant rendition of 'God Save The Queen' by a middle-aged lady clad in a sparkly red blouse and a floor-length, Union-Jack wrap/skirt so puzzlingly awful that it left most of us frowning at our iPhones and conducting a Google Images search on Lesley Garrett, just to check this lady wasn't an imposter.

Then, when she'd finally relented, Wiggins was handed his microphone, even though he was already juggling a glass vase, a bouquet and a cuddly toy, like a serial winner of the Generation Game. He first had to deposit all of these items at his feet without them falling off the podium, then he cleared his throat, and smartly turned his back on France.

Now he faced west, looking down the length of the avenue towards the Arc de Triomphe. Here, the British had gathered in huge numbers. Manx flags with their Masonic-looking three-legged star, poking up like tall poppies in a field of Union Jacks. The ferries from Dover had been booked up for days. They stood ten deep, from the Avenue de Marigny right up the length of the boulevard.

It was to these people that Wiggins turned. From their patient, sweaty ranks, a great cheer went up. And without so much as a nod to his hosts, who were now treated only to a view of his yellow-clad bony spine, he delivered the most exquisitely judged line I have ever heard.

'Right. We're just going to draw the raffle numbers . . .'

Paris shivered, as if someone had just tapped it on the back. He'd just turned the Champs-Elysées into a village hall. It was perfect.

CHAPTER 1

DEPART

It was an embossed card with my name on it: an invitation to a posh dinner. This, I wasn't expecting.

In February 2010 British Cycling was celebrating fifty years. They were to hold a gala dinner in Manchester, at which they intended to 'induct' (a curious word, that) fifty British cycling legends into their Hall of Fame, one for every year of their existence. Would I like to attend as their guest?

I very much would. I replied post-haste (or at least by email) that I would be delighted to accept their kind invitation.

I did not know, as I hit send and wrote the date in the diary, that the dinner I was about to attend would set in motion a chain of events, chance encounters, visits and inquiries that would become something of a preoccupation, and at times even, an obsession, for the following two years. This simple email was the harmless-looking digital key to a hitherto hidden world. At least it had been hidden to me. It would prove to be a world peopled by fulsome characters, quiet fanatics, feuds, pettiness, injury and ambition and as it slowly revealed itself to me, so my curiosity grew.

But buffing my black schoolish shoes and fiddling with an iron in a Manchester hotel room on the evening of the big event, I was, not unreasonably, filled with doubt.

There would, I anticipated, be hundreds of people there, all of whom would have played a significant role in the history of this sport in our country; people who had achieved greatness, coached greatness, fostered greatness or simply dedicated their lives to the furthering of the cause of the bicycle.

And then there would be me: a bloke vaguely from off the telly.

I felt fraudulent, and a little nervous. After all, I had needed fully seven years to acclimatise to the demands of covering a three-week stage race in France. It had taken me a long time to begin to understand Le Tour, its associated cast list of characters, and the intricate web of ritual and tradition woven around the race.

And with the Tour my cycling knowledge stopped. For those other eleven months of the year, it pretty much went on without me, while my day job as a reporter for ITV Sport kept me busy with football matches. As far as the history of cycling was concerned, I was still a bit stunted. For me, the Tour began in 2003, not in 1903.

I'd been learning in a microwave, trying to acquire a sense for the nuances of a very particular sport, in a very particular country as quickly as I could. But the intuitive understanding which normally takes a lifetime to develop, this was still beyond me. However much I grabbed at its coat-tails, all I came away with were torn fragments as it slipped through my fingers.

From time to time, my work had brought me to races in the UK. I had flirted sporadically with domestic affairs, but my heart still lay overseas. The Tour de France seemed a very long way from that cold winter evening in the north-west of England.

No matter. My shoes were polished to the best of my ability, and I had wedged my oversized cardboard invitation into my jacket pocket. The wheels were in motion.

When I got to the venue in the middle of Manchester (a vast impersonal aircraft hangar of a hall) I realised, to my horror, that my suspicions had been well founded. There were indeed hundreds of people there, all of whom had absolutely played a significant role in the history of the sport in our country. The invitation hadn't extended as far as my partner, Kath, so there was no one whose greater ignorance I could occasionally exploit, no one who knew less about cycling in the room, whom I could now and then refer to as 'only a nurse'. I was quite alone, it seemed.

I walked in and, fearful of being engaged in conversation, headed for the information board. Finally spotting my name amid the vast matrix of the seating plan, I identified the round table at which I was to be seated. I paid scant attention to the other names clustered around mine, before snaking my way through the slalom course of chair backs and tablecloths to where my dinner was to be served.

Only then did I realise that this was no normal table, and these no normal guests.

To my left, already seated, and waiting for the others to arrive, were a well-turned out couple in their late sixties. They looked for all the world as if they had just stepped in to the venue from some exclusive dinner dance in Mayfair. She greeted me with a regally outstretched hand, dusted a little with silver and diamonds, and he, with a white bow tie and perfectly manicured hair, smiled at me and introduced himself.

'Barry Hoban. Pleased to meet you.'

Barry Hoban! Prior to Mark Cavendish, the British rider with the most stage wins ever on the Tour de France, a contemporary, and sometime rival, of the great Eddy Merckx!

What was I doing sitting next to Barry Hoban?

'Hello. My name's Ned Boulting.'

Never has my name sounded quite as lame as it did then. It flopped onto the tablecloth, and lay there, uncomfortably occupying the space between us.

'And this is my wife, Helen.' Of course it was! Helen married Barry in 1969, two years after she was widowed. Her first husband, also a cyclist, had died on Mont Ventoux riding the 1967 Tour de France. His name was Tom Simpson.

This couple were British cycling royalty.

I took my seat, and looked around the table at the other

guests, sneaking glances when I could at the name cards in front of them. Most names meant little to me, but the preponderance of grey hair at the table hinted at Achievement, with a capital A. The great Brian Robinson was at my table, the first British stage winner at the Tour de France. He was sitting on his own, fiddling with the little enamel '50 Years of British Cycling' badge, which had been placed next to our knives and forks. He looked lost in thought. Perhaps he was reliving the 1957 edition of Milan–San Remo. But it was much more likely that he was just trying to figure out where he'd left his room key, and what time they might finally get round to serving the soup.

And to my right, sat a former World Champion.

His name didn't ring a bell, at least not to me. He didn't say much, except at one point, when, out of the blue he started to ask Helen something about Tom Simpson, and a replica Rainbow Jersey that he'd requested from the late, lamented icon. Helen, in the nicest possible way, tried to cut the conversation short.

For a moment, everyone, or maybe just I, felt a little awkward. Other than that, Graham Webb was quiet.

And so the dinner took its course. Hoban kept the table amused, a constant source of cycling-related anecdotes featuring a flood of significant names, not one of which meant anything to me. Defunct teams, oddly named races both on these shores and abroad, famous duels between forgotten men, skulduggery and comedy: this was the stuff of the evening. Brian Robinson occasionally looked up and smiled at some shared memory, before returning to his soup. And every now and then talk returned to the current crop of riders, their shortcomings, their talents, the money they earned. I hung on their words, amazed at my good fortune to be sitting alongside some of the greatest cyclists our country had ever produced; the real hard men of their time. Pioneers.

It was hard to square these men and their times with the sleek sport that cycling had become in this country. Their achievements were all the more remarkable given their unre-markable origins. Their self-sufficiency was a badge of honour, to be worn right next to their badges of enamel. I gazed around the room, and saw it all repeated at every table: a collision of the generations in microcosm. While some more senior guests banged flat-palmed on their tables to emphasise a point, or fiddled with the butter knife in their boredom, their younger counterparts held court in brasher tones or secretly checked their phones for messages.

They talk of British cycling's 'Perfect Storm'.

I've even used the phrase myself, often. The tornado of growth whipped up in the early twenty-first century by the three colliding winds of recession, environmentalism and health, and brought to a frenzy by the headlong rush for medals, jerseys, titles and honours. From the grass roots to tree tops, change was howling across our island. British cycling was being blown more quickly towards the future than anyone in that room could have imagined. Indeed, just over two years later, Bradley Wiggins was going to win the Tour de France.

One by one, all my dinner companions were called up to the stage for the Hall of Fame Induction. The names rang out. Some were no longer with us, such as the great Beryl Burton. Others were there in spirit only, such as Graeme Obree and Robert Millar. Finally, those who were in the hall, all posed for a picture. I sat alone at an empty table, my lack of belonging made visible.

Who were these men, really? My ephemeral status as a TV presenter had brought me to their table, where they had accepted me with grace and warmth. Their stories dripped with heritage; a culture at once rich, different, homely, ribald and largely at odds with the polished, corporate cycling world to which I had been introduced. Theirs was the history. Their collective experience and their considerable achievements had somehow got us here, to this rare altitude of success. They were the pathfinders. But how? And what had driven them on, in pursuit of such a madly marginalised career? British cyclist. It used to be an oxymoron, or a sort of silliness. Like French cricket.

They surely must have rumbled me. My understanding of their feats was thin, as palpably inadequate as a two-line entry on Wikipedia. Something hardened in my imagination, a thought, an impulse to shine a light, for my benefit, on this mysterious subculture. I should tackle this feeling of otherness head on. Put simply: I decided that I would like to know more. I felt for the collar of my jacket that was slung across the back of my chair.

Before I left, though, I bumped into Chris Boardman. He, at least, was a familiar face. Half-a-dozen Tours de France, on which we had worked together for ITV had seen to that. His induction into the Hall of Fame was done, and he was looking, as he often does, for a way out of the spotlight.

'Ned, what are you doing here?'

That was a very, very good question. And it had taken a man of Chris's direct wit to pose it.

'To be absolutely honest, Chris, I have no idea.'

I pushed through the door to be greeted by a pelting of Manchester rain, and went off in search of a taxi, wishing I'd ridden a bike for a living.

CHAPTER 2

CB

'Always believe in your soul, you're indestructible . . .'

The early 1990s, when Chris Boardman was in his record-breaking, medal-winning pomp, were still very primitive times for televised sports coverage.

The notion of a 'montage' was very undeveloped and exciting; a daring, edgy appropriation from the brave new world of MTV. Nowadays we take for granted the highly polished, fast-cut subliminal imagery that forms the glossy packaging around major sporting events. In fact, the 2012 Olympics were so stuffed with them, we had to invent an entirely new first-world ailment: 'montage-fatigue'.

Not so long ago, though, this kind of thing was a very young science. In fact, by the time I first started to work in television, at Sky Sports in the late nineties, 'music pieces', as we rather quaintly referred to them, were still very much embryonic and, by today's standards, almost unwatchably naïve.

Working away in windowless edit suites at Sky's soulless HQ as an assistant producer on football shows, I diligently matched moving images to lyrics from popular music. No literalism was beyond or beneath me. Over a shot of George Graham leaving Highbury, Abba: *Though it's hurting me, now it's history* . . . or, slightly more unusually, Newcastle United's famous demolition of Manchester United set to XTC: *One . . . Two . . . Three . . . Four . . . Five . . . Senses working overtime* (and here it was very important to move on to something else before the rest of the chorus kicked in: there was no obvious match for . . . *trying to tell the difference between a lemon and a lime . . .*)

Never such innocence again.

Half a decade later, when I first got to know Chris Boardman who had joined us on the Tour de France coverage, we took a childish delight in teasing him about his gold medal from the 1992 Barcelona Olympics. We were working on the fairly plausible supposition that at some point the BBC's coverage of those games must have featured a musical montage of Sally Gunnell, Linford Christie and Chris Boardman variously crossing the line, waving the flag and kissing the medal, set to the tune of Spandau Ballet's 'Gold'. This amused us endlessly, and left Chris baffled. Undaunted by his lack of enjoyment of the joke, we would try to pass off lines from the song as everyday conversation.

Thus, ordering dinner at the restaurant: 'Are you going to have the fish, Chris? *Always believe in your sole.*'

And, slightly more obscurely: 'Come and join us over here, Chris. *Sorry that the chairs are all worn.*'

You get the drift.

At a time when Chris was actually winning gold, we were all mostly hollering the chorus in smart-arse post-modern student parties.

If men like Graham Webb and Brian Robinson had cut somewhat marginal figures that night of their induction into the Hall of Fame, Chris Boardman, reluctantly, was right in the thick of things. I say reluctantly, because Chris doesn't do popularity very comfortably. Small talk is not his strong suit. Ludicrous talent, boundless application and unfettered ambition? Yes, he's quite good at all three of those.

Although I have known him for many years now as an ITV colleague, a man of the telly, a pundit, it is only when he is set in his proper context, among folk who were vanquished and/or inspired by him, that I am reminded of the over-whelming importance of his contribution to the sport. It is on nights like that dinner, when people will come up to him, saucer-eyed and very nearly kneel at his feet, that his iconic status is laid bare. It's not just the public who recognise his genius. There's barely a British rider of the modern era who won't reference him as a touchstone for progress, Wiggins foremost among them. Chris's discomfort at all this attention is as palpable as it is amusing.

His role in changing the face of British cycling, in leading the way out of a patchy past and into a holistic future, could hardly have been greater, even if it was born of little more than his prodigious will to win. A career that straddled the eighties and the nineties, as well as straddling both the track and the road, was driven by the application of inventive thinking. Simply doing things a certain way, because 'that's the way that we've always done it' meant nothing to him. To borrow a phrase from *Blackadder*, he tweaked the nose of tradition and poked a stick in the eye of convention. And he won. World Records, Olympic Gold Medals (the first Briton to do that for seventy-two years), and Yellow Jerseys on the Tour de France.

I had been meaning for some time to meet up with Chris. He was a friend, but also, I guessed, a decent starting point. If anyone could guide me through the curiosities of the British cycling scene, its stuffiness and inspiration, then surely he could help me understand how it changed from something cast iron into something carbon fibre, from woolly jumpers to sweat-wicking Lycra. It wasn't just because his achievements on a bike had helped to kick-start the whole reinvention of the sport from happy amateurism to ruthless professionalism. He had also, through his bike business, correctly identified and ridden the new wave of enthusiasm for participation, being smart enough to do an exclusive deal with Halfords at a time when bike snobbery prevented most serious brands from that association. Tens of thousands of new punters, armed with unprecedented levels of cash, suddenly wanted to splurge it on a new bike. And where would they go to spend their money? The same place they went as kids: Halfords.

Bike purists can shiver all they like. But that's the truth. And that was the genius of it.

In that sense, he was a revolutionary. And in another, slightly far-fetched sense, if GB Cycling supremo Dave Brailsford is Stalin, then that must make Boardman Lenin. Without the mausoleum, obviously.

Although there is a burger bar named after him at the Manchester Velodrome.

Of all the people I wanted to consult, Chris was not only one of the most obvious, but also one of the easiest to contact. Never without his iPhone, and more often than not juggling his iPad and MacBook for good measure, he is always within reach. So much so, that we have never quite settled on our preferred method of communication. Emails and tweets are interchangeable with text messages, always signed off with a neat, digital, 'CB'. Why waste characters?

Either way, I discovered that I would be up in Liverpool one Sunday night. I wondered whether he might fancy going for a ride the following day, perhaps near his home on the Wirral.

Good idea.
CB

That was our arrangement.

Then, an extraordinary thing happened. It was the day before the ride and I was driving north on the M40. Just as

I was pulling into Cherwell Service Station to grab a coffee, my phone pinged with an incoming, and paranormal text.

I parked up, and read the message.

If you are travelling up the M40 let me know. I've just woken up in a Travelodge near Oxford. Will meet you for a coffee en route.

CB

I looked up. I had parked in front of the exact Travelodge from which Chris had just texted me. I could have been no more than fifteen yards away from him. This was a GPS with more than a hint of divinity, as if He Himself had programmed the sat nav. It was very Chris Boardman to be that precise, however accidentally.

Five minutes later, over a coffee, we made plans for the following day.

'What kind of ride do you want to do tomorrow?'

'Oh I don't know. Hills? I quite fancy a climb.'

I thought this would stand me in better stead than simply gasping for air behind his relentless back wheel along some flat windswept stretch of the Wirral Peninsula. I had some experience of riding long straight lines with him, or rather behind him, and knew the casual pain he could inflict without even realising it. I remember once, having lost contact with his rear wheel, and fallen back by some fifty yards, looking up to see him raise his right finger in the air, and then move it backwards and downwards, so that it pointed quite unambiguously at the piece of flying road just behind his bike. I think he meant well, but there was no doubt I was being ordered to heel. He was like a giant cradling a butterfly, unaware of his power to hurt.

'OK. We'll do the Shoe.'

I nodded, sagely. What, I thought to myself with dread, was 'the Shoe'?

I tried to steer the conversation round to other things, to start to tap his considerable brains. But, for some reason, I kept losing my thread. All I could think of was 'the Shoe'.

At some point a fan sitting at the table next to ours, who had kept his counsel up till then, came over to greet Chris. He shook both our hands enthusiastically.

'Two cycling legends!' He beamed. I looked down at my coffee. He went on to tell Chris how great he was. Then we all went our separate ways.

Later on that afternoon, I received another, this time very clever message, the likes of which I have never been able to master on smartphones. When I opened it, it automatically fired up the map function on my phone, and dropped a pin near a place called Llangollen. It looked remote. It looked like there were mountains all over the place. It sounded Welsh. This was to be our meeting spot.

At 10 o'clock the next day, we pulled up virtually at the same time in a dusty car park on the side of a hill. I, in my filthy ten-year-old Renault with my bike wobbling around on the roof rack; Chris, in a squat, immaculate Audi sports car.

I frowned at him as he climbed out of the driver's seat. 'Where's your bike? Have you forgotten your bike?' I could see no evidence of it.

He grinned and popped open the boot. There it was, wheels off, not a millimetre to spare. Within seconds, it was out and assembled while I still struggled awkwardly to free my bike from the rack.

All around us, mountain bikers were fiddling with their huge, clunky-looking contraptions and padding up with body armour. Then, they would set off uphill, infinitely slowly, but in the tiniest gears that made their legs spin laughably fast. I watched them go.

It fascinated me to see how little notice they took of Chris.

He could hardly have been more conspicuous. His bike displayed his name, his helmet bore his name, and his bright yellow and white jersey had 'cboardman' written across his chest. His face looked, for all the world, like Chris Boardman's face. The mountain bike variety of enthusiast either had no idea that they were in the presence of greatness or cared not a jot. Chris told me he often came to ride out here. Perhaps that had something to do with it.

Chris makes a great play of being a sociopath. 'I don't really do people' is one of his mantras. And certainly, I have seen him negotiate early exit strategies to extract himself from encounters that he considers a waste of time. On one occasion at a function we both attended, another guest came up to where Chris and I were standing and mistakenly addressed me as Chris Boardman, something which happens fairly often but not usually when I am actually standing next to the real Chris Boardman. I grinned sheepishly, and Chris just sidled off into the distance, leaving the lamentably misguided individual to tell me all about how great an achievement my Hour Record was.

But, for all that, he is a determinedly chatty presence on a bike, keeping up a flow of conversation, which is often 'tech' related (and when this happens, the only sensible course of action is to agree with everything). Not only that, but he greets everyone on the route: riders, ramblers, farmers. They all get the same matter-of-fact 'Morning.' He doesn't expect a reply, and he doesn't always get one. Not even from sheep.

Once, back in his racing days, a sheep had darted out in front of him on a vicious descent somewhere in Yorkshire riding the Pru-Tour. He'd hit it, catapulted off his bike, slid across the tarmac and had come to a rest, only to hear the screams of some poor American rider who'd been chasing him downhill and who had no alternative than to smack into the prone figure of Boardman and his bike and execute his own somersault dismount.

It had been a narrow escape. 'If I'd hit a stone wall there, I'd have been smashed to jelly.' But because the incident involved a sheep, his teammate, the legendary German rider Jens Voigt, still recalls the incident with undue hilarity. His funster teammates stuffed wool in Boardman's spokes as a practical joke the next day. Every summer on the Tour de France, when Jens sees Chris, the story gets revisited. I guess he must believe it to be the archetypal British racing incident: Chris Boardman, the Benny Hill of the Chute. Just too funny.

People do not think of Chris as being funny. But they are wrong.

During the 2012 Tour, he received a series of emails from LOCOG. Their contents were considered so confidential, that they contained a legal threat, in the form of a NDA (non-disclosure agreement). However, this didn't stop him from sharing them with us. I am so glad he did.

It started simply enough.

The first communication came from a lady working closely with Danny Boyle on the running order for the opening cere-mony of the London Olympics. Plans were being finalised for the big night, and both former champions and cyclists would be significantly represented. Danny would be personally honoured if Chris would agree to make an appearance.

Chris thought about it briefly, and although he might instinctively have held some reservations, he recognised the importance of the event. So he replied: 'I am available and would be happy to take part.'

That was the precise moment at which it started to go wrong. The next email, after a gushing expression of delight that Chris had agreed to participate, went on to detail what this might involve.

It seemed that the IOC regulate the content of opening ceremonies more than you might imagine, and that there are certain compulsory elements. One of these is the use of doves, the international ceremony shorthand for peace.

Alarm bells started to ring.

'Are there costumes involved?' wondered Chris.

There certainly were costumes involved. It seemed that the cyclists had been earmarked for the role of the doves. Further emails revealed that they would be riding bikes and flapping wings. A peloton of 'Dove-Bikes'. Inside Chris Boardman's head a warning klaxon sounded, which in turn was accompanied by an air-raid siren. But that was not all. Given Chris Boardman's status as the godfather of modern British cycling, he had been pencilled in for an even greater honour.

Was he comfortable with heights? 'I should perhaps warn you that there will be some aerial work.'

The email elaborated again. From the Dove-Bike peloton, a single Dove-Bike would emerge, flying high across the stadium. This would be known as the Hero Dove-Bike, or Bike-Dove (I forget which way round it was). This would be Chris Boardman.

'Oh no.' That's what I remember him saying. 'Oh. No.'

He was consumed by crisis. How could he now withdraw his cooperation? Because withdraw he most certainly had to. I do not think I have ever seen Chris so worried.

Of course, none of this was helped by the fact that wherever he went for the next few days he found that he was followed by the gentle cooing of doves, a sound which, by the end of the week, almost everyone on our team had perfected, and probably also some of the riders on the Tour de France.

I don't know how he managed to swerve his obligations in the end. But, in my opinion Danny Boyle's show was just a bit poorer for the non-inclusion of Chris Boardman, dangling from the roof of the Olympic Stadium in an aero helmet and skinsuit, trying to reduce his wind profile, while all the time flapping his huge feathery arms and smiling.

We set off into a headwind for the first six or seven miles. Chris advised me to ease up a little. Unconsciously, I had been pushing myself too hard so as not to fall short of respectability in his eyes. He had warned me about this before, back in France when we first rode a little way together. That was the day he taught me the cycling phrase 'half-wheeling', which means forcing the pace just a little too much for comfort by riding alongside someone, but persistently half a wheel ahead. Such subliminal forcing of the pace is considered bad form, and very inadvisable for those who do not know their limits.

I took his advice though, and eased off. Already I was breathing much harder than him, my conversational gambits punctuated by frequent pauses . . . in which I took an almighty . . . gulp of air before I could . . . continue. As if to force home his Olympian effortlessness, he was riding his own design of cyclo-cross bike with a heavy profile on its thick tyres, built for sliding around in the mud, not for barrelling along tarmac roads. It slowed him down, but not so as you'd notice. I was on a carbon-fibre bike with stupidly slick racing tyres. This bike sped me up, but, again, not so as you'd notice.

There was so much that Chris could execute effortlessly, which I would only mimic with added clumsiness. Changing gear from the big to the small ring at the front involved me free-wheeling for a good minute, while I looked down at the chain and fumbled repeatedly with the gearshift levers, trying every combination seemingly at random before the right configuration appeared at my feet.

But I was most jealous of his ability to blow snot from his nostrils.

With a subtle move to the side, and the application of a

thumb to the nostril, he was able to clear his airways of prodigious amounts of mucus with a precision and vigour you could only applaud. I didn't dare expel it with such aplomb, for fear that it might backfire (literally) or, worse still, wrap itself around the shins of a former Olympic champion. Instead, I opted for discreet dabs and wipes here and there. Not, it transpired, the right policy.

'You're covered in snot,' Chris noticed. 'I've been watching you going about getting rid of it. It's been fascinating.'

I glanced down. It looked like I had gone to sleep overnight in a cabbage patch, and the slugs had chosen me as their observation platform.

'My nose won't do the thing that your nose can do,' I protested, unimpressively.

I was woefully unprepared in other ways, too. 'Did you bring any food?'

'No.'

This was perhaps the greatest sin of all, a bit like forgetting to fill your car with petrol. Chris had a plan though. He often does. It's one of the things that make him great.

'Did you bring any money?' Yes! Yes! I had a fiver in my pocket. 'Right, there's a café at the top of the Horseshoe Pass (I was beginning to figure that this was the mythical 'Shoe' he had mentioned back in Cherwell service station). We'll stop there and get a cereal bar.'

This sounded like a good plan.

First though, Chris had to get me to the top. There was a hiccup en route. Just as the road started to rise before the climb, I punctured.

'Have you got a spare inner tube?' No. 'Did you bring a pump?' No. 'Tyre levers?' No.

Luckily, he'd planned for just such an occurrence.

We pulled over to the side. There was no way that I was going to fumble my way through the tyre change with Chris

Boardman MBE watching over me. It wasn't even up for discussion, so rather pathetically, I simply said, 'Can you do it, please, Chris?' I very nearly called him Dad by mistake. He did. And was ever so faintly not amused by having to do it, as well.

And then we started to climb. After a while, the road bent left into the Horseshoe itself, and, more significantly, into another, but this time howling, headwind. I gritted my teeth and put my head down, and although I was in my easiest gear, simply turning the pedals at all had become surprisingly hard. The ribbon of tarmac unwound horribly before my eyes.

At the bendy extremity of the horseshoe, the gradient ramped up significantly. It was almost more than I could bear. Chris kept chatting, although God knows what about. All I could hear was the wind, and the blood battering through my ears.

'I may not . . . talk much . . . for a . . .bit.'

We did reach the top. There, on an exposed moorland shoulder of land, sat a sprawling white café. There were lots of motorcyclists, a few earnest-looking rambling couples and a gaggle of pensioners. But Chris and I were the only cyclists there that day. I stumbled in, fumbling for my chinstrap, dripping sweat from my nose and hunting for flapjack.

'Shall I fill up your water bottle, Chris?'

Mine was bone dry – sucked empty by the exertion of that ghastly monochrome climb.

'No. Still full.' Chris was checking his iPhone.

When we set off again, Chris dropped like a stone, travelling down narrow, single-track roads and round blind corners with poise and control. He wasn't even trying, he was just harnessing gravity. I saw his balanced form hurtling away from me. Way, way behind him, I teetered down the mountainside, and, when I knew that Chris was so far ahead that he wouldn't be able to hear me, I whimpered to myself. 'Shit shit shit shit . . .'

*   *   *

On the first day of the 2012 Tour de France, Chris Boardman and I took the canal path to Liège for the Prologue. This ride should not have been epic, and indeed, by any realistic measure, it wasn't epic. But the tangible presence of a nagging headwind, which was aligned with great mathematical precision right in our faces all the way, made it much harder than it should have been. For me, at least. Even Chris seemed irked by it, as we approached the sapping halfway point. Apart from anything else, the rushing of air past our ears made for very difficult conversation.

'There's a simple remedy to riding into a headwind.' He glanced across at me, as I grimaced my way forward, leaning into it at an unusually ungainly angle.

'What's that, then?' I asked. Chris had spent years of his life conducting research in wind tunnels and looking in minute detail at airflow diagrams. He was about to tell me how to tame nature itself.

'Go a bit slower.' That was his answer. I obliged.

Then we hit town, and somehow managed to blag our way onto the race route itself, joining it for the final two kilometres. All around us, riders out on their morning reconnaissance were effortlessly overtaking us. It must have been very strange for Chris Boardman, three times winner of the Tour de France Prologue, to be stuck with me, at my humble pace, on the actual route of the actual race. Perhaps that was why he suggested that I sped up.

'Go on. Race it.' I heard from behind.

I stepped on it, in as much as I could. There was already a sizeable crowd gathering for the start of the race itself in a few hours. They watched on in bafflement. I wondered if any of them recognised Chris. I did my best, hugging the barriers where I thought I should, trying to make my gear changes as smooth as possible, and listening all the time to Chris's instructions from behind me.

'Easy . . . easy . . . now turn in . . . and go . . . over to middle, tuck in . . . and maximum effort . . . now!'

It was exhilarating. I abandoned all embarrassment and relished every second of it. I must have looked like an idiot, but I felt like a champion, having been steered home by a man who redefined the art of Prologue riding. I crossed the line, and came sliding to a halt.

Chris pulled up alongside. He was smiling. He'd enjoyed it.

'That's the first time I've done that since I stopped racing.' He pulled out his media accreditation, and we both pushed our bikes in the direction of the TV trucks. 'I actually feel a bit emotional.'

And for a second, I almost believed him.

We were nearly done. The sun poked out from behind white clumps of springtime clouds. Now we had a tailwind. Gradually I regained my voice. I wanted to tell Chris how wonderful it felt to be zipping along, with so little effort, blown by the wind at our backs. But I felt that this would make me sound naïve and childlike.

'It feels great with this wind at your back, doesn't it? You feel like you're flying along.' It was the last thing I was expecting Chris to say. I glanced at him to see if he was taking the piss. But he looked earnest enough. I acknowledged once again that it is hard to know people well. Especially Chris Boardman.

We climbed again, this time up a steep, wooded road to a place known mysteriously as 'World's End' (which in fact appeared to be nothing much more than a lay-by next to a cattle grid). At one point, halfway up the slopes, the road switched back sharply, and at the apex of the corner, there was a ford. Water streamed over the surface of the tarmac. As we both turned to ride across it, I noticed that Chris took a very wide line, and I just had time to hear him ask, 'Ever ridden over a ford before?' when my back wheel flipped out from behind me, and I fell instantly and very painfully onto my side, as if I had been shot by a sniper hiding in the World's End lay-by.

'Ah. That's what you should never do when riding over a ford.' Now he tells me! 'I was going to tell you not to turn the wheel, but I didn't want to patronise you.'

'Oh, please patronise me, Chris. Please do.' I was scrambling up from the water, my left half, from arse to ankle, soaking wet.

We made it back to the car park, not without getting temporarily lost, and having to ride up two or three impossibly steep little ramps in and out of Welsh villages.

We had only been riding for three hours, if that. But I shook Chris warmly by the hand, thanked him for his time, and just collapsed into the driver's seat of my car, declining Chris's invitation to lunch at a nearby pub.

'You look like a man who just wants to get driving,' said Chris. 'Actually, you look like a man who doesn't want to get driving.'

I smiled weakly at him. Four hours later I was home. I can recall nothing of the journey other than running into Corley services to buy some grapes, without which I might have suffered from complete systemic shutdown and buried my Renault Scenic into the central reservation.

At home, I fell into the bath, only just managing to peel off the layers of Lycra, which had dried to my skin over the length of the M6.

It was only as I lay there soaking in the tub, that I realised I had forgotten to ask Chris anything that would get me closer to the heart of the matter: the mad impulse which makes people like me ride up 'the Shoe', and the even madder impulse which makes people like him want to *race* up it. To make a career of such masochism!

They were, I imagined, all terribly familiar to him: long, long hours spent, often alone, on autumnal roads, made slippery by fallen leaves and the mud from tractor tyres, dank and remote and shrouded in a mist, into which your breath disappears as you huff and puff along. The life of a British pro was so far away from the glistening come-hither of the Mediterranean. What *was* the appeal?

All those unanswered questions, about his background in cycling, his relationship with the public and the institutions of British cycling, the phenomenal success of his bike brand.

All the substance, which had made me set up the meeting in the first place: clean forgotten in the unending hurt of keeping pace with him.

Later that night I received one more text:

It was a lovely ride. You really are much stronger on a bike than you realise.

CB

I slept very well that night, with my phone and its precious message under my pillow. But I was none the wiser, really.

CHAPTER 3

NOBODY WOULD GO WITH ME

There came a time when I needed to take my dinner jacket to the dry cleaners. Patting the pockets for debris, I found a replica cigarette card that I had been given on the night of that gala dinner for British cycling. It bore a photo of a little-remembered champion, in touched-up Technicolor and sporting a reluctant smile. I flipped it over, to see the name and email details neatly written out in biro: Graham Webb.

I placed the card next to my laptop.

Graham and I had spoken a little as the dinner had broken up, over his half-eaten dessert bowl (his neck bows forward at an uncomfortable angle, perhaps from those long years spent hunched over handlebars). He had told me some things about his life, which I had found fascinating, and had left me wanting to know more. He had been the 1967 Amateur World Road Race champion, three years after the great Eddy Merckx had won the same title before the Belgian's unique talent was unleashed on the world. But like a sizeable number of amateur world champions, Webb's professional career never really took off.

He had retired young, frustrated, in Flanders. And he had never come home.

I looked again at the card. Then I dropped him a line, just to say hello. He responded almost immediately with good wishes, and beautiful grammar. And then, through neglect on my part, our contact went cold.

* * *

Many months later, I finally got round to writing to him again. The reason for the delay had been my conscience. I had long been ignoring a nagging guilt. At the dinner, I had promised Graham that I would use contacts in the TV industry to get hold of as much footage as I could of his World Championship win. Pathé owned the clip, that much I had found out. But they were being decidedly unhelpful, even when I told them that I was trying to procure it for the man himself ('He won the race. Can't you do him a favour?').

Despite all the string-pulling, I could not get any more than a heavily pixelated, downloaded thirty-second clip of the race, worse indeed than the stuff you could watch for free on YouTube. And even that had cost me a small fortune to buy. The old tape still exists, in some vault somewhere, but they simply wouldn't get it out for me. I felt bad for Graham, having promised him more.

Still, I kept returning to Graham Webb, in curiosity. No rider in my experience had ever spoken to me with such start-ling intensity. Something about his clarity of expression, his deep-set, frowning eyes, disarming in their glare, and something of what he said, made we want to get his story down.

When I did contact him again, his reply came with a warning. This was his email:

Hi Ned,

Glad you liked the story and I hope that I'll live long enough to tell more, I'm not being morbid but my health has never been up to much and after this last lot I have to be very careful. Please check with me before you plan to come to Belgium because of the above.

I've found you on FB (I think).

Greetings,
Graham

I liked the way that a man of his generation and general serious demeanour could so casually reveal himself to be a Facebook user. That little detail only piqued my interest further.

The next correspondence revealed that he had suffered a massive heart attack in 2005. His aorta had split as he was out riding his bike with a friend. But he had struggled home before collapsing. A year later, it had split again. This time he had had to undergo a terribly dangerous operation to repair the damage. He only just survived.

He wrote about his time in hospital on a Belgian Internet forum, to which he sent me the link:

> *After a seven-hour op and long coma I awoke in the intensive care unit, this time with severe pneumonia from the under cooling. Because of all the water on my lungs they had to shove a tube down my nose and suck all the water out, this several times a day. Sucking the water out also sucked all the air out of my lungs; it was like being strangled to death. Because I fought against this 'murder attempt' they had to tie me down, hand and foot. I was fighting for my life.*

It was time I got over to Belgium.

The first thing I noticed about Graham Webb, when we finally sat opposite each other in his modern bungalow in Wachtebeke near Ghent, was his silence.

It was a dark day outside, and the half-occluded windows were shrouded on either side by heavy brown drapes, swallowing most of what remained of the light and the sound from the room. Every surface in his ornate front room groaned with pictures and knick-knacks; grandchildren, medals, crystal ashtrays, all shining softly.

Behind a door, just next to where we sat in their living room, Graham's wife Marie-Rose lay, confined to bed by a bout of illness. I may have been jumping to conclusions, but I guessed that she was the homemaker, not Graham. I never got to meet her, although I was there for most of the day. Occasionally a cough or a sigh would filter through the fabric of the wall. Otherwise, when we weren't talking, the silence would rush back in to fill the space.

Time, according to Graham's own internal sense of foreboding, was running out. But it also felt like it was in abundant supply, over-represented. It saturated the airless room. I imagined the wordless minutes Graham might have spent waiting for the sound of my car to pull up outside (there had been an exchange of emails about my exact time of arrival).

'What is it you want to know?' he asked.

'Whatever you want to tell me.'

He grew up in post-war Borsall Heath in Birmingham. His memory suggested it was actually Spark Brook (itself hardly more prosperous), but Graham claims that his mother never liked to say that they were from Borsall Heath, deeming it to be a notch lower still.

He describes it as a slum. It was just that.

The area, composed of back-to-back Victorian terraces, like Leamington Road where he grew up, had suffered badly during the war. His playground was the broken landscape of streets surrounding his house. Bomb craters. Acres of bricks that once were houses. Roofs, blown to pieces and leaning out their shattered joists at unnatural angles.

Graham shared a house with his mother Lilly and with four older siblings, two boys and two girls.

Lilly's husband, Edwin Webb, had been called up to fight in General Montgomery's Tank Regiment. At the advanced age of thirty-eight he died in the opening exchanges of the Battle of El Alamein. 'Because the British tanks were rubbish compared to the German ones', as Graham puts it in his deadpan Brummie. 'The Germans had ammunition which could pierce the armour, and he was blown up in his tank.'

News of his death reached home. 'They found postcards addressed to mother in his pocket. They were covered in blood, and they just sent them off to her. That was how she found out that he'd died. Postcards from Egypt, covered in blood.'

That was in 1942. Graham was born in 1944.

Graham doesn't know whether he's been told this, or has imagined it, but he tells me that Edwin Webb had put plans in place should he be killed. 'I think he knew he wouldn't come back. And he asked his brother (Dennis) to look after his wife and his kids if anything should happen to him.'

There is a pause. 'That was how I was conceived.'

Uncle Dennis didn't hang around long though, before he disappeared from their lives, too. By VE Day, he was gone, leaving behind a boy who had no idea (despite the arithmetic of dates) who his father was. In fact, for the next thirty-five years he believed that Edwin had been his father.

'I didn't know, until my mother died in 1977, that Dennis was my dad. On her deathbed she gave my sister a picture of Uncle Dennis, and said, "Tell Graham it's his dad."'

Graham has only one memory to treasure of the man who he never knew was his real father. One afternoon, when he was 'very, very little', he was playing in the backyard, when he heard the shout of the rag-and-bone men walking down the back alley.

'I remember that one of them looked too well dressed, he was too well turned out. He came to the back fence, and he called my name out, "Graham!" He'd come to say goodbye. That's all I remember of him.'

'Were you very close to your mother?' I ask.

'Not really. No.' He thinks about it for a moment. 'I can't say we were close. She never talked to me. She never said anything. Sometimes she would be crying all the time, and I'd ask her what the matter was. She'd never answer.'

Like many women of her generation, she had reason enough; not only had she lost her husband, she had also lost her father in the First World War when she was just six. In fact, her dad had died in a German prisoner-of-war camp a month after Armistice Day. All this, Graham only knows because of research he has undertaken since her death. Nothing of the sort was ever discussed during her lifetime.

All throughout his quietly fraught childhood, a pervasive silence characterised his everyday life. His mother, a machine operator at the BSA Motorworks plant, worked every shift she could to put bread on the table for her growing family of five, but showed no inclination to indulge the demons of the past. Ignorance was this family's default position, although the difference between Graham and his older siblings, and their subsequent behaviour towards him (he is only just dealing with very damaging, long-suppressed memories), suggest that they knew all too well that the 'runt of the litter' was only a half-brother.

'That's why I like living here, you know. When I am in England, the memories come back.' The geographical distance works. 'It depresses me when I am in England. As soon as I get back to Belgium, everything just clears up, really.'

The family occupied what was known as a 'back house', which gave onto the back alley, rather than the road. Smaller and cheaper, it had only two bedrooms. Graham would sleep in the same bed as his mother, and the rest somehow made do in the other room.

Serious illness was a fact of life. In his first three years, he spent prolonged periods in hospital with repeated bouts of pneumonia and a near-fatal episode of meningitis. 'They had to pump penicillin into my spinal cord between each vertebra. I think I've had to fight since day one just to stay alive.'

Sometimes, Graham describes himself as autistic. I do not think that this has ever been actually diagnosed, but it is telling that he has hit upon this word as he looks to make sense of his past. Certainly, by the time he reached boyhood, he had completely turned in on himself. And that's when he first stepped on a bike.

'I was eight years old. One of the kids on the street had a bike. I'd never been on one before, but they pushed me off, and I just rode away, you know.'

That was it. He saved, and ended up buying a rusty old wreck of a bike, stuck in the hardest of its three gears, for nine pence from his cousin. He never looked back.

'It was my magic carpet.' The first ride he ever did was the ten miles there and ten miles back to Earlswood lakes, just outside Solihull.

He immediately got a reputation among the kids he rode with for going further and faster than any of them had attempted. They would complain that they couldn't keep up.

'That was the story of my life: nobody would go with me.'

When he turned ten, he, along with all the other kids at school who rode bikes, hatched a plan. They would ride a hundred miles. By looking at a map, they realised that Gloucester was exactly fifty miles away: there and back then, all along the same road.

But no one went with him. 'Come Sunday morning, I turned up. But no one else did. So I set off for Gloucester on my own.' He got the shock of his life when he hit the Malvern Hills, which had not been marked on the map. Over the top of the hills, he got 'terrible abdominal pains', which ended in a bout of very bloody diarrhoea – but still he soldiered on. 'I'd have rather died, than walk.'

He reached Gloucester, where he found a big roundabout in the middle of town, went round it, and started to head back.

Listening to him recount the adventure, I am astonished to learn that he had not packed a thing to eat or drink. 'Not even a sandwich Graham?'

'I never took anything to eat. There never was anything to eat. Five kids and no money? When we got up in the morning, the cupboards were bare, you know. Some days we never had anything to eat at all. That was no issue.'

About twenty miles from home he collapsed, and lay by the side of the road. Occasionally, people would come over to him and offer help. 'Leave me alone!' was all they got for their concern.

After four hours, he remounted his bike, and finally made it home. The next Sunday he went out and did it again.

I look at the retired rider sitting opposite me as he nears his seventieth birthday, and try to imagine the ten-year-old boy pushing himself into ruin. I wonder if I am to believe it all. The tales of post-war poverty are so familiar-sounding, so conforming to the archetypes of the era, that they are almost too perfect.

Yet, this is no self-dramatist.

Could his mother really have allowed him off on such an adventure so hideously ill prepared? I realise that she almost certainly knew nothing of his solitary rides. He would leave at three o'clock in the morning, before it was light. He'd be home in the evening, but wouldn't tell a soul what he'd done.

He ventured further afield. Aeroplane spotting had become a passion. As he explains, 'The only way I could see aircraft was to go to the airfields on my bike.'

I think of my own childhood, some of which was spent in the spectator lounges of Luton and Birmingham airports, listening to the indecipherable chatter from the control tower on my tiny transistor radio. My dad would sit opposite me, reading his paper patiently, as I noted down the registration number of each jet that taxied past and took off.

Then I thought of those twelve British plane spotters who were sentenced to three years in prison by the Greek authorities for indulging their passion near the Kalamata air force base. The Greek judiciary simple couldn't accommodate the notion that people might want to watch planes taking off and landing as a hobby. This is a very home-grown, very boyish madness.

It came as no surprise to me that, sooner or later, Graham's particular upbringing would lead him to a hobby like plane spotting, at which the British still excel. But the difference between his 'passion', and my 'interest', was vast.

At the age of twelve, he set off for Heathrow on his little rusty bike, a journey of almost exactly one hundred miles.

'How did you plan to get back?' I ask him.

'I never thought about that. I never thought about it.' There's a flicker of a smile as he remembers this now. Or perhaps he's remembering the Lockheed Constellation, or the Bristol Britannia.

'When I'd quenched my thirst looking at the aircraft, I

realised it was too late to get home, so I crawled into a ditch under a bush at the back of the BOAC hangars at Heathrow. I slept in that ditch. The next day, I watched the aircraft again and rode home.'

This became a habit.

One Easter, he rode to Heathrow and then on into London to find a Youth Hostel. There were only three in those days, and they were all fully booked. Not knowing what to do, he happened upon Euston Station, where a train for Birmingham was about to leave. He jumped on, paying for the ticket with the money he'd saved up for the Youth Hostel.

'I rode from Birmingham New Street station. I got home quite knackered at about teatime. Somehow, my mother knew what I'd been planning. She said, "I thought you were going to go to London?" I said, "I've been!"'

At a conservative estimate, the twelve-year-old Graham Webb had probably ridden one hundred and fifty miles, stuck in top gear, on a rusty bike, all on his own, without anything to eat.

Throughout his childhood, as he recalls, his family expressed not the slightest bit of interest in his cycling.

His mother, Lilly, had remarried. But not happily. Her new husband was an elderly neighbour called Albert Whitton. Graham suspects that she did this to free up their own house so that his sister's young family had somewhere to live.

But Graham joined the new household on sufferance only.

'You can bring that kid with you,' Whitton had told Lilly, 'but you'll have to go out to work for him. I'm not keeping him.'

'He was a terrible bloke. He'd pin mother up against a wall with a big carving knife against her throat. I couldn't say anything. I thought he'd go after me with the knife.'

At fourteen, he left school and started work on an assembly line building imitation log fires. Everyone else in the factory was a woman. Perhaps his isolation grew more pronounced. Certainly his disappearing acts grew more ambitious. He saved up money, and he took two weeks' holiday, intending to ride round the entire coast of Wales, pedalling all day until it got too dark, and then pitching his tent wherever he stopped.

All the while, he knew nothing of the sport of cycling. 'I didn't even know it existed.'

'So if someone had talked to you about the Tour de France . . .?'

'I wouldn't have known what they were talking about, no.'

The only competitive cycling he'd ever seen had been dirt-track racing in a bombsite in Birmingham. 'Road racing, time-trialling, track racing? I didn't know they existed.'

A chance meeting with a member of the Solihull Cycling Club changed all that. He suggested Graham went to a club meeting at Knowle Village Hall.

'There must have been a couple of hundred people milling around, just chatting. I sat there, not talking to anyone, wondering what it was all about. People thought I was thick.' By now he was seventeen.

He was asked if he was going to do the 'Club 25'. He had no idea what the 'Club 25' was. But they took his two shillings and his signature. He was entered.

'I got the start sheet. I was number 22. It was a time trial, but I didn't know what a time trial was. I thought everyone started together in a race. We were given a changing room, which was like someone's garden shed. All these blokes were getting into racing gear. I'd just got some cut-off jeans and a T-shirt and a pair of pumps.

'I got a bit fed up with sitting in this garden shed, so I went to have a look at the start, and there were blokes being pushed off.'

Eventually, despite him missing his start time, they let him start. But still he didn't understand the race.

'I thought, 'Christ! I've got to catch all the blokes in front of me, to win this race!"

He caught his 'minute man', and eased up so that the rider could get on his wheel, and they might work together.

'But he started shouting, "Bugger off! Bugger off!" I thought, that's nice, you know! I'm offering to help him, and he's telling me to bugger off. So I did.'

At the finish line, he was still none the wiser. He knew he'd not caught everyone, but couldn't figure out what was supposed to happen next.

'I thought, bugger this, it's still early. I'll just go out for a ride on my bike. It's got to be much more enjoyable than what these blokes are doing.'

Needless to say, he set the fastest time that day. They told him the following week when he returned to the village hall. He remembers the embarrassment. 'I went blood red. I hated any sort of spotlight.'

From that moment on, his presence on the local scene was established. The cycling community became aware of this taciturn kid with the cut-off jeans and the tennis shoes, an entire tool kit strapped to his seat post by a spare tyre. Bit by bit, he shed his naïvety, and inevitably, the prospect of a career in cycling presented itself.

In 1963, at the age of nineteen, in his own words, 'I was an aeroplane, I was a jet. I could do nothing wrong.'

Having ridden with great success as a junior, he now started to take out bigger and bigger races. He rode the Beacon mountain time trial, taking seven minutes out of the established star, Hugh Porter, who accused him of riding a two-up time trial with another rider to get the better of him. 'He was unforgiving, you know. Very, very nasty.' (Porter, now a hugely venerated television commentator, remembers the race well, and stands by his accusation to this day.)

On the final climb of that race, and as a portent of things

that lay in wait many decades down the line, his heart stopped beating, then started again of its own accord. But for a while, 'I was dead', he recalls. 'There's a pain barrier. And you can go through it. And then you get wings, you fly!'

In the 1960s a lack of understanding from the general public, and a lack of tolerance from the authorities, meant that roads were seldom closed to traffic for a 'mass start' road race. This resulted in a prevailing culture of time-trialling: races that could, by their nature, co-exist with the traffic on open roads.

Webb became prodigiously good at them. He rose to the top. At Brentwood, he rode the fastest 25-mile time trial of the year, a significant feather in his cap. But he remembers that day for a very different reason. When he returned home in the evening, he walked in to the house to find his step-father, Albert, dead on the couch. Albert had succumbed to the effects of chronic alcoholism and bronchitis. He'd 'coughed himself to death', in Graham's no-nonsense words.

Despite his bitterness towards Albert, this discovery had a profound effect on Graham. He attributes a life-long battle with depression to this moment. But he cannot explain why.

In 1964 and '65 he raced on, but his heart wasn't in it. He tried his hand at the insurance business. He married his girlfriend Karen. He was drifting away from cycling.

Then, in 1966, an old friend came to stay, after being thrown out of his own family home. The Webbs put him up. He used to cycle to his factory job early every morning. Since Graham's job in insurance didn't start till ten, he used to tag along for the ride. That rekindled his enthusiasm. He got fit and started racing again.

Under the guidance of the 1948 Olympic bronze medallist Tommy Godwin, he broke a significant British record, completing the furthest distance round a track in one hour. He bettered Les West's Hour Record by 414 yards. It was a major achievement.

'It was so easy. That night, I said, "I wonder if I can make a career out of cycling."'

That then was the moment when the penny dropped. That was the moment in which Graham Webb embarked on the journey that led him to his homely bungalow in Wachtebeke, and voluntary exile. He knew that the road to success lay overseas. The money and the races just weren't there in Britain. 'It was hopeless in England trying to make a career of cycling.'

So, he worked all winter without training, then rode the Good Friday Meeting at Herne Hill ('I cleaned up there') and the Butts Meeting in Coventry on Easter Monday ('I cleaned up there, too') and then on the Tuesday, he and Karen 'found ourselves standing in Amsterdam Central Station with two suitcases, not knowing where we were going to sleep that night'.

'Did it work out for you?' I ask.

'Perfectly.' And just this once, a smile sweeps across his features, unknitting his brow.

We break, while Graham makes a coffee for me. It's decaf, for which he apologises.

That year, 1967, the Amateur World Road Race Championships were in Heelen; fifteen hilly laps, two hundred kilometres in total. The field had been whittled down to an elite bunch of a dozen or so, and on the final lap, he just rode away from them. No one could touch him; as he crossed the line, he was still pulling away, and he won by a good hundred yards; the first Briton to win that medal in forty-five years.

He pulled on the Rainbow Jersey, and stood awkwardly on the podium ('a necessary evil'), shyly scanning the sea of faces in the crowd. Suddenly he spotted someone he knew.

'Who came pushing through the crowd towards the podium? My mum.'

She'd never before seen him race. But here she was, as far as Graham knew, on foreign soil for the first time in her life, watching her son being crowned World Champion. The British cycling fans who'd also made the trip lifted her onto the podium.

'Did you two talk to each other at all? Do you remember what she said to you?'

'Nothing was said.'

'Nothing was said?'

'No.'

There was an abnormally long pause. I tried to discern what he might be thinking about this. He stared fixedly back at me.

'And then what happened?'

'I imagine she just continued her trip home. Because she was the queen of the trip. Her son was a World Champion.'

The very next day, he turned professional with Mercier. It should have been the start of a glorious career. But that's not the way it worked out.

That winter, accompanied by Karen, he went off to a training camp in Sardinia. He was scheduled to ride the early season races in the South of France. But a general strike in Sardinia shut the place down, and kept him effectively imprisoned on the island. He missed all the races the team had wanted to enter him in.

Eventually, at the end of February, they got off the island. But in Turin, everything was stolen from the back of his car, including, significantly, his racing shoes, whose plates had been assembled just right for his pedal stroke.

That had a bad effect on his form. 'I had a lot of trouble. My bike had a bent pedal, too.' It all led to a debilitative knee injury.

Carrying this pain, he was nonetheless entered by the team for Paris–Nice. He had to abandon on Stage 2. The team stopped paying him and, despite returning to fitness and resuming his racing, eventually he was summarily dismissed. There was little to stop them doing what they wanted with riders in those days.

And that, put simply, was that for his professional career. Gone before it had even got underway. Money problems piled up. His marriage to Karen fell apart. Together with their son Jean-Paul she returned to England in 1968.

Beset with debt, and labouring in a furniture factory, Graham remarried eventually, this time to a Flemish lady called Marie-Rose Verspecht. Together, almost in the tradition of retired English footballers, they opened a pub called De Neeuw Derby, in a village just north of Ghent.

In cycling-mad country like Flanders, the very fact of Graham's career, however brief, held considerable prestige, enough to guarantee the success of the business. They paid off the debts. But the racing was gone.

Then Graham Webb tells me the story, which he first told me over canapés and champagne at that British cycling dinner months before. I hear it again. But to hear it in context, sitting in his living room as the November night has closed in outside, surrounded by photographs from 1967, I now understand that this is why I came to talk to him.

The 'Rainbow Jersey' is a particularly potent icon in cycling, perhaps even more rich in association than the Yellow Jersey of the Tour de France. Although Graham Webb had won the amateur competition, it was still a huge achievement. It was certainly the apotheosis of all that his career yielded. This beloved jersey hung on the wall of the bar, slowly turning yellow from the smokers and from the wood stove below. There it remained through the years, testifying to his ability, telling anyone who cared to ask about it that the proprietor had pedigree, real class.

One day, in the winter, when he was elsewhere, one of his

least favourite drinkers came in. Marie-Rose was on her own in the pub.

'He was a very bad criminal. He'd been released from jail. My missus served him and he made a comment about the jersey. My Rainbow Jersey. He said to my wife, "What would you think if I tore it down?" She didn't have an answer.

'When I came home later, she told me what had happened.'

Something within him, already frayed, must have snapped. In an instant, he knew that it was over. His attachment to a past, which only pointed to an unsatisfactory present, broke free. The jersey, its brilliant white fabric jaundiced, was the problem.

'I said, "Well, he won't have the chance." I tore it down, and stuffed it in the stove. I burnt it.'

It lit and then ignited. In seconds, maybe a minute, it was gone. Not many world champions have deliberately incinerated their memories.

'I had a happy childhood.'

'Did you?' There is a trace of scepticism in my question.

'I think so.' Graham pauses. 'Maybe because of my bike.'

In the morning I left early, to drive the distance back to Calais without recourse to the motorway. I also wanted to visit the Menin Gate in Ypres. It was Armistice Day.

11/11/11.

I drove for an hour through the November fog. Yesterday's clear blue skies had led to a still, grey Flanders morning. At times it seemed to be getting darker, rather than lighter. Turning off the main road I negotiated a path to the centre of Ypres and, on sighting a group of veterans, I pulled over and parked. They seemed to know the way, so I dropped in behind them and followed as they walked cheerily to the main square and the vast monument that was to stage the centrepiece of the day's Remembrance service.

I listened to their chatter.

'I can't bloody push you straight. Can't you bloody get up and walk?' One elderly man laughed at his much younger friend who was in a wheelchair and had lost both his legs from below the knee. 'What's the matter with you?'

'Oh piss off, and do your job will you?'

For some reason, I thought of Graham. He would not have looked out of place in a uniform. And as a veteran. He belonged to that kind of Britishness. In fact, he told me that he could never forgive his mother for refusing to lie about his age so that he could begin an RAF apprenticeship. It was the alternative path his life never took.

The veterans, in increasing numbers as their ranks were swelled by comrades, walked past pretty Flemish shop fronts, some of which exploited this annual pilgrimage and its associated year-long trickle of tourists. Tommy's Spirits and Cigarettes. The Old Bill Pub. Poppy's Pizzeria.

After Ypres, I meandered through Flanders as I crossed into France. These were the routes that Graham, as well as scores of other British riders, had ridden. He still rides them to this day, tentatively now, because of his heart.

The roadside was clustered with signs to military ceme-teries. I had always thought that these had been constructed after the event, moved to appropriate locations, chosen for the purpose. But the names suggested otherwise. Many, many smaller graveyards were created at the site of the loss of life. There and then. Red Farm Cemetery. Hop House Cemetery.

All along the straight roads, with their mountains of sugar beet harvested and awaiting transport, the Flemish had taken to their bikes. Armistice Day amounts to a public holiday in Belgium. As the British lay wreaths in their towns, so many Belgians take advantage of the free time and quiet roads to get out for a long ride and a chat. The first opportunity of the year to don the winter clothing.

At the mouth of the tunnel, there was an almighty queue. For three-quarters of an hour we inched forwards to the UK Passport Control. Belgian cars, French cars. There was a German BMW to my right from Cologne. Tempers flared, as people started to miss their departure slots.

I was the next car in line for passport control when we all stopped moving completely. I could make out the immigration officer in her hut, dealing with the Belgian sports car in front of me.

She appeared suddenly to be standing motionless at her desk, staring ahead. I glanced at the clock. Twelve midday in Calais, but it was eleven o'clock on the other side of the channel. She did not carry on her work for the full two minutes, and along the line, nobody moved.

It was a weird re-enactment. A thin line of determinedly different islanders facing down waves of Continentals. From the battlefields of the First World War, to the retreat at Dunkirk, this narrow strip of water, and the passage of British youth across it, has been a step into the unknown, a step into, or out of no-man's-land.

I thought of Graham's emigration. I had seen how Britain unsettles him, and how his peace of mind only returns when he reaches home again in Flanders.

He's a Dunkirk soldier no one went to pick up. I'm not sure he wanted anyone to pick him up.

CHAPTER 4

MICK'S GRAND TOUR

The Tour of Britain is not the Tour de France in the same way that there is no adequate translation into French for 'Sausage Roll'. There are no Alps; there are no Pyrenees. And sometimes, there is no race.

While 'le Tour' came into being in 1903, its British counterpart stumbled into existence many, many years later. The late forties witnessed the regular running of an amateur race from Brighton to Glasgow, which sufficed for a time, but it wasn't until 1951, when the *Daily Express* bunged the race organisers a decent amount of money (and a great deal of free publicity), that a proper Tour of Britain was up and running. Astonishingly, and ingloriously, one of the riders that year was Jimmy Savile. He didn't win it.

Eight years later, the Milk Marketing Board got involved, and their eponymous, mostly amateur, race became a fixture in the calendar. The Milk Race then briefly coexisted with the professional Kellogg's Tour in the 1980s, creating a perfect fusion of the two primary requirements for a nutritious start to the day. Breakfast, at least for those Britons who followed bike racing, was sorted.

But by 1993 the milk had run dry, and, a year later, the cereal box emptied too. Four years of Tourlessness then followed, before the Pru-Tour (sponsored by Prudential) sputtered into life in 1998. Just one year later that particular insurance-based party was over, presumably because we'd fallen behind on our premiums.

After a five-year abstinence, in which the British cycling scene licked its wounds and decided what to do next, the modern Tour of Britain was born. And that's where, for the purposes of simplicity, we join the story.

Learning about the Tour of Britain, and the army of people who make up the wonderful, bizarre sitcom of the race, was a challenge and delight. I was first introduced to it when ITV signed a contract to televise it. Without wishing to resort to hyperbole, I would go so far as to say that in the spring of 2008, my life took a new, entirely unexpected and seriously pleasing twist, when I was called to a meeting room high up in ITV's glass and steel headquarters on the Grays Inn Road in London. Tea was served, and there was a clutch of chocolate Hobnobs on a plate, as there often is when there is momentous news to impart.

It wasn't without its awkwardnesses.

'Hello. My name's Ned Boulting.'

I was talking, as periodically I am forced to, to that particular type of efficiency-exuding lady that sits behind reception desks at major institutions. I wither visibly in the face of such authority. Hers are the laminated visitors' badges. Hers, as a consequence, is the power to withhold or impart both the prospect of happiness and the prospect of future happiness, my children's prospects, and those of their children, too.

'I'm here to see Mark Sharman.'

Mark Sharman was the Head of ITV Sport. My livelihood depended almost entirely on his munificence. I thought about the word 'munificence' as I watched her tucking in the plastic folds of my visitor badge and handing it over.

'Thank you,' I said, my voice a little too high.

And soon I was following her lead, walking through open plan offices and down corridors, trundling towards a minor junction point in my life, a rumbling and grinding of wheels over railway points, a slight diversion, or at least the arrival at a different platform from anticipated. I walked through the door.

'Ah Ned, I've got a special project for you,' said the Boss when I was finally admitted into his glass and steel tomb. He looked like a man who had special projects up his sleeve. He had a way of doing things like that, which marked him out as boss material, that and the grey suit, with sleeves that were specially tailored to conceal the special projects they had hidden up them.

'Oh yes?' I sat forward on his leatherette couch, in a style loosely based on James Bond, but at the same time managing to knock my bike helmet from the couch onto the ground, in the style of Rowan Atkinson.

I glanced down at it. And so did he. We locked eyes briefly over the upturned shell of the offending headgear. He shot his cuffs, and resettled himself on his couch, in the style of Alan Sugar.

'Ned, do you ever turn up to meetings looking smart?'

'I rode here. On my bicycle.' I threw my head slightly back and slightly sideways, a nod to where my bike stood locked up on the busy London street outside. 'Sorry.'

Mark Sharman, the poker-faced, crisply suited TV executive that he was, sighed, in precisely his style. It wasn't a generalised sigh. He actually sighed *at* me, but then momentarily appeared to have lost his thread. A slight cloud passed over his reptilian executive gaze. Let's call it nostalgia.

'I used to time trial when I was a kid. Around Derby.'

'Did you?' An image of a teenaged Mark Sharman, dressed in a suit and tie, on a Raleigh, flashed past me. 'Really?'

'Yes.' There was another one of the awkward pauses, which occasionally characterise meetings with Mark. He picked up a Hobnob, and then put it down, distractedly. I couldn't help noticing that there was still no mention of the special project.

'What gear set have you got on your bike?'

This was not a question I was expecting. 'Campagnolo.'

I hoped that I had pronounced it correctly. It was a word I had only ever read in glossy black-and-white literature about bikes (well, *Rouleur* magazine, to be precise), or glimpsed on the 'mech' as I tried to untangle the mess of chain and cogs, which resulted whenever I tried to change the tyre on my rear wheel.

'Good God. Are they still going? And Shimano?' His face lit up.

'I think so, Mark.' And then, simply to fill the empty noise that whistled in to fill the gap in this sparing conversation, 'They make gears.'

He looked disappointed at me, not for the first time that day. Then, suddenly, he was down to business. 'Tour of Britain.'

This was neither a question, nor a proposition, nor a threat. It was cut and pasted straight from some niche cycling website into our actual conversation. It sounded a bit like the Tour de France, only over here. But beyond that, I couldn't have told you much.

'O . . . K . . .' I said, with some hesitation.

I thought about a map of the UK (excluding, for the sake of practicality, Northern Ireland) and imagined animated routes wriggling all across it. I had an image of a rain-soaked finish line, and clutches of people in kagouls standing by the side of the road eating fried chicken from oily red boxes. For some reason, I had a fleeting mental image of Northampton, the county town of Northamptonshire.

'Great,' I said, massively unconvinced.

That meeting was five years ago.

The first edition of the Tour of Britain that I presented was in September 2008. It started in bright sunshine on the Victoria Embankment in Westminster.

The chimes of Big Ben set the tone for a race richly bathed

in post-Olympic euphoria. The British Cycling team had taken the Beijing velodrome by storm, and catapulted Victoria Pendleton and Chris Hoy onto the back of cereal packets, from where they now beamed down at bowls full of sugary milk. That was partly why ITV got involved, I'm sure. Suddenly, cycling was as mainstream and wholesome as Bran Flakes.

That year I had as my wingman/pundit the newly retired, marvellously phlegmatic West-Midlander Paul Manning. He had been part of the quartet of riders (along with Ed Clancy, Geraint Thomas and Bradley Wiggins) who had won the gold medal in the Team Pursuit at the Olympic Games.

Before the Tour of Britain got underway, and because I had hardly heard of any of the teams or the riders on the race, I paid Paul a visit at his terraced home in Stockport. It was to be a research trip, and a chance to get to know Paul, with whom I had only ever spoken on the phone. We sat in his tidy, tight front room (barely big enough to fit a bike in), drank tea, and spoke about the race.

Although he had devoted his career to riding the Team Pursuit on the track, Paul had also ridden a fair amount on the road, by no means an automatic choice for riders of his generation and pedigree. In fact, as we sat slurping from giant mugs while the rain rattled against his front window, he informed me that he himself had won a stage on the Tour of Britain, a solo breakaway into Glasgow in 2007.

'It was good, that. I enjoyed it.' Paul cracked a huge smile.

Then, feeling like a fan and not a hard-headed journalist, I plucked up the courage to ask him if I could see his gold medal. I had not often met gold medallists before, and had certainly never seen a medal face to face.

No sooner had I popped the question, than he bounded upstairs, his long legs leaping the steps three at a time. I could hear him scrabbling around under his bed, which I thought would be the first place I'd keep a gold medal too, but probably the last place any burglar would expect to find one. I liked Paul for putting his medal under his bed. He returned with a box.

'Can I take it out?'

'Sure, go ahead.' Paul looked down at it, as if he too were seeing it for the first time. Gingerly I prised it out of its cloth berth. It was as big as a small saucer, and half an inch thick. It was magnificent. I told Paul I thought it was magnificent.

As awestruck as we have been by our Olympians, there is often a homeliness at the heart of their character that sits at odds with the grandeur of their achievements. It's a phenomenon best witnessed every four years, where the nation, through the BBC, watches a procession of British athletes crossing over the track to talk to their reporters. Seconds earlier, they've been flowing gracefully down the finishing straight, chin purposefully set and eyes menacingly vacant. Now, in the glare of the camera, they melt into hyper-normality.

'It was, like, just amazing? I mean it was awesome? I just knew when I hit the home straight that it would be, like, incredible . . .?' On and on they gush, grinning, twinkling, loving the moment. If you or I gave a post-race interview, that's exactly how we would sound, too: uncomposed, raw, wonderful.

Many hundreds of Britons (across the breadth of the summer games) have come, won medals and gone. Some have won a solitary bronze medal. Walk down the street, and there'll be no golden post box to mark their location. They're remembered by a select few, their achievements painted in gold ink on wooden boards, or up there on home-made websites, maintained by enthusiasts. But beyond that, there's not much, save for a medal wrapped in velvet, locked up in a safe or placed carefully under a bed. A lifetime, cast in metal.

Everywhere we went on the Tour of Britain, Paul took his medal. People were always asking to see it, and he would always oblige. They didn't always know who he was, or what he'd won a medal for. In fact, sometimes, they didn't even know there was a bike race on. 'Why've they bloody shut the bloody high street, then?'

But at the sight of a gold medal, encased in red velvet, its ribbon neatly folded above it, all opposition to the high street being temporarily out of bounds would swiftly fade away.

'That's bloody brilliant, that. Here, Keith! Come and have look at this bloody medal. It's real gold, that.' And Paul's expression would reflect their awe, as he gazed at it for the thousandth time. 'What was your name again, mate?'

'Paul Manning.'

'Bloody well done, Paul.'

It worried him, carrying it from hotel to hotel, from Gateshead to Taunton. He was terrified he would lose it, or it would be stolen. Nothing bad happened, though.

The race finished in Liverpool where I met up with Chris Boardman, a man whose isolated, splendid gold medal in 1992 had set the tone for all these things to come.

'The class of 2008 have stolen a bit of your thunder, haven't they, Chris?'

'Just a bit, Ned. Blown out of the water.'

We sat down by the Liver Building with the race closing in on us. Despite the late summer sun, a wind picked up, and the Mersey winked its agreement. Things were indeed moving on. And that included the Tour of Britain.

To the casual observer, the Tour of Britain looks a bit like a value-brand Tour de France. It is not three weeks long, but eight days. The teams are not nine men strong, but six. It is not ridden in the blazing heat of a Provençale July, but in the mellow sunshine, and occasional torrential storms of an Atlantic September. In 2009, when 'Le Tour' started in Monte Carlo, 'The Tour' started in Scunthorpe. Twice in two years, the stage into Blackpool has been accompanied by a cyclone. Once it had to be cancelled.

I could go on, but you get the picture.

And yet, over the course of the five years in which I have presented ITV's coverage of the event, I have fallen a little in love with it. So too have many of the riders who pop their heads above its mossy dry-stone wall, and go on to forge greater careers elsewhere: Mark Cavendish, Edvald Boassen Hagen, Michael Albasini, Thomas de Gendt. I love the Tour for the crowds who brave often atrocious conditions to stand at the side of a windswept moor and watch the race go past. The tens of thousands of primary school children who, under instruction from their class teachers, clutch homely crayon-based exhortations to encourage some spuriously adopted local team ('Go Node 4-Giordana!'). The hyperactive stewards. The RAF crews who volunteer to help out for the week. The policemen on their motorbikes who close the roads. The motorists who sit at T-junctions and wait patiently for the insanity to pass. All this, I love.

We always go to Stoke-on-Trent. It's an unwritten rule. It's a hard city, battered by macro- and microeconomics, ruined by successive generations of town planners. At its heart is Hanley, perched on top of a hill, with a richly carved Victorian town hall gazing out in dismay at the messily composed dog's dinner of concrete precincts and tower blocks that surround it. Those who know Stoke well are appropriately fond of it, with its canals and hills and pound shops and kebab joints. Those who see it with an outsider's eye, like the Dutch rider Lars Boom did in 2011, can feel humbled by its obvious plight. 'I want to win here,' he told the race organisers. 'I want to put on a show for the people who live here. I think they don't have it so easy.'

He did, and then he went on to win the overall race.

Each day, and for good financial reasons, the Tour of Britain highlights show is contractually bound to include a short sequence of shots from whichever region we are in. After all, the local authorities put up a good deal of money, and want something back for their sponsorship. These thirty-second clips, it goes without saying, are an onerous obligation, both for viewer and for presenter. They invariably include shots of a clock tower, a pedestrianised shopping centre, a church, a canal, someone flying a kite, eating al fresco in a pub garden, and riding through a park with some kids. That kind of thing.

When I first started on the Tour of Britain, I tried to distance myself from these clips by being a smart-arse. In my voice over, I'd concoct arch little phrases, and sarcastic little quips to accompany the stream of touristy schmaltz being paraded across the screen. 'Gosh, windsurfing!' Or 'Oh look, a horse!' I did this in order to withdraw myself from the process, a knowing wink, a post-modern nod to an audience that I imagined felt similarly uncomfortable with being force-fed the mantra of a regional development agency.

It didn't endear me greatly to the Tour direction, the men charged with raising the money from the regions to get the race on.

I couldn't keep it up, though. I started to bore myself. Year on year, my metropolitan knowingness gave way to a nobler intent, until I reached the point where I now happily embrace the simple, wholesome script I've been handed. I have become their mouthpiece. I am happy to sell you any county you care to mention. Insert the name of your town into the paragraph, and off I go:

'Dating back to the sixteenth century, the town of XXXXXXXXX has always enjoyed a thriving town centre. Its peaceful parkland and thriving town centre offer the perfect location for a weekend break or a family holiday. First-class recreational facilities, and a thriving town centre mean that there's never a dull moment. XXXXXXXXX's thriving town centre blends traditional values with a modern, thriving town centre.'

The race does its best to get around the country in the eight days allotted to it. We've variously been to Norfolk, Devon,

Liverpool, Gateshead, the Borders, Wales, Somerset and Essex during my years on the race, and many more places besides. The locations vary in their characteristics, as much as cloud follows sun, follows cloud, blown horizontally across the island by September's prevailing westerlies. The quaintness of the South-West with its painted cottages and rose gardens couldn't be further removed from the South Promenade at Blackpool (another perennial favourite), out of season and underpopulated. But all these strips of tarmac make up the tapestry.

Local hills come to prominence, and are spoken about with reverent hush and awe, as if we were invoking the names of deities. Constitution Hill in Swansea, Gun Hill near Stoke, Shap Fell in the Lakes and Caerphilly Mountain. I have learned that in the hearts of the British cycling community who pound up and down our lanes, these carry as much mythical significance as the Tourmalet does to the French.

People often come up to me, and without a word of introduction, but with an evil glint and a head cocked to one side, they'll say things like 'Bar Hatch'll sort them out, I reckon.'

Will it? And, have we actually ever met?

The Race Manual testifies to these obscure, sometimes unloved locations, putting down in black-and-white print the extraordinary banality of the race route. The epic, unmasked for what it is; just a humdrum sort of place.

'2nd Intermediate Sprint: 68.2 k, opposite ASDA.'

'3rd Intermediate Sprint: 97.4k, between Harvester Pub and ESSO Station.'

Even the signage suffers from an identity crisis, borrowing language from the Tour de France and translating it straight into English. Red signs, hanging from lampposts, point the way the team buses and other Tour traffic should follow so that they can park up at the stage start, or 'Depart' as it is called on these signs. Not 'Départ', you understand, the French noun with its acute accent. The English word 'Depart' is the imperative form of the verb 'to depart'. It's an order, and rather an abrupt one at that.

One man sits at the helm of all of this. Mick Bennett. He is the race director, the man who decides who races and what the race looks like. Every day you will see him stalking the finish line in a hi-vis jacket, ensuring the barriers are perfectly aligned and that the press are marshalled to within an inch of their lives. He rules with absolute power.

I had no idea, when we were first introduced, that he'd been a talented rider, that he'd represented his country, that he'd won an Olympic bronze medal in the Team Pursuit at the Munich games of 1972, and again in Montreal in 1976. At first, I took him for a cantankerous curmudgeon who just happened to be in charge of the Tour of Britain. What I least expected was that he and I would become friends, which, via a circuitous route, is what we've become.

Friend is overstating it, perhaps. Mick and I seldom text each other; he is almost exactly twenty years my senior, and pretends not to understand things like mobile phones and emails. He has a certain amount of enemies or, more accurately, people with whom he has fallen out. It's hard to gain his trust. He's an ex-rider, and they're almost all a bit suspicious and, in Mick's case, pathologically defensive when it comes to the media. By nature, he's guarded. He has a well-founded reputation for autocracy. He can be off-hand, imperious, unreasonable, even ungracious. The race is his, and must run to his rules. He and I have crossed each other often enough. Or rather, I have crossed him.

But I like Mick a great deal.

The more I speak to British riders, whether they are from the online here and now, or from the black-and-white yesteryear, the more I detect a commonality. They tend to brood. Accustomed to passing endless hours trapped in their interior monologues, with only the whirr of ball bearings and the swish of rubber on tarmac to accompany them, they often betray the signs of a fundamental unease with their circumstances, as if reinventing their physiologies day by day at the coal face of a punishing bike ride will somehow release them from who they are and what they are faced with. From the cards they've been dealt.

This is not, perhaps, uniquely British. The badge of honour that suffering bestows on the professional bike rider is the minimum requirement for entry into their elusive club. To hurt is to be. That much is clear.

But on these islands our small clutch of pros have it harder than most. Even now, when the wider public has suddenly started to embrace the sport, they battle daily against ridicule, isolation, incomprehension and the occasional assassination attempt. It's not just the white vans and rogue cars that try to force them off the road (Bradley Wiggins and Shane Sutton), not just the tiresome puddles and potholes and the jostling for space at traffic lights. It extends beyond their lonely training rides, into their everyday world. The pro-cyclist, on admitting to his profession in the pub or at dinner with friends, will be counting down an internal clock until the inevitable question is asked, with a sneer and a chuckle. 'Why do you shave your legs? Is it more aerodynamic?' They have their answers honed to perfection, and are scarcely aware of responding.

It takes determination, and a very thick skin to fly so obdurately in the face of the prevailing culture. Perhaps it also requires a particular sort of motivation.

I wanted to know Mick Bennett away from race day. So I made an appointment, went to his office, sat down opposite him and waited to see if I could find out what forces had shaped him; what motivated the motivator, or better still: what agitated the agitator?

I squinted at him. The sun shone through some slatted blinds directly behind him, so that I was not so much looking at the director of the Tour of Britain, as at a black-and-white cut-out of the director of the Tour of Britain.

I offered up my opening line of enquiry.

'Mick, so many of the riders seem to tell me the same story, that as a child they got on their bikes to put distance between themselves and something that they wanted to run away from—'

I am interrupted. 'Can I just stop you there. That's absolutely spot on.'

Our early years working together were characterised by a certain mistrust. He thought I was a bit of an upstart, and couldn't get a handle on my instinctive desire to raise an inquisitive eyebrow wherever I felt it needed raising. In 2008, for example, he'd invited Tyler Hamilton, who would later blow the whistle on Lance Armstrong, to come and ride for the Rock Racing team: a villainous assembly of dopers, ex-dopers and serial deniers, who traded heavily on their 'bad boy' image. I wanted to ask Hamilton all sorts of difficult questions, Mick wasn't so sure.

Perhaps he's just given up on me. But for whatever reason, these days, he just lets me get on with it, and seldom interferes. Except where money is involved.

Once, during the 2012 Tour of Britain, I won a bet I had struck with him. I was staggeringly right. And he was appallingly wrong. I can see steam coming out of his ears as he reads this now. But if he examines his heart, he'll know I'm correct.

The previous day, trying to predict what time the race would finish (a very necessary skill, especially when it comes to TV schedules), I had shaken hands with Mick Bennett. I'd predicted the winner would finish at 15.05, and he'd gone for 15.10. We wagered ten pounds on the outcome, nearest time wins.

When Mark Cavendish eventually crossed the line in Blackpool, it was exactly 15.06.27. I know this. It is precise to the microsecond, because we cross-referenced a shot of him finishing against the time code in the TV truck. That 'time of day' code is accurate to a tiny fraction of a second. It is the international standard.

You might infer from that, that I had clearly won the bet.

But the next day, Mick was still refusing to pay. He'd consulted the finish-line judge (an old mate from years gone by, no doubt), and between them, they'd concocted some bizarre calculation involving average speeds, the movement of the tides, the influence of Halley's comet and relative tyre pressures on Cavendish's bike, and produced a work of utter fiction, to which Mick was still clinging. (A little childishly, I thought. And told him.)

'You've bloody colluded with the guys in the TV truck, Ned. Bloody conspiracy. He came in at 15.09, and you know he did.'

He was smiling, just. So I thought we were still 'joshing'.

'If I give you my sort code and account number, you can send it to me over the Internet, if that makes it easier, Mick.'

He looked sternly at me, and then broke into a very sudden, very unsettling attack of laughter. At the same time, he cuffed me 'playfully' around the back of my head, nearly breaking my neck. I can still feel the bruising.

'Ha ha ha ha,' he laughed at me, loudly and robotically. 'You cheating bastard.'

He stomped off into Stoke, without paying up. And that was the last time I saw him that day.

And now Mick Bennett was pointing a pencil at me. It had been sharpened to a murderous degree. He's a trim, upright silver-haired man in his early sixties. He has an intense stare, and a cautious delivery edged with an accent that bears witness, just about, to his Birmingham upbringing.

Mick was born in 1949. 'I'm from a very poor background. No hot water. No bathroom.' His story was not uncommon in that regard, but nonetheless remarkable.

'Where did you grow up, Mick?'

'Spark Brook.' That rang a bell. It was a curious sounding neighbourhood. Like Tower Hamlets, or Westward Ho!, it sounded like the careless working title that some junior draughtsman in the town planning department had dreamt up over a cup of tea.

'I was given a bike by my next-door neighbour when I was young, and it saved my whole life. It was as if someone had gone, "There you are. That's changing your life."'

Mick was miming someone handing over a gift, imparting a treasure, stretching his arms across the table at me.

Just then, his BlackBerry suddenly chirruped on the desk at his side. Without even minutely averting his gaze from where it was fixed across the space at me, he deftly reached out with his left hand, switched it off, and returned his outstretched arm to the point where his neighbour had just handed him his life-changing bike. I was transfixed, and very nearly reached across the empty space to receive the notional bike.

As he recalled his childhood, I saw a landscape of brick-work, gutters, washing out in the backyards; all the post-war clichés made poignant by the reality of their existence. And I saw Mick, out on his BSA bike, rattling over the cobbles. 'One day I stopped this guy, this Graham Webb, and he said, "Come round to my house", which was two streets away from my house.'

Graham Webb. So, half a century ago, Mick Bennett and he had been neighbours!

'I knocked on his door. And I went into this "two-up two-down" like all the terraced houses were, and he showed me a laundry bag full of medals and he put them on.'

I pictured the two of them. Graham, maybe eighteen years old, proud of his haul, but modest enough to keep them bundled up in a laundry bag. Perhaps he would have found it hard to look for praise, for recognition among his peers. But maybe he'd discovered a kindred spirit. Mick, at thirteen, was still too young to be a threat or to pass judgement. And so here was an audience, his singular audience. In that upstairs room, the older boy could feel like the champion he was becoming, and the younger boy could soak it all up. It was a moment fitted to both needs perfectly. For every rider, embedded in the narrative of their careers, there is a definable Eureka moment. Mick had just experienced his.

'This is what I want to be. This is what I want.'

What followed was, by the standards of almost all of us, quite exceptional.

He became a track rider. He was very good at it, winning races, and competing nationally and internationally at the highest of levels. Those two Olympic medals testify to that. But we judge men like Mick Bennett not in isolation, but against the achievements of others, unfairly perhaps, and he would acknowledge that he was not the greatest, and although he was conscientious, solid, dependable and valued, he did not tear up the record books.

He had a fastidious nature that earned him respect and affectionate mockery in equal measure; beautifully turned out, manicured almost. A 'softy' as a noisy incoming generation of road racers, like John Herety, would have described him. In fact that's exactly how John affectionately describes him when I ask him what Mick was like. He had an easy-going nature, and took things with good heart.

One day that all changed. It was the day he stopped racing forever.

In 1984 at the age of thirty-five, Mick and his fiancée

Mandy had bought an old house together, which they were renovating. Financially, it was a bottomless pit, and they were permanently flirting with solvency issues. Mandy was fretting about money, and Mick had just finished riding in the now defunct French race, the Etoile des Espoirs. But, as she delighted in telling Mick over the phone to the South of France, they'd had a little windfall.

The BBC had finally paid up for his appearance on *Superteams*, an offshoot of the now legendary *Superstars*. They had money in their account, for a change.

'I said, "Why don't you fly out? We'll have a holiday after-wards,"' Mick tells me.

And so she did. They embarked on a week's driving holiday. They were just near to Châteauroux, where they were going to meet up with his new teammate John Herety, and his future wife, Margaret, when their sponsored Peugeot car was hit, side-on by a French couple on a motorbike.

'Mandy was killed, and I was the only one left alive in the accident.'

'Did he tell you that?'

John Herety is surprised, when I speak to him later by telephone. 'I don't think we've ever spoken about it since. I don't remember ever speaking about it.'

John is a stocky, warm, amiable and completely bald Mancunian from Cheadle. A trained chef (just like Mick Bennett, curiously) he rode in the 1980 Olympic Road Race, and had a long career which yielded a National Road Race title. After his racing career, he went into coaching, at one time as British Cycling's race director. He resigned from that post in 2005 after allegations that two of Britain's repre-sentatives in the World Championships, Tom Southam and Charly Wegelius, sold their loyalty to the Italian national team. Since then, John has managed the über-cool Rapha Condor team. For some time now, he has been operating right at the heart of the British domestic scene.

My phone call has just taken him back almost thirty years in time. And I can hear from his voice, that it's caught him slightly off guard.

But he remembers clearly. 'They went off on a week-long trip. About sixty kilometres from where they were going to meet me and Margaret, they changed driving positions. Mandy started driving. On the way from Châteauroux to Tours, they saw one last chateau. As she was turning round in the road, a motorbike came speeding over the brow of a hill. It went straight into the car door and killed her instantly. Mick was admitted straight to hospital.

'Mandy loved France. She wanted to visit all the chateaux.'

Mick Bennett spent a week in Châteauroux hospital, recovering from wounds that instantly ended his racing career. Then he returned to Britain, and slowly started a new life. He has since married, and has a family.

Châteauroux. Why does that place name keep recurring?

There is an affectation, which was briefly fashionable among the chattering classes, for a 'science' called psychogeography. It's all about psychological ley lines, the meaning in maps, the spiritual meta-text of places, and their mysterious alignment to history. I used to think it was nonsense. And it probably is.

But then, Châteauroux would suggest otherwise. And, having visited it often in the course of my duties, I am strangely affected to hear its beautifully wrought name crop up again in the life story of another British cyclist.

Bradley Wiggins in 2011, arm in a sling, swaying slightly and woozy with morphine, talking to me in the car park of Châteauroux hospital, his Tour ended by a broken collarbone. Mark Cavendish, on the very same day, winning for the seventeenth time. Back home, Mick Bennett would have been watching on TV.

Three years previously, Mark Cavendish, in the dark blue of Columbia's 2008 kit, fists clenched in wonderment, crossing the line in Châteauroux to take his first ever stage win on the Tour de France.

Once again, Mick Bennett was at home, watching. And, without a shadow of doubt, cheering.

It's the flip side of Mick Bennett. The one that, for all his occasional bluster, is too rarely glimpsed. But I've seen him taking time out in the middle of the most hectic part of the day to return a free sponsor's flag that some kid has dropped on the road. Then he'll spend more time than you might think talking to the youngster, until, with a ruffle of their hair, he's off to make the race work. When he looks at the future, he has one eye on the past.

'Now it seems the heart's almost gone out of it.'

Mick squints at me from behind his desk. It is obvious where this conversation is heading. The march on progress has stolen the joy. The spirit is in danger of being bludgeoned out of the sport. Mick Bennett, despite his reputation, is capable of disarming sentimentality, an affliction that I suffer from too.

'As a kid, I just had this passion and this yearning to get out on my bike because it was a release. It was independence. I could go twenty or thirty miles on this bike and get away from it. I suddenly realised, and it was like a bolt of lightning: my God, I'm thirty miles from home in this countryside and it's incredible. It's amazing. I am in complete control of my destiny. It was the start of a journey that I'm still on.'

Mark Cavendish is a favoured son of Mick Bennett. Mick's eyes light up when he talks about him. Every year, regardless of which team Cavendish is riding for, Mick goes out of his way to cajole, persuade and ensure the Manxman's participation in his race.

'Cavendish is fantastic. That's what I call a professional bike rider. Because it's in here.' He thumps his heart. 'He genuinely can attach himself to the other side of the barrier. He's a bit old school.

'He's the best in the world at what he does. But that was how he started. He felt that independence and that freedom. And I wonder how many kids have got that. And that's why he's pissed off and he's passionate, because it's from here.' He points, again, demonstratively at his heart.

'It's almost as if that bit has gone somewhere. And I don't seem to see it anywhere else now.'

On the last day of the 2012 Tour of Britain, Mark Cavendish, who had suffered like a dog for a week through wet and wild hills and a terrain that punished him every day, rode up the cobbled high street of Guildford for the last time in his cherished Rainbow Jersey. With two hundred metres left to race, he'd torn an unbridgeable gap in the bunch, and had time to look over his shoulder, sit up and coast into a wall of jubilant noise.

The crowd had stood ten deep all day waiting for just this moment. It placed a perfect full stop at the end of an extraordinary summer.

No longer was the Tour of Britain an oddity, a quirky secret, an irritation to the flow of traffic and a financial basket case. The mainstream, for better or worse, had washed in.

'We're on a tidal wave of support for cycling. We are pushing on open doors.'

I put it to Mick that he's sometimes not as hard-nosed as people think he is. 'You're quite sentimental,' I tell him.

'I am.'

Then I make a confession. I admit that, driving past the dozens of primary schools on the route of the Tour of Britain, whose children have been lined up to watch the race go past, all cheering, I sometimes start welling up.

'I do! I do, too, Ned!' And his eyes, now I look, are watery. We both sit there in his office, surprised by each other and surprised by ourselves.

There came a moment on the 2012 Tour of Britain, when I knew that I had finally, perhaps definitively, been accepted into the bosom of the British cycling family. Interestingly, it happened standing on the top of a truck in Stoke-on-Trent, which is not the place you normally would start when you are trying to track down rites of passage.

I was standing (on the truck's roof) in front of a camera, a microphone in one hand, and touching an earpiece with the other. To my right, bolt upright, and deferring to me, stood one of British cycling's most grizzly hard men, Rob Hayles, a rough geezer, by outward appearance, with the slow heart rate of a Buddhist monk. The recently retired former World Champion and Olympic bronze medallist was as popular on the roads of this country as any man who has ridden a bike in anger over recent years. I was somewhat in awe of him. We were both concentrating hard, as the voice in the truck below counted down to our 'on air' time.

'One minute left on the break.'

Rob momentarily broke his pose. I could see from the corner of my eye, that something had caught his attention. He was staring intently at me, or more specifically, at my nose.

'What?'

'Thirty seconds to on air.'

With great care, Rob reached out towards my face and gently, almost lovingly, stroked the end of my nose with the back of his hand. I watched on, wide-eyed.

He withdrew his hand. 'There. That's better.'

'What, Rob?'

'A bogey, Ned.' We both looked down, and sure enough, a small offending crust still clung to the back of his non-microphone hand.

'. . . in ten, nine, eight, seven . . .'

'Thanks, Rob.'

'Pleasure.' And with the merest hint of a frown, we both assumed our on-air smiles.

Just out of shot, and with great subtlety, Rob Hayles, shook his left hand free of its encumbrance.

But as for me? I knew I had arrived on the Tour of Britain.

'. . . . cue Ned.'

'Hello, and welcome to Stoke-on-Trent.'

CHAPTER 5

SOMETHING TO MAKE YOU CHANGE YOUR MIND

I hold my hands up. This book is not even slightly comprehensive. Without justification, or remorse, it ignores shamefully large swathes of the country. The heart of my cycling experience resides elsewhere.

My story pays only lip service to the Union-Jack waving melodrama of the velodrome, skirts the Olympics (haven't we heard enough about them?), only occasionally mentions the Tour de France and leaves BMX racing and cyclo-cross entirely alone to entertain those who understand their peculiar appeals. And, just as it also fails to engage with the important and hugely successful women's cycling scene, so it becomes clear that I am writing with only one particular type of bike rider in mind: me.

Not only that, but it is a story generated in a particular place (London) for a particular audience. Me, again.

Cycling connects the dreamer with the expert practitioner. On my bike, I could be, in my own deluded imagination, a little like the champions I had met, and continued to meet. That's why I found myself drawn over and over again to the same sort of men (and they were, exclusively, men).

The more I bored down into what I sought to understand, the narrower the hole became. But it was no less rich a seam for that.

My own personal history with the bicycle is unremarkable, and features a considerable time out, during which Margaret

Thatcher stepped down from power, the Eastern bloc collapsed and Take That came and went. I think Mickey Rourke's pre-comeback career fitted neatly into that void, too.

Before that, some indeterminate time after the end of the Second World War, but before *The X Factor*, I clearly remember standing with my dad in a back garden in Bedford frowning at a skinny blue aluminium bike that some bloke was flogging for fifty quid. Dad had read a small ad in the *Bedfordshire on Sunday*. It was to be my birthday present.

'This bike was used in the Tour de France, you know.' The bloke in the back garden was perspiring in the July heat, or maybe because he was lying through his teeth.

He seemed very authoritative, very knowledgeable, as he hauled it out of his shed and leant it against a wall. Dad and I were impressed, as much with ourselves for knowing that there was a bike race called the Tour de France as with the bike itself.

'Really?' Dad looked at the machine in muted wonder. He pinched the back tyre, testing all-knowingly for pressure. Once again, I was impressed, this time with Dad, for knowing stuff about tyre pressure.

'How about forty-eight?' Dad said, and the deal was done with an instant handshake. He was good at haggling, too. I noticed how very suddenly the bloke had stopped perspiring.

It was a great bike, though. I rode it for many years. Even after it had grown fractionally too small for me, I still loved it, and went to college with it. Then I promptly got it nicked, swapped it for a pizza or set fire to it as an act of genre-breaking installation art, I forget how it went.

But that was that for me and bikes for a long, long while.

I left college, moved abroad, drifted around, ran up debts, phoned home for help, then came and settled in London, not knowing where else to go, nor what else to do. Eventually, circuitously, fortuitously, miraculously, just as middle age was finding me, I found the bike again. Luckily.

This renewal of acquaintances followed only after I had been introduced to the Tour de France. That was ITV's fault. It's normally the other way round, of course: first comes the passion for cycling, then the interest in the Tour. But with childlike simplicity, having spent a month watching young men ride bicycles unnaturally fast, I decided, on my return to these shores, that I needed a bit of the action, too.

So I went to Harry Perry's in Woolwich and came out with a mountain bike designed, as its genus suggests, for mountains. The fact that Woolwich and its environs presented nothing more challenging than a gentle slope down Thomas Street to the ferry seemed not to cross my mind. I liked the bike's bulk and the proper heft of its chunky tyres. It felt serious, appropriate. Its dead weight was made even more unequivocal by the addition of a day-glo orange child's seat attached to the seat tube.

I sat unhappily on this thing, all the while trying to convince myself that I was enjoying the experience, my thirty-something legs feeling themselves back into some sort of usefulness after a decade of sedentary motorway miles (my pursuit of a career in sports reporting had taken me up and down the M1, but it had not done much for my cardiovascular system).

Nonetheless I enjoyed the views of the lower reaches of the Thames as I rumbled along the riverside path. It was the movement that made it all worthwhile, a cold wind forcing water from the corners of my eyes; the sounds, even the smells (there are dog food and syrup factories nearby – a heady mix).

I used to ride along a twenty-minute waterfront stretch from my old house in Woolwich to the Underground station at North Greenwich. This is a long, ostensibly ugly reach of very tidal river, not the prettified riverside setting so beloved of ramblers further upstream where the Thames tickles Berkshire. There are no quaint pubs, nor creaking locks to negotiate.

Instead there are industrial units, a giant concrete-clad storage depot for Sainsbury's, mysterious, villainous pubs. Fred's Wood Workshop used to stand along the river, next to his son's metal yard. Cory Barges still go about their business, letting fly sparks as they cut and weld their floating stock, the barges that carry garbage from the City to the incinerators. Along this wide stretch of river, shingle and gravel from the sea bed are brought to shore and sifted into their constituent parts. Rusty conveyor belts rumble overhead as dredgers are unloaded. Their cargoes hold the dank smell of the North Sea's greyish depths. Now and then, the footpath silts up with lifeless sand, carelessly dropped from the boats.

Here, the river is broad, tidal and grey. At high tide it comes rushing towards London, slowed only by the silvery buttresses of the Thames Barrier and cut in two by the churning of the Woolwich ferry, whose two boats criss-cross the river in perfectly executed synchronicity, thundering their old diesel engines against the ebb and flow as they hold their position on the river. Built in 1963, they are great anachronisms, with names like *Ernest Bevin*, and *John Burns*, who led the great Dock Strike of 1889, and coined the marvellous phrase 'The Thames is liquid history'.

One day, someone will connect the North Circular to the South Circular road by building a giant new bridge, and the ferry will stop running forever. But in the meantime, this was the awe-inspiring backdrop to my earliest commute on a bike.

Some friends from Paris came to stay with us once. We lent their teenage daughter and her boyfriend some bikes, and suggested they rode this stretch of the Thames Path and that we'd meet them in the beautiful surroundings of Greenwich Park for a picnic. They set off full of youthful verve. By the time they reached us all waiting by the Royal

Observatory, their faces had clouded over. They had found the experience, in their words, 'apocalyptique', 'dégolace'.

They were right, in their own way, the little Parisian prigs. The dull sweep of the estuary with its prosaic surrounds happens to be a source of constant wonder to me. But, if you are used to pinching aubergines for ripeness, scribbling poetry and sniffing flowers amidst the prettiness of the rue Mouffetard in Paris, then you are a long way from your comfort zone when you are cycling through Charlton. London is a brute, frankly.

My ride left behind the industrial remnants of the working river, and as the Greenwich peninsula drew its shape ahead of me, so too did the toy-town architecture of the Millennium Village, and its centrepiece, the Dome. That was my final destination. From there I would hop onto the Tube.

It was, I guess, about three miles, all in all. It was a great revalation to me that a bike ride on this scale was even possible.

I rode it, at a very gentle pace, in something like a quarter of an hour. And, arriving slightly breathless, I padlocked the bike and made my way underground, feeling glowing and virtuous. Within minutes, I was whisked into Central London.

Back at the station though, and while I was up in town working, my bike did not fare well. Malevolent forces went to work, picking over its aluminium carcass, harvesting the usable parts. Time after time I would return to find my lights missing, the saddle gone, a wheel nicked. Each time this happened, I would take the bike back to the workmanlike setting of Harry Perry's with increasing malaise.

'I need a new saddle.'

He would look up from whatever bike was upside down in front of him. 'Not again. Can't you leave it somewhere else?'

'There is nowhere else.'

One week, and one new saddle later.

'Back again, then, Ned?' He put down his spanner and wiped his hands on a cloth, as if he were a barman in a French bar, not a mechanic in Woolwich.

'Why would anyone try and steal handlebars?' I wheeled in my decapitated bike.

He sighed and shook his head.

And then, he said it. Life-changing words, muttered innocently over a till as he racked up the price of the new set of handlebars.

'Why don't you just ride all the way into London? It's not that far.'

Was the man insane? I had an instant vision of vast distance, like a Dalí landscape, an unreachable horizon. This was a journey of such prodigious length that it needed to be executed by subterranean electric trains, hurtling along at great speed through the blind, dark tunnels underneath London's sprawling mass, and overhead, mile after mile of Victorian streets blindly flashing by. It was an act of faith and hydraulics. It was not something you could accomplish by bike. That much, surely, was obvious.

'Eight miles, door to door. Take you forty minutes.' He picked up his tools and returned his attention to the job in hand, leaving me gaping in the doorway to his shop, with the shape of my life already, imperceptibly changing.

My first trip into Central London by bike was my Road to Damascus. Actually, it was the road to Bermondsey, but I wasn't going to be fussy. It didn't take the predicted forty minutes, I was too slow for that back then, and besides, the half-deflated, heavy tread of my mountain bike tyres made the ride feel like driving a car with the handbrake still half-engaged. But it was a huge adventure.

On returning home late that afternoon, I felt as if my legs would seize up forever. They ached in a way that they had never ached before, my thigh muscles, my calves and lots of nameless tiny little fibres that make the joints bend. My body had been stunned into usage. I sat down on the toilet, as the bathtub filled, and then didn't have the strength to stand up unaided, having instead to fall off sideways and crawl to the bath, so I could haul myself up from floor level.

Then, washed and pomaded, and slightly full of myself, I sat at the head of the family dinner table, and held court on my considerable accomplishment. I kept my audience in thrall, like a solo polar explorer in human company for the first time in six months. I had seen things which required a telling. I had wrestled metaphorical bears, and vanquished them. My family hung on my every word.

'The remarkable thing is it's actually not that bad once you're past Deptford. I suppose you even get to go through that bit of Surrey Quays which you normally can't drive up around the one-way system and there's a cycle lane the whole way through and actually the traffic could be worse and did you know about Southwark Park? Well, that's a whole thing in itself, never been there before and there's a bandstand and tennis courts and an art gallery right in the middle of it and you can turn left onto Tower Bridge, which cars can't do, and then when you're coming back you can stop off outside the Cutty Sark and grab a coffee without worrying about your bike because there's an open air café . . .'

My eldest daughter shrugged. My youngest banged a plastic spoon on the table and grinned at me toothlessly.

An awkward silence fell across the family table, and then they started talking about something else. I was left alone with my thoughts, which were now mostly played out in the muted pastel shades of an A to Z map.

London had opened up to me. The city that I had called home for the important part of my adult life had started to make a different kind of sense, and pose questions in entirely unexpected ways. And it did this, I understood, simply because of the movement of a bicycle.

My wonderment at the human body's ability to propel itself eight miles there and eight miles back was only the start. It wasn't long before my desire for greater bicycle-related adventure led me to embark on ever more ridiculous journeys. I upgraded my bike, buying a second-hand Shogun aluminium thing with a Campagnolo chain set, and allowed the Saracen to give itself over to rust under a tree in the garden.

The Shogun was a game-changer. I loved that bike with risible ardour. It cost me £350, and when it finally succumbed to a hairline fracture and had to be dismantled six years later, I honestly felt like I had lost a friend. It was skinny, gold and fast.

I fitted it with normal pedals at first. Then I bought some pedals with toe straps. Then I went the whole hog and bought cycling shoes with cleats. Naturally, I succumbed to a catalogue of slapstick tumbles while I got used to riding 'clipped in'. The silliest of these involved turning right in front of three lanes of traffic on London Bridge, realising that they had the green light, trying to stop, and slowly falling sideways onto the tarmac, locked to the bike and smiling apologetically all the while. I lay on the tarmac for some time, blocking the entirety of London's southbound traffic heading over London Bridge, before my feet finally wriggled free and I was able to exit the scene, chastened and bruised.

Most of the miles I clocked up over the happy six years my Shogun and I shared together were ridden around London. Rarely did we venture out. Once we rode around the Scottish borders for a few undulating miles, and on another occasion we rode in and out of Edinburgh from my parents' house near Livingston. Both times, I found the lack of traffic, the noise-lessness and isolation of the country road unsettling. Left alone with just the act of turning pedals and pushing onwards, I found my mind wouldn't settle. It couldn't break free from the narrow confines of the act. There weren't enough distractions. I needed a Ladbrokes and a Costcutter's within arm's reach.

No, London, with its ever-changing backdrop, its appalling dangers and its thousands of fried chicken shops and hair salons, was my cycling Nirvana. I enjoyed the cut and thrust and puncture, the elbows-at-the-ready nastiness and surprising camaraderie of the commute. I developed instincts for the rogue left-turning white van who overtook you simply to cut you up. I became wary of pedestrians, one of whom had stepped into my path and sent me to hospital with concussion. None of it deterred me though. The city drew me in. I am never more content, more distant from my everyday neuroses, than when I am perching on my saddle between the throbbing scarlet flank of a Number 53 bus and a parked black cab, or jostling for room alongside delivery vans and courier motorbikes in the green space reserved for cyclists at junctions.

Riding a bike over many years around a city as vast and intricate as London is like being a spider spinning a web. Scuttling off in every possible direction, leaving a silken trace of memory where it has been. For me, those traces connect Lewisham with Wembley, Richmond with Canning Town, Hammersmith with Croydon.

Like so many other London men and women of a certain age, I have discovered the unreserved joy of pushing past the capital's great, wind-picked water on a bright spring morning, or riding in the early-onset gloom of a November dusk through Hyde Park to London Bridge to see the hubris of the Shard tower rising month by month, or watch the shifting scenery, the shop fronts renovated, burnt out, gentrified, or boarded up for ever.

Few cities open up to the bike like London does.

*   *   *

The riding grew stranger, more niche. It became organised, almost becoming a pastime. Things were morphing fast into something new, and, as my curiosity grew, so London's sweeps and curves, lumps and bumps continued to amaze.

In the spring of 2011, I was invited by some complete strangers to take part in a gentle Sunday ride known as the London Classic. It was a bizarre London homage to the Belgian Classics, those one-day road races that invariably feature sharp climbs and long stretches of cobbles. After briefly scanning their website and watching a cheerful little film all about the 2010 edition of the ride ('The Bone-Shaking Cobbles and The Lung-Busting Hills'), I contacted them back and gratefully accepted their invitation. It sounded fun. Sort of.

So one crisp Sunday morning, I rode over, with my friend Simon, to the pub in Crystal Palace where we were all to meet. We arrived too early. They were just setting out the trestle tables and starting to fry bacon. We drank a coffee and watched the organisers of the London Classic go about their work. They had entry forms to set out, race numbers to pin on jerseys and souvenir stickers for the bikes. They were secretly enjoying the administrative banality of it, while giving off the impression that they would rather have been anywhere else. I liked them. As they tut-tutted and joked with each other, I wondered how many other disparate hobbies were being pursued that morning (with tut-tutting and trestle tables) up and down this country of tut-tutting hobbyists.

When eventually we set off, we dropped down into Central London through Dulwich and Brixton. That much was fairly straightforward. Then, after crossing the river, the route became tortuous. Somewhere near Covent Garden it started going crazy, doubling back, looping round, zig-zagging and circling: doing nothing that so much as resembled a straight line for anything more than a hundred yards.

There was a reason for this. The organisation had scoured images of London on Google Earth for signs of cobbles. And everywhere they found them, they routed the ride. Little arrows were pinned on lampposts all along the thirty-seven miles. Some sections of pavé were only a few metres long. Others, such as those in Wapping, were a few hundred. All in all there were twenty-six sectors of cobbles (graded from one star to five), and seven 'bergs', short, sharp climbs up and away from the river as we headed back to Crystal Palace. They bore iconic names: Maze Hill, Gypsy Hill, Honor Oak.

At the fearsome Vicar's Hill (a Category Two climb), my family came out to cheer me on, it being just around the corner from my house.

This was a big moment for me. My home turf, my family out to honour me as I passed. How many times had I seen this enacted on the Tour? The local hero riding off the front of an indulgent peloton and into the bosom of his family at the roadside. But that's not quite how it happened.

Simon (an actor who you may remember from his defining role in a Bananabix advert which aired briefly in 1997), had the audacity to attack. It was an unforgivable breach of cycling etiquette. The jobbing thespian, whose stagecraft had helped to shift a banana-based cereal, crested the summit before me, and drew cheers and whoops from my turncoat children.

And then it all went wrong for the theatrical artist. From my perspective, a few dozen metres behind him on the climb, I was delighted to see him slow down to take the applause, lose balance and fall in a ghastly sideways arc towards the road before he could unclip his shoes. He landed with no dignity left to his name in front of my children. The cycling gods had exacted an instant and terrible revenge. By the time I lumbered to the top, my family had stopped laughing at Simon and were looking rather pityingly at my effort. In case I needed a reality check, the looks on their faces told me that

I wasn't in fact racing the Tour of Flanders. I was wasting a Sunday morning in the company of a bunch of South London misfits pretending to be somebody else, somewhere else.

But no matter. I loved it all. It was a ride masquerading as a race, an eccentric nod to one of cycling's great Continental institutions, executed with perfect earnest, British, dottiness.

I instigated still bigger and bolder adventures within the M25. Sometimes I had to dream them up. Sometimes they were breath-taking in their simple-mindedness. The eighty-odd miles it took me to visit every football ground in the capital was a high-tide mark in futility.

At each ground (Crystal Palace, Fulham, Brentford, Chelsea, Arsenal, Tottenham, Barnet, Leyton Orient, West Ham, Millwall and Charlton; in that order), I self-consciously took a picture of myself to prove that I'd done it. It took me hours and hours to complete the loop.

Somewhere in Edmonton, I bonked (cycling-speak for ran out of energy), staggered into a newsagent and stuffed two Turkish Delights straight into my mouth before I'd even paid for them. I had to sit down on the pavement for a minute or two after that while the world turned into a pink chocolate-coated jelly. Barnet nearly killed me. And by Leyton Orient, I had given up looking for back routes, and ended up ploughing down the A12, buffeted by the passing turbulence from three lanes of thundering trucks.

Eventually, but hours later than I had imagined I would, I arrived home exuberant. I swiftly uploaded the photos, and emailed the whole series to my dad on the bizarre assumption that my adventure might somehow impress him. I was in my forties. Other things might have impressed him, but not that.

He replied by email the next day.

'Where's QPR?'

*   *   *

But I am not alone. The madness is not mine alone. In fact, I would hazard a guess that I am only mildly afflicted.

The last time I rode over Lambeth Bridge at 8.45 in the morning, I burst out in spontaneous laughter. Three self-organising lines of cyclists, each ten bikes long had formed at a set of traffic lights. Each rider failed openly to acknowledge the absurdity of this event. No one nodded at anyone in recognition, nor in wonder at the sight of so many other like-minded cyclists on the road. But one by one, and a little po-faced, the commuters took their place in this new pageant, becoming a very British affair. The 'slow lane' for hire bikes, heavy mountain bikes and Brompton folding bikes, the 'middle lane' for fixies and hybrids, and the 'fast lane' for white middle-aged men on carbon-fibre bikes worth more than their houses. The cars didn't stand a chance. It was remarkable. People are remarkable.

Something good has happened here in London, which perhaps has found an equal reflection in towns and cities the length and breadth of the country: the number of people using bikes has gone from 'negligible' to 'something'. And sometimes, that 'something' amounts to 'really quite a lot'.

Car drivers rail at cyclists riding two abreast. I get into arguments at dinner parties with car drivers who rail at cyclists riding two abreast. Then, when I am out on my bike with friends, I find myself riding single file so that car drivers will not rail at me and my friends for riding two abreast. It's a first-world problem, I suppose. And cyclists can be every bit as sanctimonious as motorists can be unreasonable.

I took the kids on a cycling protest ride shortly before the 2012 mayoral election, thinking it would be a family-fun happy/smiley kind of affair. It wasn't. It was freezing cold, drizzling and militant. Before I could object, one of the organisers had draped a hi-vis marshal's gilet on me, and charged me with cycling ahead to major junctions and blocking the road by sheer willpower while our long stream of protesters cycled past. I spent the morning in agonies of discomfort, quite unable to discharge my duties with anything that even faintly resembled conviction. I must have looked like a vegan in a pie shop.

'Critical mass, mate!' my fellow partisans would yell at me. 'Reclaim the streets!' Oh, whatever. I weakly grinned back at them, and then looked at the motorist I was inconveniencing, with a cringing countenance. Wrong man. Wrong job.

But the cyclists are here to stay. They are a day-glo visible presence, with LED lights winking out their pious Morse code. They jump lights, they enrage drivers, they hug the gutter, they slip through the traffic, they slosh through puddles and they ring their bells in moral outrage. They race, they trundle, they rock from side to side. They puncture and they ride on. In all their manifestations, suddenly, they are everywhere.

The explosive and unheralded interest in cycling has penetrated previously inaccessible recesses in the capital. Places like the Village Barber's, at the end of my road.

This very unpretentious Turkish barber shop, run with occasional zeal, but mostly *Daily-Mirror*-reading, Lambert-and-Butler-flicking carefreeness by Ahmet, a second-generation Cypriot immigrant in his late twenties, is where I have been going for years to get my hair hacked off. On every one of those visits we have observed the same, barren, routine. Until last summer, that is.

Normally, up till now, I cycle to the end of the road, and lock up my bike outside his shop. He watches me, as he pauses briefly over the TV guide in the paper. Then I go in and ask for a 'number four'.

And always, when I am seated, and he has tucked in the red nylon sheet thing into my collar, the same question. 'Natural neckline? Or square?'

'Um . . .'

Since I have never seen the back of my head except in those awful seconds when a mirror is held up at the end of the cut, I am never sure what the correct neckline answer is. 'Oh, just the normal.' I hedge my bets.

'Not working today, my man?' This, too, always gets asked, since I am invariably the only customer and it's normally a Tuesday lunchtime, when upstanding, productive citizens are at work in offices.

'Yes, I am. Kind of.' He looks sceptical. I try to tell him about my imminent trip to Northumbria to cover a bike race. But it doesn't work. Ahmet has not registered a thing. He never does.

Until suddenly, last summer, the summer of 2012, when there was a confluence of two events. The first was an almighty traffic jam. It took him an hour to drive the three miles to work (no Olympic lanes in Sydenham).

The second was the arrival of his new neighbour, Mark.

At the side of Ahmet's shop, there is a tiny little room that has variously been rented out to all manner of chancers and shady entrepreneurs. The last tenant operated an IT Solutions and Web Design Service, which mostly unlocked mobile phones and did the odd photocopy for 10p a sheet. They didn't last long.

Then Mark, a wiry young bloke, took on the lease and, implausibly, opened a bike repair service. Instantly, it started to thrive. One day Ahmet looked up from his *Daily Mirror*, took notice, and promptly bought a bike.

Mark told him that there is a cycle path almost all the way from his house to the shop, along a river and through a park. It came as a revelation. Ahmet now rides with delight and pride into work every day, and no trip to the barber's shop is complete any more without a discussion of London's cycle network, the speed of commuting, and his elaborate preparations for the onset of the cold winter weather.

But it goes further than that. He's had new bike racks installed outside the shop. He takes a solicitous interest in how securely the bikes are locked. He recommends Mark's service to his customers, and Mark has brought new customers to Ahmet, middle-class men who would normally never have considered the Village Barber's at the end of the road, where a cut costs £9, and has done for as long as anyone can remember.

The two things, hair and bikes, have become movingly symbiotic.

When I lived in Hamburg, during a worryingly long directionless period of my life in the early nineties, there used to be a shop called 'Wein und Schuhe'. As its name suggests, it sold wine and shoes. You'd pop in for a bottle of wine, and end up buying some shoes. Or, while trying on a pair of pumps, you'd be tempted by a South African Chenin Blanc. It was odd, but perfect. Now, at the end of my road, Ahmet and Mark have created the same perfect storm. It is equally miraculous.

But, if my claim to be a London cyclist was really going to stand up to scrutiny, then there was one pilgrimage I had yet to complete. It seemed inevitable that one day I would make my way to London's Herne Hill Velodrome, and quite shaming that I hadn't yet done so.

Its name, spoken with affection and reverence, kept cropping up. Every time I talked, either idly or with intent to anyone with a feel for the history of the sport, and in particular with a London connection, the place would get a nod and a name check. The only surviving stadium from the Austerity Games of 1948, Herne Hill has been in continuous use ever since. It reeked, even from a distance, of 'heritage', which is what you get when your 'legacy' acquires wrinkles. It had a holiness all of its own, that much was self-evident.

I had been skirting it, literally, as well as figuratively, for long enough. Given that my home is no more then three or four miles away, the fact of my non-visiting seemed increasingly to be preposterous. Indeed, it was becoming a source of *mauvaise-foi*; a deep-set shame that I would try to hide from the wider cycling family.

'Remember the "Good Friday", Ned? Not last year's, but the one before that?' This was the sort of casual testing gambit that would often be sprinkled into conversation with cycling folk, a group to which I scarcely belonged, but with whom I had more and more occasion to deal.

'Sure.' (Bluff.)

'Well, who won the scratch race?'

'The scratch race?' (Playing for time.)

'Yes. I can't remember.'

'Oh, I know who you mean . . . Damn! What was his name?' (Playing for time and a bluff all in one.)

Enough of the deceit!

It was time for me to find out why it was that so many of the paths I'd followed in the lives of riders and fans of all generations seemed to meet and cross at Herne Hill. I would go and pay my respects at the oval-shaped tarmac cradle of Bradley Wiggins's career, and the bluff would no longer be so naked. I would fill in the bald spot on my map of the known cycling world.

As it happened, the Good Friday meeting was just around the corner. This, I had learned, was the very centrepiece of London's track calendar.

I had nothing else in the diary. I checked the weather forecast, not without trepidation. It seemed to suggest heavy downpours, a howling wind and occasional glimpses of watery spring sunshine: 12 degrees, but feeling like five. My resolve took an immediate knock. Perhaps, I plotted, if I exploited the almost certain reluctance of my nine-year-old daughter, I could use that as my excuse to stay at home instead.

I looked at her over the Cheerios one morning. 'Fancy going

to the Good Friday meeting? You don't have to.' I added the last corrective rather over-hastily.

'Is that like the Olympics?' she crunched.

'A bit like that. But not much like that. Although there will be chips.' Why was I suddenly trying to sell it to her? 'It's a bike race,' I told her, more realistically. 'Well, in fact it's lots of bike races.'

'Cool.' She loaded up another spoon.

'It might rain. Heavily.'

'I hope Liquigas are there.' Crunch. She had a curious passion for the Italian superteam, mostly comprised of more-or-less reformed dopers. I hadn't the heart to tell her that the two-time winner of the Giro D'Italia Ivan Basso probably wouldn't be too sure what to do with the £50 Homebase voucher on offer for the runners-up of the Madison.

So, when the day of the races dawned, we set off. We rode there, through more and more salubrious parts of London until we dropped down into Dulwich village itself, manicured and affluent and a long way removed from Lewisham, which we had left behind us. As we freewheeled downhill, coasting past the unfathomably expensive organic babywear shops and cutesy bakeries, I felt suddenly unsure that I had taken us in the right direction. We stopped so that I could consult the map on my phone. It seemed scarcely conceivable that there could be a bike track tucked away anywhere near here, still less an Olympic venue.

But, turning onto Burbage Road (average property price £852,977), we stumbled across just that. Herne Hill Velodrome, as good as invisible to the passing motorist and set back from the road by some hundred yards, accessible only via a pot-holed track, is a patch of pure history, modestly disguised as nowhere very notable.

We chained up our bikes, paid a few quid at the gate and walked in.

It was a wide, shallow track, recently, and expensively refurbished in smooth dark tarmac. It was nothing like the tight, gleaming, polished bowl of the wooden bankings in Manchester or Stratford. It was low and menacing. Around three sides there were mature trees, swaying a little at the top. Behind that, some of London's most exclusive houses ignored the bicycle shenanigans just over their garden walls, and turned their brick backs to the scene. On the home straight, ugly, plastic-seated, temporary stands occluded the real gem: Herne Hill's old wrought-iron-and-wood grandstand, built with civic pride in 1891, boarded up and made unsafe at the hands of corporate neglect in the late twentieth century, a no-man's-land of listed decay. But there it was, the link to the past: cycling's Lords.

A tannoy was announcing the upcoming race, with a nasal amplification more commonly reserved for platform announcers in Ealing comedies. Someone was selling cup cakes and slices of fruit loaf from a trestle table. The programme sellers were fumbling clumsy fingers in their pockets to change down fivers. Along the railings stood a healthy smattering of a few hundred folk, huddling chins in scarves, nudging one another, and casting worried glances skywards. Riders came and went from parked cars to the interior of the track, carrying bikes, and walking pigeon-toed on cleats. A judge in a blazer climbed a ladder, and with a sharp 'crack' from the starting pistol, the next race got underway to a polite ripple of applause. We went off in search of chips.

I watched the day through my daughter's eyes, deeply glad that I had her with me. She took in the sprints, loving the dead arc, the still moment of the cat and mouse chase when the riders dare not show their hand. She went saucer-eyed at the sight of a Devil race in full cry, she thrilled to the stink and noise of the Dernies, with their fat old men turning pedals in slow motion as their antique-looking motorbikes farted around the track. She passed chips unsighted from hand to mouth, her gaze fixed on the action.

Two hours in, but only halfway through the proceedings, I asked her if we should go home. She looked at me as if I were simple. 'It's not the end. The scratch race is the end.'

She threw a chip in her mouth.

We stayed another two hours, then rode home, secretly pretending we were in a scratch race. I let her win. I'm good like that.

CHAPTER 6

THE SIX-DAY EVENTIST

He's been standing by the barriers for hours, along with his wife, Mia. Both of them are exhausted since their Paris hotel caught fire the previous night, and they had to evacuate. But despite the lack of sleep, the excitement of the day has carried them through. Maurice Burton is straining to catch sight of the newly crowned champion walking up the Champs-Elysées, and waving to the crowds. He would dearly love to make eye contact, a nod of recognition, anything. That's the reason they've come to Paris, after all.

Mia stands at his side, her iPad poised. She is ready to film the moment.

But Bradley Wiggins, walking slowly back up the finishing straight, having just won the Tour de France, doesn't appear to notice him. The cobbles are washed over with sound, and besides, on either side of the road, thousands of faces are turned towards him. The fact is that Maurice is just one of many.

So he just walks by. I glance at Maurice to see if he's feeling hurt. I can't tell, really. But then I've never really been able to figure out what Maurice is thinking.

Maurice Burton's bike shop, De Ver Cycles, is on an unlovely main road in South London. As his business has started to thrive, so too has his brick-and-mortar empire. The canary yellow and black signage now straddles two properties, and the interior layout of the shop boasts three separate show-rooms. One is for everyday bikes. One is for road bikes and another displays accessories and clothing. Behind that, there are workshops, two offices and a large space in which bikes get unpacked and stowed. But that's only the visible part.

One day, Maurice takes a set of keys and he walks me still further into the remoter reaches of his territory, through storeroom after storeroom, each one crammed to the rafters with all manner of bikes and bike parts. Back and back we go, opening doors, switching on lights, scrambling over boxes, through room after room. I lose any sense of the architectural integrity of the place as we turn through unlikely angles and move further and further back from the street. It's like potholing, without the safety measures. Eventually, we reach a backyard of sorts, piled high with old wheels, the odd frame and assorted bits. It's fair to say that he has a lot of space at his disposal, and perhaps not a great deal of control over its use.

We stand there briefly surveying the chaos and speculating about how it could best be put to use. Maurice has been considering setting up a custom frame-builder's workshop. I look around the place imagining it. There was a time when a variety of independent frame-makers used to populate British cities. Up until a few years ago there was one very close to my house. Whitcomb Cycles of Deptford used to build beautiful handmade cycles, finished off in purple and silver and chrome. I often used to gaze through the window, but seldom got up the courage to walk in. And when I did, they tended to look at me like I'd just walked dog shit into their premises. They must have smelt my difference, instantly sized up my lack of belonging, my ignorance of their ancient artisan code.

Anyway, they sold up, eventually, and disappeared. It seemed a bit perverse of Maurice to want to buck the trend towards mass-produced, imported bikes, a sentimental, rather than a commercial enterprise.

Instead, in this ramshackle hinterland, I am seeing a café. I imagine tables, TV screens, the cough and gurgle of a coffee machine, and South London's cycling community chatting away amiably. Instantly I have a plan in place. Book readings, film showings, social evenings.

'A bit like the Rapha Club.' I make reference to a very smart, very minimalist cycling café just off Brewer Street in Soho. Maurice frowns. 'But a down-to-earth, South London version, Mo,' I suggest, trying to make it sound more appropriate to the surroundings.

He doesn't look too impressed. And instantly I wish I'd kept my thoughts to myself.

'I don't know if that's me.' He thinks for a moment. 'That's not really me, Ned.'

He turns the key, which closes the automatic door to the yard. My guided tour has come to a close, and we are turning to head back to the shop. It occurs to me that Maurice thinks of himself as an outsider. I later find out that the same thought, I am relieved to hear, has often occurred to Maurice too.

'No, I don't fit in any mould. I don't want to fit in any mould really.'

We're sitting down with two cups of tea between us now. They are perched on the only free surfaces on Maurice's otherwise overflowing desk. Invoices, orders, brochures, magazines: all the flotsam of office life. Maurice peers at me with his head bent to one side, and a half-smile. 'But then, I don't think you quite fit in, do you, Ned?'

'Oh I don't know about that,' I mutter, thinking guiltily about my suggestion about the Rapha Club, my über-middle-class upbringing and my university education, in fact, the whole of my utterly conforming life.

'Well, in certain ways, Ned, I don't think you do. Sorry if I have to tell you that, mate.' Maurice Burton looks at me and chuckles. I have no idea what he means. But, coming from him, I take it as a huge compliment.

'Anyway, what do you want to talk about today?'

'You, Maurice.'

My café idea never gets mentioned again.

One day in the middle of the 1960s, young Maurice Burton spotted something in a front garden in Catford that caught his eye. It was a touring bike. He stopped on the street and looked more closely at it. He could see that the forks were a bit bent, but otherwise it looked in good enough nick. He walked up to the front door and knocked on it.

The lady who opened the door to Maurice explained that it had been in an accident, and that they were waiting for insurance money to get it fixed. He listened attentively to every word.

But then, as he walked away, he already knew he had made a defining choice.

'My dad wouldn't let me have a bike. He was a bit anxious, and didn't want his son squashed by a lorry. He couldn't see the point of me riding a bike. That's for kids, he'd say. He wanted me to be a doctor or a lawyer.'

His father Rennal had come to London, via the USA, from Jamaica in 1948. Once here, he'd found employment as a tailor's presser, working for big fashion houses such as Jean Muir. By the 1980s he was preparing the clothes for Margaret Thatcher and Princess Diana to wear.

It was at work that Rennal met his future wife, Grace Spires. She was a seamstress. Maurice's parents were serious-minded craftspeople who had no desire to see their children take a backwards step in life. And bicycles were backwards.

They had scant tolerance of, and little understanding of, Maurice's growing passion. He did own a bike but it was a bit of a joke. It was the same crappy old thing he used for a paper round, and it was always landing him in trouble. Often face first.

'"Look at that boy. Look how he mash himself up again. Look at him!" That's what Dad would say.' Maurice, impersonating his dad, breaks into a treacly Jamaican patois, at odds with his soft South London cockney.

Not that he took any notice of his father's warnings. He spent whole days rattling around London's much quieter streets, enjoying the adventure, relishing his speed, getting to know his strength.

But, it was true: he needed a decent set of wheels. So, standing outside that Catford front garden, young Mo knew already what he was going to do. There was no chance his parents would get him a nice bike like that, and there was no chance that he would ever be able to afford one either.

'I kind of felt that I needed that bike, so I sort of, kind of . . . half-inched it.' He figured that since it was insured, it would be a victimless crime.

It was, in fact, a trademark Burton scam. Ten years later, when he was living and riding professionally in Belgium, he used to cross back and forth on the ferry, changing his registration plates to Belgian numbers on the way home to London, and vice versa on the way back to Belgium. He figured that with foreign plates he was virtually immune from prosecution for traffic offences.

Until one day when he thought he was being watched. 'I'd unscrewed one, but there was someone walking around the deck, and I hadn't changed the other one yet.' He drove off the boat with one British and one Belgian plate. It was another victimless crime.

But, back in Catford, back in 1966, all that mattered was that he had his bike. He was up and riding.

'I never got off the bike the whole day. Nobody could beat me. They couldn't come close to me.' It changed everything. 'Me and my cousin Dexter, who lived in North London, used to meet on Blackfriars Bridge and just go off riding for the day. Chessington Zoo. Kew Gardens. We never went to the [country] lanes that much cos we never knew what to do, or where to go.'

But the world of professional racing, the possibility that you could make a career out of messing around on a bike, remained hidden and alien, as it did to almost the entirety of the British population.

One Saturday afternoon, as always, *World of Sport* was on the TV.

'I remember watching the 1969 Tour de France. Ten minutes, they used to show on there. I told me dad, "I want to be like him. That man there."' He was talking about Eddy Merckx.

'And Dad said, "You have to eat steak every day if you want to do that." I told Mum that I wanted steak every day after that.'

It was the following year that his school organised a trip to the Herne Hill Velodrome. He sat in the old wrought-iron stand and listened to a man called Bill Dodds tell him and his classmates from the Roger Manwood secondary school, 'From here, you can go to the Olympics.'

He gazed down from the wooden seats and looked at the wide, shallow track, the trees behind the back straight catching in the wind. He accepted the challenge.

He would go on to win many races at Herne Hill. And then he would win even more elsewhere. But the Olympics? That bit never happened. Something much more interesting awaited Maurice Burton.

'You've heard of Major Taylor?'

I nod. Maurice looks knowingly at me, a look that signifies something.

Although the name Major Taylor means something to me, I cannot say I could tell you with any certainty who he was or what it was he did. But thankfully Maurice takes my nod at face value. Talking to Mo often feels to me like a test of my inadequate grasp of cycling history. I have to judge when to feign familiarity and when to own up to ignorance. Too much of either, I reckon, will make him suspicious.

But I'm grateful to Maurice Burton for pointing me in the direction of 'The Worcester Whirlwind'. Some time later, I get hold of a biography of Major Taylor and start to read. His story, I discover, bounces around between the boundaries of the credible. The more I read, the more I am astonished that his name doesn't sit alongside the most celebrated in the history of sport. The perfection of Taylor's narrative arc almost makes me doubt its veracity. Is he a fable?

As the nineteenth century drew to a close, there was no bigger sport in the USA than cycling. Even small cycle meetings would regularly be attended by 20,000 or 30,000 spectators. And Marshall 'Major' Taylor was the undisputed star of the scene.

Taylor broke multiple world records, in 1898 holding seven simultaneously. He dominated the track cycling scene in the USA and travelled widely in his latter years. His appearances in Australia, New Zealand and continental Europe, most particularly in the velodromes of France, attracted huge publicity and he commanded proportionate fees. There is documented evidence that his earnings totalled $35,000 per annum. And in 1904 that was a great deal of money.

Two things marked him out as extraordinary: he was brilliant, and he was black.

His entire career, and what remained of his post-racing life (he died, prosaically bankrupt and living in a YMCA during the Great Depression, having lost his fortune in unwise business ventures), were played out against a backdrop of what he called 'that dreadful monster prejudice'. Repeatedly he found that access to races and to the institutions around the sport, from colleges to clubs, was blocked to non-whites. But worse was to come on and off the track.

As the Worcester journalist Albert B. Southwick documents: 'They would crowd him off the track, hem him in "pockets", rough him up off the field, curse and threaten him. There is no telling how often he heard the "N" word, and other vicious epithets. After one close race (in Boston, no less!) a burly cyclist got him in a choke hold that made him black out before the police dragged the assailant off. In Atlanta, where he had planned to race, he was warned to get out of town in forty-eight hours or else.'

Taylor was immensely capable, extremely articulate (his autobiography is a model of dignified prose) and largely forgotten, even by a soppy American public hungry for legitimate heroes. Where Jesse Owens will be remembered for ever, Major Taylor has mostly vanished from history, just as his money melted away in the 1930s. And like Owens, he too found his most accepting public was not necessarily at home, where the discrimination was overt, but overseas, where it was couched in the beguiling language of paycheques and plaudits; in Europe, he found adulation, albeit at arm's length.

One hundred years later, in the pleasantly chaotic office at the back of his bike shop, Maurice Burton drops in his name, no more than that. It's in the context of illustrating a point he's making about the lost glamour of the Continental track scene. And what a scene it was.

In 1904, Taylor rode a triumphant tour of Europe, challenging the best that the Continent had to offer on the track. He raced fifty-seven times, more often than not against fields including national champions. He beat forty of them.

Such domination. Such an appetite for success.

Exactly seventy years on, in 1974, in Maurice's debut season on the European circuit there was a rider like that, too. His name was Eddy Merckx. Maurice and Merckx did not meet on the roads of the Belgian Classics, nor in the mountains of the Grand Tours. They did battle on the boards of Europe's great velodromes. 'Six-Day' meetings, festivals of gladiatorial track cycling had never been more popular.

Although the format had originally been a Victorian British invention, it had been the Americans who had glamorised and formulated the template for Six-Day racing. After the Second World War, it migrated back to Europe. Earls Court, in London, regularly staged Six-Day events, but it was Germany and Belgium that took the races to their hearts. Ghent, in particular, led the way. That's where Maurice crossed Eddy Merckx.

'My first year was Eddy's last year.' We are talking on Maurice's home soil now. These are the events and the stellar names that illuminate his career.

'It was my first Six-Day. I was keen to do well, I was hungry. We went for everything. We had a car race [a race with a new car as a prize was always a feature of the meet]. It was a Madison Devil, in which teams of two riders alternate laps. Each time the race passes the finish line, the last-placed team is disqualified, and so on, until there is a winning duo, and "the devil take the hindmost".

'It came down to two teams,' Maurice continues. 'Merckx and Patrick Sercu, and Paul Medhurst and me.'

In front of a partisan Belgian crowd, largely inebriated and infatuated with their great champion, there could only be one result. The Cannibal, Eddy Merckx would *have* to win. That's how things played out in the highly choreographed world of Six-Day meetings; the story always had a happy ending. But, almost by mistake, and quite against the spirit of the event, Burton and Medhurst won the race. It was a major breach of good manners.

'We shouldn't have done it. But we won by half a lap.'

But the great champion had one more chance to save face. 'Later in the evening, in another elimination race, there was just me and Merckx left. So I think he decided he'd better have a little quiet word with me, you know. He came along-side and said, "You let me win this one, yeah?" I said, "OK." It was the man that I'd seen a few years before on the *World of Sport* and my dad had told me that I had to eat steak.'

He grins. 'I let him have it, Ned. But I made it look good.'

Just then Jason, one of the Maurice's mechanics, pops his head round the door, with a question about a bike build for a customer. And then the phone rings.

'You'll excuse me, Ned.'

Before Belgium called and the glamour of the Six-Day circuit gripped him, back at Herne Hill in the early 1970s, a teenage Maurice Burton began to tear through the categories. He had a name, a reputation. 'Slow-Mo' was a formidable opponent, with great tactical nous and a turn of speed that few of his peers could match.

It would be fair to say he fell off a lot. In fact, he was known for it. But if he stayed on, he often won. And he delighted in winning. Actually, not much else mattered.

'You imagine when you ride against somebody, and when

you beat them, you see them throw their bike on the floor. How do you think that made me feel?' The grin is back. But this time, it's unambiguous. Winning, he recalls, had been a visceral pleasure.

'Were you quite a hard bastard?' I ask him.

There is a long pause. 'I think I probably am quite a hard bastard.'

He switches my past tense for his present tense. Perhaps he has to be. He certainly *had* to be. London's mostly white cycling scene didn't exactly embrace its latest recruit.

Maurice had a close friend from the same South London secondary school near Lewisham. Joe Clovis was from St Lucia. They got to know each other after that first visit to the velodrome and under the protective wing of the coach Maurice had met on his first day at the track. They adored Bill Dodds, the avuncular figure they both credit with looking after their interests. They were, along with another guy called Jim Robertson, pretty much the only black riders competing at Herne Hill at the time.

Jim Robertson still races there. Now well into his sixties, he has not missed a Good Friday meeting since 1970. He is well known, feted even, for doing the same trick each time: attacking early on in the showpiece 'scratch' race, the simplest event of the day, in which the first rider across the line wins. Robertson has always ridden on his own off the front for as long as his legs will allow. These days that means maybe only for a lap. Then he drops like a stone through the field. Joe and Maurice had a fairly low opinion of this kind of show-boating back when they were young men, and thought that it smacked of tokenism, the acceptable face of black partici-pation. Their contention was that Jim was not perceived as a threat, and was not taken seriously, according to Joe, whereas they were there to win.

Among that group of young riders, there was sporadic violence. From time to time, it would all boil over. On one occasion Joe and Jim came to blows, with Maurice trying to separate them. 'How did that look to everyone at the track?' Maurice remembers with wry amusement. 'The only three black cyclists trying to knock each other out?'

But, much more seriously, the occasional covert beating was administered, I am told. The context was never defined, but the suspicion was that there were times when it had to do with skin colour.

'Kamikaze' Joe Clovis who, by his own admission, didn't quite have Maurice's talent ('I only once beat him and he absolutely hated it'), still lives in Catford. He gave up riding a long time ago, and has only recently taken one of his sons down to the track. 'He wants to be a doctor. I can't stand in his way.' It's a curious reversal of the way things were. He goes on, 'Besides, I wouldn't want him to have to go through what we went through. And I'm not sure how much has changed.'

It must have been, amidst the fun and games, an alienating experience. He remembers Maurice and him getting a lift back from racing at Leicester with the father of another white friend. As they left the M1 at Brent Cross, they were discussing the best route across London to get to Catford.

Maurice told the dad, 'If you go through Brixton, that'll take you straight to Forest Hill, and then you're nearly there.'

Then his friend's dad said, 'Why would I go through that coon country?'

Joe Clovis can remember the insult as if it were yesterday. 'Maurice and I sat in the back of the car, totally silent. We were shocked. What was the response? We were in the man's car!'

There was another occasion when Maurice went out for a sixty-mile ride with two fellow members of the same club.

They rode two abreast in front of him, leaving him to ride the whole way on their wheels and in silence. Not a word was spoken to him. He is certain, with hindsight, why they never spoke to him.

The occasional overt act of racism was one problem, but what both riders felt almost more keenly was the systematic prejudice of officialdom.

Track cyclists would have to glue on their tubular tyres, known as tubs, making sure that they wouldn't roll off the rim during the race. This happened quite often, and invariably caused injury. So, as a safety measure, riders would have to present their tubs for inspection by officials before being allowed to race. The officials would try to roll them off with their hands to see if they were firmly stuck down.

Joe Clovis had noticed that his tyres were being rejected more regularly than anyone else's. He grew suspicious, and mentioned his concerns to a white rider.

'One day I told my friend Paul that I thought my wheels weren't going to pass because I was black. It was the first time I ever raised the issue.'

Paul reacted with consternation. But Joe was adamant and, to prove his point, he borrowed his friend's wheels, which had just been passed fit for the race. He took the very same ones for re-inspection. And in his hands, apparently, they were no longer good.

'They just rolled the tyres right off. Both of them.'

Perhaps their riding styles didn't help much. Both Burton and Clovis were strong sprinters, and would sit in, seldom going to the front. It didn't endear them to the crowd, nor did the other riders like it much. But it got the job done. And the more he won, the more Maurice began to feel that they'd all rather he just disappeared for good. They nearly got what they wanted.

'I was training at Herne Hill. A couple of guys were just riding in front of me, sprinting, and one of their tyres came off. He crashed, and I crashed into him. I went over both of them, and I ended up with one of my teeth in the track at Herne Hill. The tooth was actually in the track. The whole tooth.'

He ended up in hospital, where his parents came to visit him. 'My face was hardly recognisable.

'I heard that after that accident some of the people at the track thought that that was the last of me, that they wouldn't see me any more. And that's what they were hoping. That I'd just go away.'

On another occasion he won a race at Crystal Palace by half a wheel, and was immediately congratulated by the rider he beat. But the judges saw it differently.

'They said that he won the race. I got second place, and he won the race.'

As he recounts this story, there is a long pause in Maurice's office, not for the first time. He's frowning and smiling at the same time. And when he looks up I am not sure whether he's angry or amused.

'But I won the race. When he heard the judge's decision the other rider said, OK, maybe I made a mistake. But he didn't make a mistake. I won the race.'

And in 1974, he won a national title, the twenty-kilometre race at Leicester. As he stood on the podium, the crowd booed. In photographs from the time, he is smiling back at them.

'If you look at my face on there, I had a little grin. It didn't worry me. It didn't upset me. It didn't make me angry. It didn't piss me off. It pissed them off. But it didn't piss me off.'

Joe Clovis watched on in the stands as his friend took the win. Back at home in Catford, Maurice's dad was watching the wrestling on *World of Sport*. The phone rang. It was Clovis. 'Switch over to the BBC, Mr Burton. Your son's on *Grandstand*.'

'Up till today, I still don't know if he actually switched channels and saw me winning the national title. I just don't know.' Maurice and his dad don't talk about those days too often.

He turned up the following year to defend his title, crashed in the home straight and was disqualified to boot. In his eyes, this was the final petty act, although it's hard, at this distance, to back up his claim that he was being singled out for special treatment. But that was the perception, and he'd had enough. As far as Maurice Burton was concerned, his future lay elsewhere.

'They didn't boo me over there. They didn't boo me in Belgium. No, it was the opposite. Sometimes I don't realise how much they appreciated me over there.'

Not everyone around at the time backs up Maurice's claims of racism. There are those, even now, who are tempted to brush it off as chippiness or as an excuse for his own shortcomings. One rider told me that 'it wasn't because he was black that he wasn't selected for the Olympics, nor that he wasn't good enough. It was because he was ugly!'

It's meant as fun, and Maurice is rightly, if not universally, held in high esteem by the London cycling community. But, the more I ask around the white establishment which still sits at its heart, the more I get the sense that the issue has never been truly addressed. It's easier not to.

Once when I go and see Maurice at his shop, he keeps me waiting for a long time. A customer has come in who is parting with a significant sum of money. Maurice has his priorities and at times like this, understandably, I am not one of them.

I have no objections to this hiatus since it grants me an opportunity to mooch around his shop, glancing at the bits and pieces on display, as well as the dozens of images covering all the walls. There are old posters from his racing days in Belgium, faded photographs of Maurice snarling over his bars in numerous close finishes. There is a framed shot of him on the podium that day in Leicester, smiling at his detractors.

Every now and again, a famous name jumps away from the print and catches the eye.

Maurice Burton raced with Bradley Wiggins's late father Gary Wiggins in Belgium. He knew him well. When Bradley was born, he had held him in his arms within a few days. Back in London, long after the dissolution of the Wiggins' turbulent marriage, Maurice maintained sporadic contact with Bradley as he grew up. He watched him with a distant associated pride. In the most recent picture of the two of them, Bradley looks young. He is wearing the red and blue of the national champion, his hair betraying some ill-advised experimental blond highlights. He is standing next to Maurice and grinning awkwardly. In British cycling, it seems, you are never more than one or two removes away from champions.

There are pictures of Maurice's son, Germain. There are spaces on the wall for more, although he has been allocated a narrow corridor towards the rear of this shop. He's the boy on the time-trial bike, the boy winning the hill climb, the boy on the podium; the sixteen-year-old prodigy.

But, in flesh and blood, he's also the boy behind the till who's just left school and now works in a bike shop. Maurice Burton's two sons (Robert is a couple of years younger) are highly rated prospects. They are good, exceptional even, in their age groups, and both have been talked about as potential future champions, although getting their stoical father to admit that is a near impossibility. He's far too cautious, modest and inscrutable.

I talk to Germain while I wait for his dad to finish. He sits at a high stool, the cash register in front of him, occasionally serving a customer. He thinks hard about what he says before

he says it. He has his father's slow, deliberate delivery. He tells me how he is devoted to the road, and has no experience of riding on the track. It's the opposite from his father's persuasion. But strangely it is having similar repercussions; he has ended up racing in Belgium. The junior scene there is flourishing, and fast; the average speed of their races often equals or exceeds the best amateur races back home.

He sits at the till, casually letting drop the names of Belgian towns, races, teams and riders. There are not many South London teenagers, I imagine, who can differentiate between West Flanders and Antwerp. Germain Burton can, just like his old man could.

In 2012, Germain was selected to ride for Great Britain in the Junior World Championships, and finished strongly in the main field. His potential seems boundless. But his father is always there to demand more, to warn of the potential pitfalls, and to put on a firm handbrake when ambitions shoot too far ahead of application.

'Right, Ned. Sorry to have kept you waiting.' We break off and I follow Maurice back into his office. He's reading a freshly printed invoice as he goes.

'That looked like a good bit of business, Mo.'

The customer has left the shop. He was a well-dressed man in his early fifties at a guess, tall and slightly out of context for Norbury. Maurice tells me he is high up in Lloyds Bank in the City. 'What was his final bill?'

'Eight thousand pounds.' Maurice barely registers any emotion. 'That man's come to me because he doesn't want to go to Evans or wherever. He wants to come to me. I know a bit about what I'm selling.'

I suddenly think about that bike he 'half-inched' from the front garden. He's come a long way. From Catford, to Norbury, via Belgium.

Quickly, we are back in the seventies.

If any fragile bond had existed between the rider and the country of his birth, the experience of being booed on the podium of the National Championships had broken it.

'They just didn't like me, I think.'

It's hard to know what the reality of the selection was. But after a solitary trip to the Commonwealth Games in 1974 in

Christchurch (from which he returned without a medal), Maurice Burton never represented his country again.

'I felt like I was a foreigner. I didn't feel like I was British. It was like I was in no-man's-land.' And so, it was only fitting that it was the original no-man's-land that drew his attention. Flanders.

It was Christmas Day 1974 when Maurice Burton arrived in Ghent. He headed straight away for the Kuipke, the legendary velodrome. Here, under this canopy, and around this vertiginous track, was the beating heart of the sport north of the Alps. This was always the starting point for a generation or two of the hopeful, the misguided and the tenacious from Britain and Australia trying to make it on the Continent. And what's more, the night he arrived, the place was in full cry.

Christmas Day racing was a tradition, the track, beery and smoke-filled. Already he was very far away from his home in Catford where his family would be quietly celebrating Christmas. The scene laid out before him was cacophonous, unruly, thrilling, a far cry from the reserve with which the sport was 'enjoyed' back home.

He sat in the stands and watched Eddy Merckx and Roger de Vlaeminck win a Madison race, drinking in his fill of these stellar names in action. In theory, this was supposed to be a two-week holiday from the apprenticeship he'd half-heartedly started, mostly to appease his parents. At least, that's what he'd told people. But he knew what was really going on.

'I had two weeks to decide what I was going to do with my life. I'm either going to be a bike rider, or I'm going to be an electrician. You can't do both.' He pauses. 'I never went back to work.'

At the end of the racing, he went off in search of the one contact at his disposal: the extraordinary Rosa De Snerck. Rosa and her husband Marcel ran the Plume Vainqueur bike shop in Ghent. She had become well known in the Anglophone scene for her helpfulness towards this shambolic trickle of hopeful immigrants. If she herself could not offer some temporary lodging for them, then she'd find somewhere else for them to sleep. Unfortunately, this occasionally meant they'd be sleeping at the 'Butcher's Shop'. This was the rather ghastly nickname for a rather ghastly place.

And that's where Maurice Burton ended up spending the first few bitter weeks of his cycling career abroad. Many British riders made the same harrowing acquaintance with the landlord of the Butcher's Shop. He was a curious man called Jan Vermeeren, or Jan 'The Papers', as Australian rider Alan Peiper remembers in his autobiography, *A Peiper's Tale*. Unwashed and hirsute, he trawled round Ghent and collected old newspapers all day, which he then brought home in a hand-drawn pony cart. Some of them he burnt in the stove (the only source of central heating), but mostly he just stacked them in huge piles throughout the otherwise unfurnished premises.

'The rumour was that Jan was rich and owned many houses,' writes Peiper. 'He just lived like a hermit, on the edge of society. He found his food in the dustbins at the back of supermarkets and I would often see him eating rotten fruit in the kitchen.'

Maurice Burton lived there at the same time as Peiper. He too remembers his esoteric landlord with a mixture of horror and fascination. 'He was a Seventh Day Adventist. He never washed and never shaved, and he used to sleep with his boots on. He never washed out his bowl, he'd just put the next food in it and eat away.'

'Welcome to Belgium?' I suggest to Maurice, as I try to imagine what this boy from Catford made of Jan Vermeeren.

'You'll soon find out whether you're going to make it as a rider in Belgium. You'll soon find out.'

*   *   *

Within a year Maurice was a professional, and within four weeks of turning pro, he'd earned enough money to pay cash for a brand-new Toyota Celica. Already he was earning upwards of £2,000 a week during the winter months of the 'Six-Day' scene. He stuck at it for the best part of a decade, too, most years pulling in £35,000 or thereabouts. This was big money. At the same time, his father retired, after a life-time's hard work on a wage that coughed up little more than £150 per week. On this score, at least, his son had emphatically won the argument.

But the track scene in Belgium, with all its showbiz connotations was complex and draining; each rider's role in it was pre-ordained to an extent, and his membership of its elite always in the balance.

The racing itself was, more often than not, a high-speed charade, albeit a murderously hard one. As in the wrestling, so beloved of his father back in London, the winner was frequently pre-determined, and the exact manner of his victory choreographed. That isn't to say that the best riders didn't routinely carry away the spoils; there was no way that a weaker member of the group would ever be allowed to dominate. It's just that the races were more like almighty ballets. Attack would follow attack, all of them pre-decided, until eventually the winner would 'thrillingly' reel them in and prevail. The aesthetics of the win were every bit as vital as the win per se.

Maurice remembers getting his instructions on a nightly basis.

'The boss would tell you how many laps you'd take. If it's your lap, and they're all riding at fifty kilometres in the hour, then you've got to be doing fifty-three kilometres an hour to ride away from them. So you've got to have it in you in order to do it. It only becomes a problem when you start to take one more lap than you're supposed to take, and that's when they start to get a bit heavy on you.'

It was demanding, from the start. First of all, to join the elite, you had to be good enough, and your face had to fit. With so much at stake, the competition among amateur wannabees was brutal.

'Once in Ghent, some Australians and British amateurs ganged up against me, and one of them tried to put me over the rail.' As he remembers that frightening assault, Maurice notes that in 2006 a Spanish rider named Isaac Galvez had been killed when he rode into exactly that rail.

'I knew what was happening. Afterwards I went down into one of the massage cabins underneath the track.' He was seeking out his assailant. 'I wrecked the cabin with him in it. I just went in there and turned him off the table. I wrecked it.'

There was, as Maurice recalls, a nucleus of fifteen or so riders who earned the big money. He was one of them. But they constantly fretted about their membership of this fraternity and were wary of newcomers. They also doped, routinely, casually, daily. Alan Peiper describes the scene. 'It was a joke, it was fun, a buzz, no different from a beer or a coffee. That was the attitude; it was as commonplace as that, just like naughty kids experimenting with beer or cigarettes in the park.'

Maurice Burton, with the benefit of hindsight, and having seen a number of his peers meet premature deaths, sees it differently. Less of a joke, all in all.

He is glad, in many ways, that a broken leg in 1984 put an end to his racing career. Had that not happened, he suggests, his health may well have shelved off steeply. Although he is no mood to talk about this in detail, he leaves me in no doubt that the drugs were endemic, omnipresent and consumed without the slightest thought for the consequences. The rewards for this rarefied gladiatorial existence were clear enough: fame, money, status, and thrills. But it was a hard, insecure and corrupt affair too.

And then there was the colour of his skin. The sniggers and whispers and boos which formed the white noise of his education on a bike in Britain had been silenced when he emigrated. But the issue had not gone away. It had just morphed into something more marketable.

Once again, I am reminded of Major Taylor.

'I was something different [in Belgium]. They liked that. They never used to say I came from England. They used to say I came from Jamaica. It sounded better. I just let them.' A shadow of a smile passes over Maurice's weathered face. 'Whatever it took, you know.'

Sometimes it took extreme tolerance, on Maurice's part. It was an unreconstructed world, in many ways lawless, or at best making the rules up as it went along. The velodromes of Germany, Milan, Switzerland and Belgium echoed to some strange sounds indeed.

Horst Schütz was one of Maurice's contemporaries. By nature a sprinter, he had also been, at one time, the motor-paced World Champion (following in the pedal-strokes, some eighty years previously, of Major Taylor himself). Schütz, it is said, had a highly particular way of geeing himself up before a race, which he at least had the common sense to keep hidden as best he could.

His teammate Roman Hermann, (who went on to become the Minister of Sport in Liechtenstein) told Maurice how Schütz used to motivate himself by playing recordings of Hitler's Nuremburg Rallies.

'I think if he saw me now . . . poor guy. Last I heard he was selling brushes and eggs and things door to door, you know.' There's sympathy in his voice when Maurice tells me this, but there is the merest trace of schadenfreude, too.

Then there was the matter of the nickname they gave to Maurice. Another German, the handsomely named Albert Fritz, one of the greatest Six-Day riders that country ever produced, came up with it and for a while it stuck.

'At one point there was a nickname, yeah.'

It takes Maurice a while to tell me what it was. 'I didn't like the name very much, you know. I don't know why they called me that.'

I have to push him a bit.

'It was Bimbo. I don't know why.'

I am stunned to hear this. And Maurice, as if aware of my surprise, looks painfully embarrassed. There is no art to this nickname. No veneer of subtlety, nothing clever at all.

It is a word that has no direct English equivalent, but its nastiness lies somewhere on a scale between 'Sambo' and 'Wog'. That's how it would have sounded to their ears, and that's how they would have introduced 'Bimbo' over the tannoy.

'Ned, it's a hard world out there. It's a hard world.'

'You remember. You were with me. We saw him go past and he sort of stopped and I think he realised.'

It's my last visit to Maurice's shop. We're talking about his trip to the Champs-Elysées. It was true: Bradley Wiggins, having strolled past Maurice, who'd been calling his name, temporarily checked his stride. He didn't come to a halt, but he did register something. Even by looking at the back of his head, as he walked away, you could tell.

I wonder what it meant to Maurice Burton, this moment in time. I wonder which bit of him was touched by the spectacle, why he'd gone out of his way to be there: the flag-waving Brit? The Jamaican? The itinerant cyclist from no-man's-land? The father to a cycling son?

Perhaps it was just that it was Bradley Wiggins. Had it been any other rider, Maurice might not have made the trip. Born in Belgium, raised in cycling, never quite conforming. Another outsider?

Wiggins turned and came back towards Maurice. He was

being flanked by TV camera crews, recording the moment. Security dogged his every step. Mia fumbled excitedly with her iPad (and to her eternal regret, completely failed to press record). There was a brief smile, as he neared.

The two men embraced over the barriers of the Tour de France. Not much, if anything at all, was said. Only later could Maurice put it into words, back in the chaotic calm of his office. 'It was a wonderful experience. It's a part of history. It's a circle, it's a full circle to me. I saw him when he was a little baby to winner of the Tour de France. To some degree I feel that I am part of that family now. More than I did. More than I did when I was younger.'

'Have you changed, Mo?' I ask.

'I haven't changed at all. The country has changed.'

There's one final pause. 'What else do you want to know, Ned?'

I tell him that I think I've got enough.

CHAPTER 7

ROMANTICS IN BRITAIN

So true
Funny how it seems
Always in time
But never in line for dreams

In 2011, the Tour of Britain ended with a split stage. Mick Bennett and the race organisation had pulled a surprisingly wonderful rabbit out of the hat. There was a time trial in the morning, followed by an afternoon race around a spectacular route along Whitehall and the Embankment in Central London.

Huge crowds packed the start/finish line, and spread out along the length of the five-and-a-half-mile course. Heavy showers were forecast for later, and would indeed materialise at precisely the moment that Mark Cavendish sprinted for the line to win the final stage of the Tour in a wet and windy London parody of his greatest Champs-Elysées triumphs. But for now, at least, as the riders rested between the two races, a warm sun beat down and the rain clouds bided their time over the horizon.

To entertain the spectators during the two-hour hiatus between events, some sponsors had the idea of putting on a 'celebrity' time-trial competition, ambitiously called a 'Hot Lap'. This being cycling, and cycling still being a minority sport, the calibre of celebrities they were able to sign up was modest at best (Dermot Murnaghan, for example, had promised to turn up but didn't show on the day, depriving the race of perhaps its biggest star) and at worst, it was laughable. They asked me to take part.

My pupils dilated instantly at the prospect. When else would I ever be cheered off a proper start ramp with a man counting down the seconds, and a proper machine going 'beep, beep, beeeeeep'? When else would I be allowed to ride as fast as I could along the Thames, sometimes on the wrong side of the closed roads and straight through red lights?

I had my misgivings, of course, since the only other time I had ridden in a 'race' (a Brompton folding-bike thing), I had tumbled backwards through the field almost instantly, and was forced to dig so deep, just to avoid the ignominy of finishing stone last, that I felt faint for hours afterwards. The exertion and the humiliation had made me want to throw up. Racing bikes, I had established after just one outing, was an unutterably horrible experience.

Nonetheless, the fragile ego of the very minor TV presenter left me very little choice. It dictated that I accept the prestigious offer to ride the Hot Lap.

We were assigned teams, each of us joining three other riders who had bid extravagantly for the right to ride with us. The fact that the bidding was extravagant (or so we were led to believe) was not only embarrassing, but also demographically limiting. It meant that the winning teams were almost entirely composed of investment bankers.

My team was called Schroders. They presented me with a rather smart blue racing jersey, with their company's name emblazoned all over it. But my identification with the team went even further because, over the previous ten years, most of my pension contributions had disappeared down a black hole expensively administered by Schroders. I had a very real stake in the team, a fact that I took some pleasure in pointing out to my team captain who failed to see the funny side. Much like I did every month.

As my allotted time grew near, my nerves increased commensurately. We milled around, waiting for the off. I bantered briefly with Graham Bell, the ex-downhill skier turned TV action man. He was dressed head to toe in Team Sky clothing. There was Denise Lewis, the heptathlete, Amy Williams the snowy medal-winning Brit. There was Dean Macey, the former decathlete. He was my 'thirty-second man', which meant that he was the last guy to set off before I took to the start ramp.

My knees actually started knocking against the frame of my bike as I sat on the saddle, held by a complete stranger, confronted by a sea of faces. I had no idea that knees actually 'knocked' when under duress, except in the *Beano*.

Beep. Beep. Beep. Beeeeep. I remember thinking, rather abstractly, about the composition of the strange ungainly cast of the Bash Street Kids as I slipped unconvincingly off the ramp, and started to pedal in the direction of Trafalgar Square. And that was the last thought I had that wasn't filled with the furious imperative to stop the pain from happening to me. By Northumberland Avenue, no more than about four hundred metres from the start, I was already at the limit. Underneath Waterloo Bridge, some five hundred metres further, I was perfectly poised on the edge of total collapse. To complete the next five miles at that speed seemed unthinkable.

I recalled to mind, through the disorder of my distress, Chris Boardman's scientifically perfect measure for determining effort in a time trial: you should ask yourself, 'Can I sustain this to the end?' If the answer is 'No', then you're going too fast. If the answer is 'Yes', then you're going too slow. But if the answer is 'Maybe', then you're judging the pace just right.

In my case the answer was 'UUUrgghnngh.'

I contemplated easing up, and allowing the remaining riders all to coast past me. I could showboat my way to the end, I thought, blowing kisses at the crowd, taking the piss, being shameless and losing all my dignity. Or I could continue to blow snot from both nostrils, groan involuntarily, suffer self-evidently, get soundly beaten and lose all my dignity.

It was during these agonised deliberations that I caught sight of the athletic backside of Dean Macey. Yes, the former World Championship silver medallist, the heir apparent to the great Daley Thompson, a man of imposing physique and eight years my junior, was coming back towards me! I was closing in on him! I was catching a proper athlete! If my heart had been capable of skipping a beat, which by now it wasn't, then it would have done.

By Tower Hill, where the course turned around a hairpin bend and started to head for home, I was just a second or two behind him. It took me an age to close out that final tiny gap, but by Old Billingsgate Market, I had unmistakably, and at the full extent of my capacity, drawn level with him. Surprised by my sudden presence at his side, he glanced across. 'Christ,' he said, 'I must be really shit.'

At that precise moment, a third rider appeared on the scene, hurtling from behind me, and ripping past us both on the outside.

It was Gary Kemp, from Spandau Ballet.

I remember thinking, 'Wow! Gary Kemp, from Spandau Ballet's really fast.' I think Dean Macey was thinking the same. Either way, his athletic self-respect was affronted by the sight of a New Romantic lead guitarist and sometime backing singer trouncing him. The knock on effect was that there was no chance of him letting himself be overtaken by a minor sports presenter as well. With an imperceptible acceleration Macey started to pull away from me again in pursuit of the rapidly vanishing Kemp.

I was powerless to do anything about it, and by the time we reached the finishing straight outside Downing Street, neither man was visible.

For the record, I actually completed the time trial a little faster than Dean Macey, but somewhat slower than my Schroders teammates, one of whom was clearly in his mid-fifties (and no doubt had a substantial and well-funded pension plan to look forward to when the day came for him to retire).

But neither he, nor I, nor Dean Macey were anywhere near as fast as Kemp. I had been humbled. Later on that afternoon, I was more formally introduced. In fact, bewilderingly, he introduced himself to me, rather than the other way round. I don't think he actually said, 'Hello, I'm Gary Kemp from Spandau Ballet', but in my imagination, I rather wish he had.

This was a man who had written the songs to my adolescence, to those long nights staggering around at the back of the Chiltern Radio Roadshow, taking crafty little swigs from warm cans of Colt 45 lager instead of actually talking to girls.

Fifty-one years old, trim, fit, and dressed entirely in the trademark black and pink of Rapha's exclusive range of clothing, he looked impressively athletic and perfectly aesthetic. His eyes twinkled with the madness of an obsessive.

'I love cycling,' he told me. 'I just love everything about it.'

It was months later that I first heard about the New Romantics' Ride. There'd been talk, of course. Occasionally it would get an oblique mention, a hint or two, in some newspaper diary, or feature in the lifestyle column of an in-flight magazine. But I knew of no one who could verify its existence, let alone claim to have been invited to take part.

I wondered what it could be.

I had visions of a peloton of flamboyantly dressed middle-aged pop legends floating around on all manner of bikes. Penny farthings would certainly be involved, as would tricycles, tandems and choppers. Helmets would surely be eschewed in favour of fedoras, trilbies and Napoleonic headgear. Most riders would be wearing greatcoats that flowed out behind them, occasionally getting caught in their spokes. It would be a carefree, debonair pageant. It would be Romantic, with a capital R.

But, did it actually exist? Or was it an urban myth to be filed alongside the secret underground tunnels that supposedly connect Buckingham Palace with the Edwardian brothels of Whitechapel? (Actually, I just made that last one up, but you can see how easily these things start.)

So I went to the source. I managed to obtain an email address for Gary Kemp from the sponsors of the Hot Lap. I worded a request for an interview, and hit send.

Barely ten minutes later, and to my wild surprise, I got a reply.

Hi Ned,

Yes, of course.

I live in town, West End. I had a new baby this week so end of next week. We could have a spin round Regent's Park. I usually have a gentle park ride with the lads on a Friday morning for an hour. And an interview after at mine if you like?

G.

This was the closest thing I had to proof of the existence of the New Romantics Ride. I read and reread the email, studying it closely for nuances. Who were the 'lads'? What was meant by the conflicting terms 'spin' and 'gentle ride'? What pace did they imply? Would I be able to keep up and, even if I did, would I be able to talk? After all, I had seen Kemp ride and had been soundly beaten by him.

Consequently, it was with great trepidation that I set off one grey Friday morning for Regent's Park. Even the clothing choice had been testing. In the end, I'd opted for the canary yellow polyester of the De Ver bike shop in Norbury (I would make Maurice Burton proud), believing that would offer the least chance of me wearing the same thing as any of the 'lads'. I doubted very much whether they'd have been clothes shopping in south London.

In that regard at least, I was quite right. Arriving at precisely the allotted hour and at the prescribed meeting point (which for reasons of confidentially, I hope you will understand, I cannot possibly commit to print), I noticed instantly that I was not the first. An impeccably clad man in his middle years already stood on the pavement, patiently holding his Condor bicycle, wearing a cap, and scrolling his iPhone as he waited.

It wasn't Kemp, I established, as I rode past him. I had been too shy to stop. This often happens to me, but normally at weddings. I fear most of all those painful reunions and cold introductions on the way into churches, and will go out of my way to postpone them until the last possible minute, even if that means driving past the churchyard half-a-dozen times with one eye on the dashboard clock, before finally parking up and entering the fray. This was no different.

Out of sight now round a bend in the road, I executed an awkward U-turn, and approached again the man in the cap by the side of the road. This time, as I neared him, I saw he'd been joined by another, similar figure. They seemed to be making each other laugh. That was enough to put me off again, and I rode past for a second time, quite unable to pull over and introduce myself.

Another U-turn, which I conducted in the full realisation that the Metropolitan Police would by now have picked up on my aberrant cycling behaviour through any one of the hundreds of CCTV cameras that bristle from lampposts all along Regent's Park. This time I took a deep breath, and I came to a halt. By now a third man, also not Gary Kemp, had joined them. My arrival made it four.

The first man noticed me, initially with blank suspicion, then with mild recognition.

'Hello,' he said, reasonably enough.

I took my helmet off, and introduced myself. 'I'm Ned.'

'Yes.' He seemed faintly amused and mildly curious. 'Good to have you with us.' But he didn't offer his name in return.

From the other two people who weren't Gary Kemp, I felt more scrutiny. I judged that it would help allay their suspicions if I offered up my credentials for gate-crashing their party.

'I was invited by Gary Kemp to join you.' This much, of course, was true. But the moment I found myself actually saying it, the less plausible it sounded. In fact, as the words tumbled from my mouth, they sounded absurd. I might as well have strolled onto the set of *Mamma Mia* and claimed that I'd been sent there by Colin Montgomerie.

But my reasoning seemed to appease them, even if, when I told them I was going to do an interview with him, it cast me out at an increased distance from their clique. I was now definitively, on the outside. 'I don't know where Gary is. He's normally the first one here.' The man with no name effected some introductions. 'This is Lee.' The second man-who-wasn't-Kemp nodded at me. 'And this is Nadav.' I instantly knew that Nadav was not a name I would be able to remember.

The bloke whose name I'd just been told was fiddling with his brake cables. He offered me a friendly enough 'Hi'. And then he returned to his bike. Since the other two men had returned to the conversation that I had interrupted, I strolled over to him, already dreading the conversation I was about to begin about bikes.

'Wow. What a great bike. What is it?' Actually, it categorically was magnificent. It was a skinny steel beauty with a custom paint job to die for. Well, maybe not to die for, but definitely to pay lots of money for.

'Oh this old boneshaker? It's just a silly thing really. But I kind of like it.' He had a strong, but very Anglo, South African accent. He went on to tell me the name of the exclusive Italian bike builder who had custom made it for him, but I was no longer taking it in. I was busily wondering who on earth this man might be in real life. He was tall and, like the rest of our tiny peloton, in his trim-if-grey mid-fifties. And, also in common with the others, well groomed and perfectly presented in ochre shades of retro woollen cycling garb, complete with kid skin gloves. I was, by now, violently self-conscious about my neon nylon top.

'You should have been here last week. This thing was off the road and I had to use David Millar's time-trial bike.'

'I really don't know where Gary's got to.' The first non-Kemp broke in. 'I guess the baby?'

We all agreed that the presence of a newborn might have detained him. It was clear that the other riders wanted to get going, Kemp or no Kemp. This presented me with a slight dilemma. Should I continue with the ride, uninvited though I was by the other remaining members, or gracefully bow out. I ploughed on.

And into the heart of the New Romantic Ride.

> *And now I know what they're saying*
> *In the music of the parade*
> *We made our love on wasteland*
> *And through the barricades*

We set off in an anti-clockwise loop on the main road, circling Regent's Park. By now there were five of us, as we had been joined at the last minute by Simon Mottram the founder and owner of Rapha, cycling's most exclusive brand. I knew Simon a little (he was often to be seen at races), so was pleased he had arrived. But now our numbers were suddenly uneven. This made the politics of the peloton fraught with complication.

The roads around the park are wide, unusually so and quiet for Central London. They can easily accommodate two cyclists riding side by side. But not three. As a result, since our group now totalled five, one rider would always be supernumerary. Quite often, and quite understandably, this was me, riding out the back, alone with my thoughts.

The pace was very gentle though, and the chatter ahead of me fluent and friendly. Old pals. Occasionally, shreds of sentences would catch in the wind and drift back through our little bunch to me at the rear.

'. . . I'd never seen the place so deserted . . .'

'. . . he's had to sell up. I haven't seen him since that thing he did at the White Cube . . .'

'. . . couldn't believe it when she showed up. Especially after what happened last year . . .'

I was lulled into a false sense of familiarity. As if I too had been meeting up in the park with this bunch of friends for years. As if I had decades of shared history to paw over as we rode. I could get into this.

The man they called Nadav (his name had suddenly come back to me. Or rather it hadn't. But for the purposes of this narrative, let's just say I had remembered it . . .) dropped back on his fancy Italian bike, and we found ourselves riding together.

'Did you feel a bit strange riding a time-trial bike round the park last week in this group?'

'Yah. It was a bit surreal. That's for sure.'

'And you said it was the same as David Millar's Cervelo from the Tour?' I asked, more as a matter of form, than from any genuine interest.

'No. It *was* David Millar's bike. He gave it to me'

That shut me up. But, unfortunately, not for long enough. 'I've just finished reading his book,' I told him. It was true.

'What did you think?' asked Nadav, with a sideways glance.

'I enjoyed it.' I thought briefly about the book, Millar's revelations and, at times, self-flagellation. The image of himself that he has embraced over recent years has an element of theatre about it. The cover photo illustrated this perfectly; moodily lit, dark and soulful, with a hint of menace. I thought it was a bit daft.

'The picture didn't look much like him, though.'

'Oh.' There was a pause that was significant enough to signify something. 'How do you mean?'

'It's just not the David Millar I have known down through the years. It looks like someone else.'

'I'm surprised you say that.' Again that pause. 'When I took the portrait, David loved it.'

And with that, the portrait photographer injected a minute amount of pace. Just enough to gap us. Not for the first time, I was left alone with my thoughts.

Without me noticing it, we were now six. We had been joined by another sprightly little chap, also of a certain age, riding a tiny powder blue chrome and steel touring bike with a hand-stitched leather saddle pouch. He rode with a very high cadence, right at the front of the group. Simon Mottram told me his name was Kadir (another name I was destined instantly to forget, even though for the purposes of the narrative . . . etc.), and that he makes these bikes himself. 'You should go and talk to him. You'd have so much in common.'

I looked at Simon sceptically.

Building bikes, it seemed, was not all that Kadir did. He had spent the previous day at a photo shoot with Mark Cavendish, supplying odd items of cycling bric-a-brac and nostalgia for the set. His private collection of bicycling artefacts had furnished the photographer with retro props for Cavendish to variously hold, clasp, throw, sit on or slap to his head.

The other surprising thing about Kadir was his speed. After about forty-five minutes of meandering round the park on the outside, the bunch instinctively headed through some gates and onto the internal ring road inside the park. Here the pace quickened. After one kilometre, there was a slight incline, and, wordlessly, everyone started to sprint. I had no idea what was happening.

When, after about ten seconds, we crested the 'summit' (Kadir had comfortably beaten everybody), the pace slackened again, as everyone caught their breath. I dropped back to Simon Mottram.

'What the hell was that all about?'

'Where there's a hill, there's a race.' He winked at me.

A hill! It must have risen no more than about six feet over a hundred yards. Before I knew it, we had nearly completed a full circuit, and the race started to heat up again, as the 'hill' approached. This time I was better positioned for the sprint, finishing second, but still some way behind the pocket rocket that was Kadir. I couldn't help it, a loud guffaw escaped me. Partly due to the effort involved in trying to catch the pint-sized cycling nostalgist. But equally, it was the absurdity, the pyrrhic nonsense of it all.

And on lap three, I got him. He didn't see it coming. I blind-sided him, and by the crest of the ascent, I blasted over the line at least three lengths to the good.

Behind me, Simon Mottram had commentated on my win. 'Kadir holding his line, but Boulting's coming, Boulting's closing all the time. Boulting takes the win!' It is worth reminding you, as you read this, that we were all professional men in our forties and fifties.

I eased off on the pedals, allowed myself to freewheel. As I rolled along, Kadir acknowledged my victory with a nod,

Nadav patted me on the back, 'Not-Kemp One' offered his congratulations in the form of a broad grin, but 'Not-Kemp Two' rode past with a stony demeanour.

Together, he and I rode in to the café towards which everyone seemed to be gravitating.

'What is it you do, then?' I asked him. I wanted to eradicate any chance of insulting his work before I knew what it was.

But 'Not-Kemp Two' simply didn't answer. He just grinned cryptically. I didn't know whether or not I should repeat the question (perhaps he hadn't heard). And I didn't know for how much longer I should hold my expression of curiosity, head half-cocked to one side. He remained silent. I eventually un-cocked my head.

We stacked our bikes up at the café, shared a little idle chat about the Belgian Classics. I produced a copy of *How I Won The Yellow Jumper* from my rucksack. I had intended to give it to the former Spandau Ballet man. Instead I offered it to Nadav, as a certain type of peace offering, which to his great credit, he politely accepted.

But that, in itself, provoked a flurry of awkwardness. He had no bag, and his beautifully tailored back pockets on his retro merino jersey wouldn't stretch to holding the book. So the cursed thing just sat on the table in front of us, its jokey type-face and primary-coloured illustrations looking tawdry and unamusing. I wished fervently that I'd left it mouldering in the depths of my rucksack, nestling against a cereal bar.

Then 'Not-Kemp One' looked at his watch, sighed and left. 'Better go. Got a bloody radio show to present.'

Of course he had a radio show to present. Didn't we all?

It had been that kind of day. But there had been no Gary Kemp.

On returning home, I emailed Simon Mottram. Who were all those other people in the park, I wanted to know? His reply, and a little Wikipedia work threw up the following cast list for the New Romantic Ride:

Bob Elms (Not-Kemp One). Wrote for the *Face* and *NME* in the 1980s. Dated Sade. Invented the name of the band Spandau Ballet. Has presented numerous TV shows, and now hosts a long-running show on BBC London.

Lee Barrett (Not-Kemp Two). A major figure in the 1980s club scene. Discovered Sade, and went on to manage her. He asked her, 'Can you sing?' She failed the audition, but got the job anyway.

Kadir Guirey. A leading light in the 1980s' skateboarding scene, Guirey also appeared on *Top of the Pops* with a band called Funkapolitan. He was their lead singer. Now a leading collector of cycling memorabilia.

Nadav Kander. A world-renowned photographer. He has exhibited in every major gallery from new York to London and in 2009 was named International Photographer of the Year.

Then another email pinged into my Inbox. It was from Gary Kemp.

Dear Ned,

I am mortified and so sorry. My wife asked me to do the school run today, and so I didn't do the ride. I forgot it was with you. So sorry as you came such a long way. Can I come over to you? Let's talk.

Gary.

'So sorry as you came such a long way' could have been a Spandau Ballet lyric, I thought. I told him there really was no need to apologise, that Lewisham was not such a distance away, and that I'd enjoyed it, anyway. I recounted my points victory over Kadir.

Kadir is fast! My God, you must be good!

Could we meet next Friday, perhaps?

Absolutely. In the diary now.

G.

Next Friday dawned. At 6.30 in the morning, I received an email. Again it was from Gary Kemp.

Hi Ned,

I've got a bloody Achilles injury that has flared up over night so cannot make it. Please let me know that you got this. We will get there.

Best
Gary

The following week, I tried again to fix an appointment. I asked him if his Achilles was better.

Hi Ned,

Yes, feeling better but this Friday I have to take my son to his piano grades. When's your deadline?

Best
Gary

Since there wasn't really a deadline, I gently let it go.

In August, some five months later, we had another near miss. He and I were guests on separate episodes of the same cycling show on ITV. He was on a few weeks before me.

One of the elements in the show was a 500-metre 'roller' challenge, riding a stationary bike very fast for a short burst. He, I noted with interest, had completed his distance in just over 26 seconds.

My target was now set. When I took to the saddle in front of the cameras, my only concern was to get close to the time set by Gary Kemp. To my surprise and delight, I managed 25.72 seconds.

The next day, after a long period of silence between us, I dropped him one last speculative line, could we finally meet? I wasn't really expecting a reply. Especially since I'd been unable to resist letting him know about the 25.72 seconds.

Hi Ned,

There's a coffee bar called Kaffeine on Great Titchfield Street. Is that OK? Say 10.45 a.m.

G

It was indeed OK.

Gary Kemp, chiselled, blow-dried, immaculate, had his hands full. He arrived at our meeting place with his baby son, Rex, in his arms, and was shoving a pushchair, from which a dozen different bags and straps were hanging, into the crowded über-hip coffee bar. His three-year-old son Kit was also part of the Kemp family's ram-raiding attempt on Kaffeine, Kit's preferred method being a scooter.

'I'm *so* sorry, Ned.' He was trying to park the buggy in a non-existent space, and prevent it from falling over backwards by standing on one leg and bracing his thigh against the frame. I wondered how long he could keep it up. 'Lauren's coming along any minute. I told her that this wouldn't work. But she's on the turbo, you know.'

Then he was off, shaking a bottle of formula, in search of a bowl of warm water to bring it up to the right temperature for Rex. The pushchair fell back against our table. Young Kit looked at me.

'Are you a doctor?' he asked.

We both looked at his toy medical set.

'No, but I feel a bit sick.'

When Gary and Rex returned, he found Kit repeatedly injecting me with a huge amount of some unidentified substance from an oversized blue plastic syringe. Then, with admirable diligence, Kit did my tests: temperature, heart rate, peering into my ears. Then, for the sake of thoroughness, he tried his own knee reflexes with a hammer. He wasn't ruling anything out, the young Kemp.

Gary and I attempted to get some adult conversation underway. But it was all in vain, as it often is when adults are surrounded by infants. Each opening gambit would be snuffed out by a small-voiced complaint or enquiry.

'So what's next for you, Gary?'

'Well, I've got a few different—'

'Didn't want that one. I wanted one with raisins in.'

Rex finally had his chops round the teat of the bottle and was guzzling away. Lauren arrived, looking a bit stressed by the sheer spread of the chaos we had invoked in the café. With apologetic smiles aimed at the staff, she then removed all the male members of her family, bar one.

'Bloody hell, you must be thinking, this isn't what you thought life would be like for celebrities!' Gary took a sip of his coffee. 'What do you want to know, Ned?'

Very quickly, we were onto the New Romantics Ride.

'Martin Fry's joined us. He was out last Friday on the ride.' I nodded. Martin Fry was the lead singer of ABC. So now, irritatingly, I had the refrain from 'Shoot That Poison

Arrow' going through my head. It turned out to be the perfect accompaniment to Kemp's everyday tale of pop star turned bicyclist, which it seemed, was not such an unusual meta-morphosis.

'You look back in the 1960s and it was very close to Mod culture. Bryan Ferry was into it, Paul Smith, Jeff Banks, all these old Mods. It was Continental, so it was sort of sexy.' And then, quite rightly, he points out that 'Kraftwerk famously gave up being in a band, basically so they could cycle all the time!'

But the Kemp brothers and their peers were more interested in other things at the time, and all this bicycle nonsense had passed them by. 'We've got a history of getting completely smashed and wrecked and creating fashions and making a lot of money selling records all over the world.' And as Gary Kemp says this, I am reminded of quite how big they were during my childhood, and of how surreal it is to be sitting here with the man who wrote the soundtrack to my life. Or at least the bit which involved hanging around unrequitedly outside Jane Woolhouse's front door on Chaucer Road.

It wasn't until Kemp hit his late forties, and was introduced to the expensive, monochrome aesthetic of Rapha that his head, with a 'cap always at a jaunty angle', was turned. He started to go online, sometimes at night, often furtively.

'My wife thought I had some sort of homoerotic secret. Suddenly I was looking at black-and-white photos of stubbly blokes with shaved legs.'

I laugh at this notion, and try to embellish it. 'With massage oils and embrocation creams?' I add, with a chuckle.

'Yes,' says Kemp, looking unengaged, and with a discreet glance at his watch. I am left with the sense that I have taken the joke a little too far.

'Cycling's a cult for older men. I couldn't do golf. I left that to Tony Hadley. He's a larger man. I'm going to wait for my hip replacement before I get into golf.'

Tony Hadley, striding around on a golf course in a black polo neck and black slacks. I could very easily imagine that. It was such a rich image that I was, temporarily, no longer able to think of anything else to ask. Fortunately, Kemp was on a roll. The words, as you would expect from a songwriter, came easily to him.

'Where do I meet my old mates again? We don't go out to clubs any more. And if we're in the Groucho, we're probably with our wives. I felt there was a vacuum. Cycling was the answer.' I imagined them all sitting around a table in the Groucho club, as the conversation dries up. The men exchange knowing glances. The women excuse themselves and head en masse for the Ladies' room.

'Of course it does suit our addictive natures. Aesthetics meet endorphins. I love that thing.' Album titles, or potential album titles seemed to spill from his every sentence.

'I find the cadence very musical. That's the rhythm, that's the key. You're in a song, and it's hard and it's fast. You can't stop. You can't slow down. I do find myself singing songs as I'm riding along. But it's usually horrible stuff like "Brown Girl In The Ring".'

'Shoot That Poison Arrow' was suddenly no longer the song I couldn't get out of my head. As ABC took a bow, I welcomed Boney M onto the stage. Kemp continued, his flow uninterrupted, his verbal cadence, not skipping a beat. *Tra-la-la-la-la!*

'I get the same buzz as I used to being in a band. Riding in a group is like being in a band. There's this thing about living in the moment, which I love. With music, you're thinking only about the next eight bars. And with cycling you're only ever thinking about the next eight metres.'

Suddenly, Gary Kemp paused. He looked down, thoughtfully, and then looked up with a sudden, fresh smile.

'I should have said eight yards, because there's a nice internal rhyme then.' He looked wistful. 'Missed that.'

Our time in the café came to a close. Gary Kemp had things to do with his family, and I had to be somewhere else to do something much less rewarding than talking to a New Romantic about cycling.

At a fundamental level, there was no difference between his passion for the sport, and anyone else's. But his was wound up inextricably with a time and a place. I liked the idea that every Friday morning, come rain or shine, a clutch of men who did their bit to shape our lives are remembering themselves and reinventing themselves lap by lap around Regent's Park. Even if I never joined them again, it was good to know that they would be there, for as long as they could be.

'We think we're really fast and really tasty. We're a bunch of blokes in our late forties and early fifties. I mean, how fast can that be?'

Faster than me.

I thanked him for his time, and we left the café together, talking speculatively about collaborating on spurious TV projects that we both knew would never see the light of day.

I had my bike locked up outside, and, as I fiddled ineffectually with the key in the lock, I temporarily lost my composure as I became aware, not for the first time, but with great clarity, that I'd finally pulled it off. I'd just spent an hour talking to Gary Kemp.

We shook hands, and he walked off up Great Titchfield Street. My final words to him will haunt me for some time.

'Bye, Martin.'

CHAPTER 8

GILLOTS AND THE THIRTY-FOUR NOMADS

'He's only gone and pissed himself, Gill!'

Ron Keeble points delightedly at the rapidly spreading damp patch on my shorts, mostly centred around the waistband and crotch. Gill, a sprightly lady with slightly more finely tuned manners than her husband, glances down at the offending area, at first alarmed, and then with carefully concealed amusement.

'Oh, leave him alone, Ron. Can I get you a cold drink, Ned? A Coke, an orange juice?'

'Yes, please,' I mutter, mortally embarrassed. 'An orange juice would be very nice, thank you Gill.' I have become twelve years old, and I am round my friend's house in the kitchen.

Ron, coming in from the garden and sliding the French windows closed, isn't quite prepared to let it rest. Not just yet.

'Looks just like he's pissed himself.'

'Don't listen to him, Ned.' Gill pours me a drink, and I manage to mumble my thanks.

I cling to my two remaining scraps of dignity; I *haven't* actually pissed myself. And I *have* climbed to the top of Alpe d'Huez. Sort of.

There is a hard core of hard men in and around British cycling in whose presence I merely shut up and listen. They are men who make little or no allowance for the fact that not everyone has been following the minutiae of their beloved sport for the past forty years.

In their company, everything is different. Gone is that certain wide-eyed delight that newcomers like me and the Spandau Ballet chap can share and see mirrored in each other's immature appreciation of the sport. Shortcomings, for newbies, are natural. Deficiencies in knowledge are accept-able, even if, in Gary Kemp's case, the clothing has to be perfect. But not everywhere I look do I find such under-standing. Sometimes it can be withering.

During the last summer's Tour of Britain (a race small enough for the teams, the organisation and the media to share hotels), I often found myself thrown to the wolves. Gathered together over a beer in the evenings, a wizened cast of cycling's principal characters would recall races that had been won in dubious circumstances, riders who had overstepped the mark or team managers who had promised much and then disap-peared into thin air. You had to know who the lead actors were. You had to be there.

Ron Keeble was invariably there, loud, bawdy, sharp and funny, a vital presence over dinner and drinks at the end of every stage. He was, to use a cliché that covers a range of attributes, larger than life, or at least, larger than me. He drove the car for one of the race commissaries on the Tour of Britain, a macho job that is normally, and for good reasons, reserved for ex-riders. He had just the right amount of acquired wisdom and instinctive recklessness to weave an estate car in and out of a peloton along narrow country lanes.

Such was his status that everyone assumed I knew him, and that he knew me, but no one had actually ever introduced us. After a few days the moment had passed where either of us could possibly have said, 'Sorry. I didn't catch your name.' I found myself trying to sneak a glance at his accreditation, to no avail.

So, we kind of drifted into a state of knowing each other through a prolonged period during which we were both playing for time, of referring to each other simply as 'mate', or still worse, 'fella'.

The 2012 Tour of Britain came and went, and we parted company as we had started, virtual strangers. All that I knew for certain of this sun-tanned, nattily dressed Londoner, was that once upon a time he'd been a rider, and that he was fizzing with obscure plans, pie-in-the-sky projects and business ideas, some of which sounded pretty plausible; like wrapping bike frames in customised vinyl to protect the paintwork, or a new pedal that would fit multiple different types of cleat. He was always onto something. I had taken a liking to him. He made me curious, too.

A few months after the Tour, and because he'd invited me, I rang him up and went round to his house.

'Bring your cycling shoes,' he'd insisted. 'You're going to ride up a bloody mountain.'

In *Orpington?* I thought. But I didn't say anything. I just made sure I had my cycling shoes. If Ron told you to do something, then you were normally well advised to do it.

The day had begun forbiddingly. I rode the ten or so miles from my place to his, misjudged the severity of the ride, and collapsed from sugar-depleted exhaustion at a Bromley petrol station on the way. One flapjack and twenty minutes later he answered his door, to find me and my (very humble) bike looking like something undesirable smeared across his doormat. He gingerly picked up my bike and stuck it in his shed, eyeing up the rust patches on the chain, and the worn out tyres with a simmering discontent he did well to contain. A neurotic intolerance of poorly maintained equipment is perhaps the only thing that unites every rider I have ever met.

'It's not about the bike, Ron,' I quipped, merrily.

'Yes it bloody is.' We went inside.

Ron and Gill had bought the house in the early 1970s. He led me through to the pleasant sunny kitchen while Gill left us to it. We could see through the French windows that autumn had just started to blow into the garden. We drank tea, and Ron doodled with a black biro as he listened to my questions. Very carefully, and with great attention paid to the shading, he wrote the word 'Cyclist' in a homespun, ornate font. That single word was it, really, that was the sole line of inquiry.

Listening to him was like an immersion in an exotic language. The flora and fauna of the domestic cycling scene informed all his memories, a mystifying landscape of names and dormant institutions long forgotten. They tripped off his tongue: the Golden Wheel, the William Tell, the White Hope and something that sounded like the Wally Gimber, and probably was the Wally Gimber. And name after name of towering figures of yesteryear from a track scene so central to Ron's life that he could barely conceive of a world in which they held little or no currency, men of the decimalisation era with names like Norman, Roy and Don. I could have stopped him and asked who they were and what the hell they were all doing in Kirkby that Tuesday night, but that would have got us nowhere. Ron's narrative allowed for little deviation.

He spoke in a code, even when asked the most superficially comprehensible question.

'Where did you meet Gill, Ron?'

'Ah.' He looked up from his doodling towards the kitchen door behind which Gill was playing with one of their four grandchildren.

'Well,' he started, with great portent. 'We was down Gillotts, and it had the Thirty-Four Nomads.'

A Dictaphone, placed between us, recorded that sentence. I have listened back to it seven times, now, hoping to understand it. But there it is, in all its naked, impenetrable glory. Gillotts. Nomads. Thirty-four of them. You know.

Ronald James Keeble was born just over the water from the Houses of Parliament, less than a year after the end of the Second World War. He grew up in the Elephant and Castle, an area that has consistently failed to acquire a satisfactory identity in the landscape of South London's town planning.

Some years after Ron came into the world, they turned the area into a vast network of dual carriageways and roundabouts, with subterranean passages and brutal shopping precincts that would define the location for half a century. Only now has the Elephant's extraordinary proximity to Westminster been reflected in the potential of its real estate value, and the developers have started to land grab en masse. Gone is the archetypal Heygate Estate that flanked the arterial New Kent Road with its endlessly long, endlessly forbidding façade. Going is the pink-clad Elephant Shopping Centre, complete with indoor market and best remembered for housing the public enquiry into the murder of Stephen Lawrence.

But, in Ron's childhood, in those years of austerity and making do, Elephant and Castle remained, at least in part, resolutely flattened; scarcely a priority for the Greater London Council. Besides, the Luftwaffe had left its calling card in the shape of a series of burnt-out shells and buildings reduced to crumbling collapse. So it came as no surprise to me when Ron, nursing another cup of tea into which Gill had slopped one healthy teaspoon of sugar, suddenly remembered where he'd got his first bike from.

'In a bomb crater, it was. The forks were bent, but I got that sorted.'

It's not quite true, of course. By now I was beginning to establish that such childhood memories often required visiting and re-visiting before the layers of obfuscation and fabrication are eventually peeled away. Before Ron had found that bike in a bomb crater, he'd already written off another one. A friend had lent him his, so that he could ride over to Millwall and visit a girlfriend who went by the appropriately post-war name of Sheila Mellish. On his way back from his liaison with Miss Mellish, he lost control of his mate's bike. 'I was coming down Blackheath Hill and I went under a lorry.'

Blackheath Hill is very steep.

I am struck, not for the first time, by the casual way in which riders recall life-threatening accidents. A few years later, and by this time he had become a proper rider, fate picked up where the lorry left off. Ron was lucky not to have been killed. 'I smashed my back up. I was told that I wouldn't walk again.'

He was at the front end of a hotly contested points race at a track meeting at Earls Court.

'I was going round Graham Webb for a point, and he lost it. And he took me up into the banking.' The track at Earls Court was a temporary structure, installed just for the meetings and then dismantled. Health and Safety wasn't a priority.

'Well, I went over the top of the banking, fell down into the stalls that they'd made, and then fell through them down to the floor.' When he opened his eyes and looked up, all he saw was the criss-cross geometry of the wooden scaffolding that supported the seating. In his concussed state, he assumed that he was lying at the bottom of a gas holder, looking up at the sky.

A hard man, then. That's what I think he is. But, it appears I am wrong. Ron Keeble smiles self-deprecatingly back at me.

'I was soft. I don't mind admitting it. I was a soft southerner. I never ever went abroad [to live]. I was a mummy's boy. If, like now, they'd said you've got to go and live in Manchester, I wouldn't have liked it.'

And so Ron Keeble, unlike others more discontent with their lot back at home and dreaming of adventure, never really chanced his arm in the big bad world. Unlike so many who went before, he remained resolutely wedded to the British scene, the world of the Six-Day track meetings (sponsored for many years by Britain's worst ever lager: Skol) and domestic honours. Not for him the privations of life on the road, he wanted his home comforts too keenly.

The only really big adventure away from home left a lasting impression. He went to Munich in 1972. He was part of the Team Pursuit quartet who came home with the Olympic bronze medal. The other three men were Ian Hallam, Mick Bennett and Willi Moore, who blew a tyre in the semi-final, allowing West Germany to gain a fatal, and decisive, advantage. They went on to win gold. But Great Britain can feel with some justification, that it could have been, perhaps should have been, them. Such things change lives.

Ron, people tell me, took a long time to come to terms with that, if he ever did at all.

The 1972 Games, as they are remembered by Ron Keeble, sound like a terrific *Boy's Own* adventure. 'Hi-jinks' and 'capers' spring to mind. Listening to him relive those two weeks of competition, it's hard not to feel deeply envious of such an experience, the shared joie de vivre, the camaraderie. Bound together by the sheer effort of getting yourself to the start line, fit and with a functioning bike, the team were held together despite, not because of, their circumstances. They had to supply their own bikes, and their own tyres, for example, and you suspect that if the authorities had found a way of getting them to fork out for their own train tickets to Germany, they'd probably have done that, too.

The preparation, needless to say, was homespun and eccentric. Mick Bennett had been entered to ride the kilometre time trial (the others had all ridden deliberately slowly in the Olympic trials to avoid being picked) as well as the Team Pursuit. He therefore could justifiably claim to have worked harder than the others and needed more pampering in recovery. He developed his own techniques, and used to borrow Gill's Novocaine cream, which she was using as a topical anaesthetic during breast-feeding. He used to smother his legs in his friend's wife's medicine, and go for a lie down in his room after a training block.

'He loved it,' remembers Ron, with a wistful smile. Knowing that their teammate would be nodding off, his legs smothered in breast-feeding ointment, Ron, Ian and Willi would sneak up to his room, and then rap at the door, pretending to be race starters.

'*Attention, messieurs les coureurs!*' they bellowed through the door (which roughly translates as On Your Marks!)

There'd be a brief silence during which the trio of athletes held their noses to prevent their giggles from snorting out. And then, from behind the door, 'Fuck off and leave me alone.' They'd run off hooting with mirth, like a scene in *Carry On Cycling*. A young Sid James would have played Keeble. Bennett would have been Charles Hawtrey.

And in the athletes' village, they devised a cyclists' decathlon. This comprised Peach Lobbing (lobbing peaches), Restaurant Racing (a bunch sprint to the canteen), Sauna Sitting (sweating stamina), as well as more conventional disciplines, like the Swimathon. This involved swimming lengths of the pool, having to reach out of the water to touch the wall before splashing back in and turning for another length. It was all well and good, before Willi, reaching for the wall, dislocated his shoulder and locked solid, his outstretched arm trapped in mid-air. He couldn't move.

'Willi! Touch the fucking wall!' they yelled at him.

'Fuck off, Ian. Help!'

'Ian was a doctor,' Ron recalls. 'He was the only one with medical training. He had to pop his arm back in the socket.' This was just days before their competition started.

Mischief. Everything about Ron Keeble implies mischief. To say that his eyes twinkle would be the second cliché in this chapter, but another one that I am prepared to indulge. He twinkles with the delight of it all. Mick Bennett once told me that Ron had found life after Munich very difficult. This may be true. But the man sitting opposite me, scribbling away and chuckling, shows no signs of anything other than rude health, and mischief.

Occasionally, he reminds me that I still have a mountain to climb. I swiftly change the subject back again. Back to Munich.

When horror visited the athletes' village, with the hostage taking of the Israeli Olympic team, the GB Pursuit Team were evacuated from their rooms that overlooked the infamous balcony on which the terrorists were, from time to time, visible.

The intervening years have given Ron plenty of time to feel the true outrage of this tragedy. But at the time, and with their own race programme interrupted and indefinitely suspended, their self-absorption made them brood.

'The whole time you were thinking about the ride, the ride, the ride. You were still thinking selfishly, "Shit. I've got enough on my plate."'

Besides, as the siege went into a second day, Ron thought they could have been of use to the authorities. One of their 'cyclists' decathlon' events had involved tossing cartons of the sponsor's chocolate drink Sour Milo onto the exact balcony they now saw on their TV screens.

'We could have taken then out. If they'd left it to us, me and Willi could have taken them out, whack! No problem.'

Appallingly, no amount of improvised British bravado would have had the slightest effect. The siege ended in bloodshed. Eleven members of the Israeli Olympic Team were murdered.

Ron shows me his Munich medal. It's not kept anywhere special; today he leaves it curled around a statuette next to the telly. Tomorrow it might be slung round the door handle of the fridge. But, if Munich and 1972 represent certain things to most of us, they mean much more to Ron Keeble. Of that you can be sure.

Now, suddenly, there is another cyclist in the kitchen. Brian Smith is a retired Scottish pro, a two-time British National

Road Race Champion, no less, and once, briefly, a teammate of Lance Armstrong on Motorola. He was a tough rider, racing clean in an era when not that many others were. He's still a prodigiously tough man, with fingers in many pies: a team manager, a commentator, a fund-raiser, a fixer. He is also married to Ron Keeble's daughter, and the grandchild with whom Gill has been preoccupied is his oldest boy.

My otherness has just been made flesh and blood. I am no longer merely 'not a cyclist', I am also 'not family'.

Brian had got wind of my visit, complete with my vaguely promised intention to ride up this mythical mountain. It transpires that the mountain in question is Alpe d'Huez. Ron Keeble has a virtual trainer, complete with a video display, in his gym. This, it seems, Brian Smith cannot miss.

'My record's thirty-four minutes,' he claims, with not the slightest flicker to give away the fact that this is utter bollocks.

'But Pantani's record is thirty-seven something!' I protest. 'And he was doped.'

'Well, I did thirty-four.' There is no trace of self-doubt. I later find out that his record is in fact forty-six, but at the time I believed him. Ron, meanwhile, has got up to boil the kettle.

It's good to see them together, the archetypal cockney and the deadpan Scot. They should have little in common, being two alpha males from opposing ends of the country and a generation apart. But here they are, cutting each other to ribbons with their barbed comments, completing each other's sentences, clearly utterly comfortable in each other's company, two peas in a pod. Or, as Brian later confesses, like father and son. They are both, after all, cyclists. I listen as their conversation weaves in and out of the sport.

Then suddenly, as the kettle bubbles up and then switches itself off, Ron remembers something about his childhood.

'Mum started working for this woman, you see, who owned

her own company.' Ron begins to pour the tea. His mother had been a contract cleaner. 'At the time, I was still crap on a bike.' I glance at Brian, expecting him to seize on this assessment. Just the merest raised eyebrow from Brian.

'Thing was, she was a clairvoyant. Anyway. I was crap, like I said, but she told my mother that she'd had this dream that I'd become an Olympic champion.' Ron declares this with a slight flourish, looking satisfied. He puts the kettle back.

Ron goes on, and tells us of the strange fate that awaited the poor lady. 'She went missing. A couple of months later, they found her in the loft in her house on Sydenham Hill. She'd ended up hanging herself.'

He strains the teabags. 'Sugar?'

'One please.'

'But, before she died, I remember that she told Mum I'd become an Olympic champion.'

There is a pause. Long enough for me to guess what Brian is going to say.

'She got that wrong, then.'

'Fuck off, Brian.'

Brian organises an annual fundraising event for the British cycling family. Big name riders, as well as all sorts of other people with a love for the sport make their way to attend the drinking-fest that is the Braveheart Dinner. Ron is always there. It seems that, in common with just about everybody else, he's often a little bit the worse for wear. And he always comes away with something from the charity auction.

That explains why his outbuilding, a small rectangular brick construction at the foot of his garden, houses such an extraordinary amount of stuff. It's not just bits and pieces that he has accrued at the Braveheart Dinner, it should be noted. There are boxes containing brand-new bikes, unopened, and, on the day I was there, a fifty-five-inch plasma TV complete with 'Six hundred pounds' worth of 3D glasses. Never used the bloody things. Nor the telly.'

But, as he explains, there's enough money sloshing around the Keeble estate (he owns a chemical firm) for him to buy things according to the principle of 'Because I Can'. This, I agree with Ron, is a very good reason to buy things, and much more sustainable than its poor relation, 'Because I Can't'.

All around the room, some hanging from nails and hooks, but mostly just stacked up against the wall, Ron has a collection of framed cycling jerseys. Apparently there are 'loads more up in the bedroom', but this assortment would do just fine. Brian, who finds the whole thing faintly amusing (but whether it's the room, my presence in the room or a combination of both of those I can't be sure), points to a signed Rainbow Jersey, which once belonged to Tom Boonen, after his victory of 2005.

'That's Tom.' Brian makes the sign of the coke snorter, with a thumb held to his nostril. 'And there's Rasmussen, look.' Sure enough, and largely inexplicably, Ron Keeble has acquired a signed Polka Dot jersey from the 2006 Tour de France, worn by Denmark's skeletal climber the year before he had to be bundled off the race in drug-related ignominy and confusion. I look around for more. There's Ivan Basso. His Liquigas team jersey had been signed just before the enforcement of his two-year suspension. It seems that Ron Keeble has unwittingly assembled a rogues' gallery of some of the most notorious riders of the last decade.

'And that's the best of all.' I look across the room. There, leaning against a wall, behind a rowing machine, is a real beauty: a signed yellow jersey of Floyd Landis, the first man ever to be stripped of his title (many more have subsequently followed where Landis dared to tread).

It's a gem; a framed scrap of cycling iconography, a Turin shroud, with the face of Floyd Landis secretly embedded into its weave, if you stare at it hard enough. I ask Ron how much he paid for it. He winks at me, but it's clear he doesn't want to tell me, either because he believes that discussing his fiscal largesse would be distasteful in such straitened times, or that he'd been too pissed to remember. I suspect it is the latter.

I could no longer delay the inevitable. An Alp rose up in front of me. It towered before my eyes, or it would have done had Ron not briefly lost the remote control. Then the screen sputtered into life, a flickering still frame of a road leading away, and up into the distance.

Ron set about getting the training bike ready for use. It was a turbo trainer; a bike whose front wheel has been removed and whose back wheel is held in place against a roller. It wasn't going anywhere, except in this particular bike's case, Alpe d'Huez. Virtually.

The handlebars were adjusted, my feet clipped in. I adjusted my Lycra, grateful for the padded seat of my shorts against a saddle which felt wooden. Last words of advice were imparted as I stared up at the computer screen. I actually knew this road for real. It lay on the outskirts of Bourg d'Oisans, a town whose familiarity lies in the fact that it is included almost every year on the route of the Tour de France. I have driven through it on many occasions. This time, in a small suburban back garden, I would ride it. My heart beat fast. Ron and Brian stood either side of me. They wished me luck, and I thought I could sense a smirk, not because I could see it, but because the urge to snigger was buried not far beneath the surface of their last-minute ministration.

I suddenly thought about the exchange of text messages with Ron I had stored on my phone from the day before:

Me: Is Alpe d'Huez going to make me physically sick?

Ron: Let's put it like this. If you get to the top I will be surprised, and it will probably be the hardest thing you ever do.

Ron: Only joking!!!!!!!!!!!!

Ron: Or am I??

It wasn't the twelve exclamation marks that bothered me, but the two question marks. Suddenly, as I perched on this unwieldy bike, flanked by a family pack of former pros, in this glorified shed surrounded by the signatures of the decade's most infamous dopers and bounders, I felt that those two question marks got to the very heart of my predicament. What was I doing here??

'Right, off you go.' The clock started to tick. I pushed off. Magically the video display sprang into life, and I started to move forward, but ever so slowly, my legs instantly rebelling against the gradient. I was wading through treacle. 'You're just on the flat now, the climb starts round the corner.'

This was unwelcome news. I tried to push on a bit. But the gradient display showed that I had now hit Alpe d'Huez itself and that the road was getting steeper. Commensurately, the resistance applied to the rollers increased. It was night-marishly stiff. Ron placed a water bottle at my side, and a towel on the handlebars.

'Just pedal. Just pedal up it.' Brian may be many things, including bright, clever and thoughtful. But 'just pedal' struck me as particularly asinine. What other choice did he imagine that I had? Not pedalling would get me nowhere. Not even out of this bloody shed.

On and on it went. The display suggested that the summit was 8.6 miles away. Eventually, after what seemed like an age, and at the cost of a sapping amount of effort, it budged. I stared at it in disbelief. It now read 8.5 miles. The sweat already poured off me.

Ron had left me to it. He'd gone to get changed into some shorts so that he could exercise on the rowing machine and keep an eye on my progress. Brian, after a few more encouraging, yet useless, words about pedalling, simply left, never to return.

And after that I can't be sure of anything.

Sometimes I was alone in that garden in Orpington. Other times I was alone on the tree-lined slopes of the great mountain. Voices came and went. The occasional laugh. The odd solicitous enquiry. My calves burnt. My thighs howled their disapproval through the medium of hurting unimaginably. At one point Ron tried to hold me still on the bike, to prevent my upper body from swaying from side to side like a Weeble. 8.4 miles, and then, an age later, 7.9 miles to go. Would this ever end?

My water bottle was dry. My towel was wet through. Sweat ran all the way over all of me. I had never seen the backs of my hands sweat before, nor my elbows, nor knees. I had not known that these areas of my body's surface had pores through which it was possible to sweat. Perhaps the subcutaneous pressure had simply bust holes in my skin.

Rivers of Salty Distress. For a while that phrase stuck in my imagination. It repeated itself on a permanent loop in my inner ear: 'Rivers of Salty Distress.' Where had I heard it before? Was it a Johnny Cash album? If it wasn't, I thought, it damn well should be.

7.3 miles to the top.

In my delirium, and to his wild excitement, Ron calculated that, at my current rate of progress, I would breach the finish line exactly seven seconds short of one hour. He showed me the readout of his prediction on his iPhone. Through a film of sweat, I made out the numbers: 59'53". So I had a target. This made it even worse.

But, as all things do, given time, this dark, dark hour came to an end. As Alpe d'Huez itself, the nasty ski resort that it is, reared hideously into pixelated view I sprinted for the line. Somehow, I hauled myself there with one last effort.

My time? Fifty-nine minutes and fifty-one seconds. Not only had I smashed Ron's predicted time by a whole two seconds, I had finished comfortably within the hour, and only twenty-two minutes slower than Marco Pantani.

Once Gill had handed me my orange juice, and Ron had stopped laughing about my sweat-stained clothing, everything started to come back into focus. Not just Ron and Gill's kitchen, but my life itself. It was time to get going.

That's what happened to Ron, too. At the age of twenty-six, just after the Munich Olympic games, he retired from cycling to start a family, only to realise after a further five years that he missed it too much, at which point he came out of retirement to race again, this time against people ten years younger than him. The lengthy time out had done nothing to diminish his ferocity on a bike. On his first race back, he declared, 'None of you little boys are going to piss over me. You're going to have to climb over me to beat me.'

But often they did beat him. His best years had gone. 'I wasted all them years. Wasted them really.'

He went on to do very well for himself, when cycling finally let him go, or he let go of it. 'Money doesn't make you happy. No. But it makes being unhappy easier to bear.'

'And this generation? Wiggins? Cavendish? Brailsford?'

'Dave Brailsford? Either he's been arsehole lucky . . . or he's been brilliant.'

He thinks about the Tour of Britain, the triumphant lap of honour for the two British superstars on the team. A few weeks after the Olympic Games, both Mark Cavendish, racing for the last time as the reigning World Champion, and Bradley Wiggins, the Olympic gold medallist winner of the Tour de France, had taken part in the race. Cavendish raced hard to the end. Wiggins, perhaps less so. In fact, he climbed off halfway through with a tummy bug, having ridden an almost invisible race to that point.

Ron and I remember how the crowds turned out in unprecedented numbers every day to catch a glimpse of their idols, who didn't always give too much love back.

'Without doubt, Sky is resented. By the way they turn up with the best bus, and the best cars. They are resented.'

'Everywhere you went it was "Cav! Wiggo! Cav! Wiggo!" You couldn't get near Wiggo for minders.'

'I've known him a long time,' says Ron Keeble, as we head out to retrieve my bike. 'Me and him are the only two London medallists.'

That had never occurred to me, I tell him.

'But I'm the only one born and bred at Herne Hill.' He laughs, and his face splits into a wide, wide smile. Then he turns to go back inside. There is packing to be done. The next day Gill and he are flying off for a short break at their place on the Costa Blanca.

The next time I see him he asks me if I have stopped 'bleeding from my arse'.

I think I now know a little of who Ron Keeble is.

CHAPTER 9

THE MAYOR WHO HATED CYCLING

The last time I saw Ken Livingstone, he was buried up to his nose in a megaphone and almost no one was listening to him. That must be very difficult for a politician. Like watching everyone dry retching at the tables of a Michelin-starred restaurant, if you happen to be the chef.

I'd quite liked him, unfashionable though that might be to admit. I had no hard political convictions to base this on. It's just that his final period in office coincided with my reinvention as a cyclist, and also with London's reinvention as a cycling city. To some extent, I had credited him with this, and had subconsciously invested considerable emotional stock in the man. I had taken an interest.

That day, I had rather forcefully persuaded my nine-year-old daughter to ride with me all the way from Lewisham to Central London along the north bank of the river. She adored riding her bike, and I had just given her a spanking, shiny little kids' 'racer', in which she took appropriate delight. But this particular ride, truth be told, had been a little tiresome. The Thames Path was made to be walked, not ridden, and we kept on having to dismount and stop for pedestrians.

Arriving, slightly irritable, at Charing Cross station, our final destination from where we planned to catch the train home, we pushed our bikes past a clump of people holding banners, and a man in an old-fashioned mackintosh, droning on nasally about five-year investment plans. It was Livingstone, approaching the fag-end of an election campaign that had stalled badly amid allegations of tax avoidance. He was holding an 'impromptu' rally, flanked by his party faithful. Not many of them appeared to be listening to him. They were mostly whirring double-thumbed over BlackBerry keypads.

'Do you know who that is?' I asked my daughter, who had stopped alongside me to watch the curious spectacle.

'It's Ken Livingstone,' she said. I was surprised she knew his name. It sounded strange to hear her say it, dragging up a name from the early 1980s and grafting it into the here and now. She seemed so young, standing there with her gleaming aluminium bike – and he with his old mac and megaphone, preaching the creed, seemed unchanged in large measure since first he stepped into office. I would have been about her age then.

Too young. Too old. The gap between their two lives, their two Londons seemed suddenly unbridgeable. I occupied some sort of space in the middle.

We pushed our bikes off towards the station. The sound of his campaigning faded as we walked.

'I loved that ride, Dad.' I couldn't help smiling. 'Can we do it again?'

The word 'Cycling . . .' drifted across the concourse towards us. I didn't catch the rest.

It was all Livingstone's doing that on 7 July 2007 I got a parking ticket on Pall Mall. I dropped it on the ground, in broad daylight, in front of witnesses, and as bold as you like. I never paid it, because it was ethically, morally and culturally misjudged.

On the odd infuriating occasions when I have found a plastic-pouched fine nestling under my windscreen wiper, I curse in as strong an expression of outrage as my middle-class parentage will allow (Oh for God's sake!), pocket the paper with the intention of appealing to the Supreme Court of Petty Injustice, and then forget all about it until time has almost run out, when, after fourteen days, I suddenly remember that the bloody thing is about to jump from £40 to £80, and I rush to the nearest computer to pay online, clutching my credit card, and repenting all my sins by entering the sort code, the account number and the three digit security code. £40 down, I may be free of further prosecution, but am left with a surfeit of smouldering indignation.

But here, I knew I was right. You see, I had the moral heft of a hundred years of acquired culture on my side. I was working for le Tour. Henri Désgranges, Lucien Petit-Breton, Fausto Coppi and Jacques Anquetil (not, sadly Jan Ullrich, as he was serving a ban at the time) were all at my side, in a highly abstracted spiritual sense, when I said to the traffic warden while holding the weather-proofed penalty notice between my fingers, 'What's that?'

He looked wearily at me.

He had just clamped the fine to the window of our French registered Renault Espace, and was probably about to clock off and go home. It was about seven o'clock on a Sunday evening. At the back of the car, the tailgate was open and Woody and Liam were stacking all their TV kit into the boot. Drifting over from the Mall a hundred yards away, we could hear the sound of fork-lift trucks growling over the tarmac while they dismantled the Tour de France.

'These are double yellow lines,' he offered, explaining our infringement. But the traffic warden, a put-upon man with a West African accent and a whole bunch of pouches and keypads strapped to his waist, betrayed a fatal lack of self-confidence.

'No, no. That's not how it works!' Liam chimed in with the kind of Glaswegian grin that can veer very quickly from the charming to the grievous bodily.

'That's true.' I intervened, hoping to sound commanding. 'It's the Tour.' I pointed at the accreditation sticker on our windscreen. The whole area had been closed to public traffic and only accredited vehicles had been allowed in for the last twenty-four hours at least. I think he was gradually becoming aware of the error he had made.

He hesitated. He was just indecisive enough for us to know that we had won. He lost, and the Tour won.

It had been a moment though. Not any old moment, but A Moment.

We had lived in sunshine and carbon fibre and huge crowds and yellow jerseys. We had turned the Mall into the Champs-Elysées. London had not so much embraced the Tour, as taken it out for dinner, taken it for a walk along the river, then taken it home and seduced it wholly. It had been a Tale of Two Cities without the revolution. For me, in my fifth year of covering the race, it was a chance to show the folk back home what I'd been banging on about all along. I had entered some sort of halcyon half-world. I had quite forgotten where I was, so befuddled was I by its charm.

So that's why the parking ticket was wrong. It didn't fit.

When the Tour de France came to London in 2007, I made a little film about riding in London. The idea came about at our regular production meeting in the spring.

'Shouldn't we do a little thing about cycling in London?' I asked hesitantly. I was still at the stage where I had little confidence in my ideas, born from the empirical evidence that they were often extremely weak. This was especially true when they deviated from covering the race itself.

Steve Docherty, our producer, looked at me despairingly. 'Go on, then.' I tried not to look surprised.

The executive producers were sent into a tailspin. The problem was insurance. I intended to ride my regular route, in rush-hour traffic, from Woolwich into Central London, accompanied by a cameraman standing up and facing backwards on a motorbike, Tour de France style.

I received an email. 'Our insurance does not allow for any filming in the traffic on open roads. You may, of course, film "pass-by" shots from a static roadside position, but on no account should you risk filming from the back of a motorbike.'

I acknowledged receipt of the email, and promptly ignored the content. This was entirely consistent with the wishes of the show's producers who were expecting me to do just that. By sending me the email, they were simply covering their own backs. Now all the risk was on my shoulders.

That wasn't the only thing on my shoulders, either. I carried a rucksack crammed with batteries, linked by cables to cameras rigged all over the bike, and a radio transmitter, connected to a microphone on my collar to record my words. I bristled with aerials. I emitted a personal electro-magnetic field powerful enough to jam police signals and change the phasing of traffic lights. I looked, in those post 7/7 years, like a genuine Central London menace.

That was how the police saw things, too, which presented problems of their own. Since the feature involved riding past significant London landmarks, we inevitably aroused their suspicions. I passed Downing Street at least three times, for example, with my wired-up rucksack. And on each occasion, policemen, either uniformed or under-cover, stopped me and wanted to know 'what the hell I thought I was doing'. Whenever I was stopped, the cameraman on the motorbike would disappear, and pretend he didn't know me, which made my excuse for a story all the less convincing. My alibi had simply disappeared round the corner.

Still, it was fun, documenting on film the particular nuttiness of cycling around the capital. We passed over Tower Bridge, swooped by St Paul's cathedral where, to my delight, a purple-shirted bishop stepped out on the zebra crossing in front of me. What are the chances of that happening right on cue? God was willing this short film about cycling into being. We were obviously filming it in His image.

I harangued motorists who'd thoughtlessly blocked the green zone reserved for cyclists at traffic lights. I 'bantered' with some scaffolders in a big beaten-up truck who offered me a can of Red Bull in Greenwich, before we raced each other to the Rotherhithe tunnel. I was cut up by a taxi, which stopped suddenly in front of me on the Embankment, and I narrowly avoided a speeding police convoy taking high-security prisoners from Belmarsh to the Old Bailey.

I rode all morning, stopping, starting, repeating little stretches of road and doing mad loops of Parliament Square. Then, as we paused for a coffee near the National Theatre, John, the cameraman, suggested I rode home, and we did it all again. 'This time, I'll film you from the front.'

It turned out to be a hell of a commute.

The Tour de France was coming to London. It still didn't sound quite right.

I think I underestimated the importance of the occasion. Perhaps it was simply a function of the fact that the Tour itself was still reasonably new to me, that I had no real grasp of what it was that I was witnessing. But, with the passing years, it seems almost unreal to me that the Tour itself had passed along the Mall. Quite glorious, it was. And the fact that it will return again to London in 2014, two days after starting in Yorkshire, is a tribute to Britain's sudden passion for the event and a reward for loving it before we were even any good at it.

Mark Cavendish, with trademark acuteness, reminded us all of the scale and grandeur of the 2007 Prologue, when he stood on an autumnal podium in 2011, enjoying the applause of a huge crowd which had gathered to witness the Olympic Road Race test event.

'Riders in the peloton who were lucky enough to start the 2007 Tour [it had, incidentally been Cavendish's Tour debut] still talk about how it was the best ever. The crowds, the whole thing, it was just immense.' And then he smiled into the crowd who couldn't help but beam back at him. They delighted in Cavendish, and they were not a little pleased with themselves, too, for being in on the increasingly un-secret secret from the start.

It is worth noting that the London 2012 test event itself was a triumph. Normally these things are simply a matter of protocol, a dry run for the technical side of the event, for the TV cameras and the finish line crews. The odd, very committed rider will turn up to recce the course, but they will ride it as part of an extended training session, watched by precisely no one. Yet, London turned out. Not just at the finish line on the Mall, but all the way along the course, and in great numbers on Box Hill and in Richmond Park. We were instantly into wild speculation about the numbers involved. There was no way of knowing, so people decided to make up figures of their own. The BBC went for 100,000, just because it sounded grand without being wildly inaccurate. Others, more excitably, went for 250,000.

What is without doubt, though, is that those who did push up against the barriers to catch a glimpse of Cavendish and Co. almost certainly would have been there four years previously, when the Tour came to town. That sun-kissed moment would have provided their inspiration.

Yet how much its gospel spread out among the wider population, in those pre-Beijing, pre-Hoy, pre-Brailsford, pre-Wiggins days, remains a moot point. The huge crowds, I would suggest, *were* the cycling support. That was it. Everyone and anyone who cared about the sport went to London, and stood there watching.

We showed it on ITV1. It bombed. Not nearly enough people watched it for the race to justify its place in the schedules. So the Tour de France disappeared from the main network to its current home on ITV4, only to re-emerge in 2012, when Bradley Wiggins actually went and won it. It took something as seismic as that to convince the number-crunchers that cycling was good business.

No, the wider populace almost certainly has no recollection whatsoever of the weekend that Britain's capital city and France's iconic bike race got caught in a compromising clinch, right under the watchful eye of Lord Nelson. And Ken Livingstone.

My kids attended a primary school in South-East London at the time, which is located just the other side of a level-crossing from the route the Tour would take as it snaked out of London and into Kent. It was safe to say that, in the build up to the Tour's grand arrival in SE7, very little was said or done that either informed, amused, excited or entertained the children about the significance of the spectacle.

In fact, worryingly, it fell to *me* to inspire a generation.

This was unfortunate, since there was little I dreaded more than having to execute any kind of public function in a school environment. I had been bullied, quite rightly, by Kath to go into Year Five and Year Six and talk to the kids about the Tour. Mercifully, for the sake of my own children, they were not in either of these classes, otherwise, I fear something permanent might have broken in our parent–child relationship.

As I gazed at the rows of blank-faced nine-year-olds listening attentively enough, but with a complete lack of reference points, I realised, with a rush of panic, that none of them so much as had an inkling of what I was talking about. Their teacher, smiling politely at my attempts to keep her charges stimulated, looked discomforted, and kept glancing surreptitiously at her watch. Every time she did that, the kids noticed her doing it, and a little more concentration went with each gesture. Clearly, they were not among our most avid ITV4 viewers; the Tour de France was as foreign a concept to them as, well, France really. Or bicycles.

Nothing that I was telling them about average speeds or time-trialling was inspiring much enthusiasm. With scarcely concealed anxiety, I upped the ante, and started to spill out all the overblown half-truths and hyperbole that often accompany well-intentioned idiots' guides to the Tour.

'In the olden days, at the beginning of every day, the riders all used to slip a beef steak down their cycling shorts, to cushion their bums on the saddle.' Giggles. Nervous glances at the teacher to see if 'bum' was a word they could laugh about without getting into trouble. This was going better. 'Bum' was a good word. I made a mental note.

'Then, after riding about four hundred kilometres.' Back to blank looks. 'That's about two hundred and fifty miles. Like riding from here to York . . .' (more blankness; time to improvise) '. . . or twelve thousand times around Charlton Park' (a lie), 'they'd get off their bikes, take the steak out from their shorts, all soaked in the salty sweat from their bums' (one more for good measure), 'and hand it to the chef in the hotel to fry up for their dinner.'

'UUUUUUUrgh!' Thirty delighted shrieks, and one relieved teacher, oblivious of the fact that her children had just been lied to. As urban myths go, this nonsense about sweaty steaks shows real staying power.

For my final flourish, I told them how many calories a rider would burn on a mountain stage, and translated that into the visual medium of dozens and dozens of mini Mars bars, which I emptied onto the table in front of me. There was instant chaos. It was as if I'd tipped a load of mini Mars bars out into a pile in the middle of a room full of nine-year-olds. The teacher, shooting me a horrified look, did well not to stroll to the front of the class and land one on me, as the place erupted all around.

I left, after that, and I have never been invited back by the school to speak on any subject. I thought I'd been rather good.

A week later, as Stage One of the Tour de France got underway, I watched the live coverage coming from our stretch of road in South-East London, hoping to catch a poignant glimpse of Kath and my girls waving at the Tour (and, by extension, at me, off for another month apart), and I couldn't help but notice how empty it was.

It is an ugly stretch of road, the very same part that the BBC never show on their coverage of the marathon, cutting out the first five miles of Woolwich and Charlton: 'Here they are at the start on Blackheath . . .' And then, the next thing you see: 'Oh, look, it's the *Cutty Sark*.'

It is a very deprived part of the Borough of Greenwich. The passage of the Tour meant precious little to anyone there, and not many of the kids had bothered to walk to the end of their road to witness the spectacle. Not even for the free Haribos that I'd told them would rain down on them, like a gelatine act of God. It was a shame.

It had been surprisingly easy to achieve, getting the Tour to London. Cheap, relatively, and uncontroversial: an idea so simple that it seems perplexing that no one had managed to bring it to life before Ken Livingtone's administration pulled the Lycra rabbit out of the aero helmet.

One freezing December day in 2011, just as the mayoral election of 2012 was gaining momentum, I was finally invited, after some badgering, to share an audience with Ken Livingstone at Labour's London headquarters in Victoria. I arrived by bike, filled up with a sense of appropriate sustainability in my transport choices, to be met by an enthusiastic political aide, a chap called Joe. He had no idea where I could lock it up. 'We don't normally get people visiting by bike. I don't know what to suggest really. Do you want a cup of tea? Ken's waiting.'

'Yes please.' I said, trying to look (or at least *feel*) like a hard-bitten political hack. I left my bike chained up to a lamppost outside, and untucked my jeans from my socks.

Ken and I had a little previous. Not that he'd remember.

The last time I had interviewed Livingstone was in Paris at the end of the 2007 Tour. He was a little bit the worse for wear, and slurring his words. London's mayor, after an extremely boozy lunch at the Jules Verne restaurant in the Eiffel Tower, had just been shown a Vélib, the Parisian bike hire scheme. He was impressed, and no doubt emboldened by the sunshine and the volume of Pauillac swilling around inside him, declared to his staff that he wanted the same thing for London. And so it was that the Boris Bike was born. The incoming mayor would later inherit a project hatched over lunch near the Champs-Elysées in 2007.

We interviewed him about it. Or at least we tried to.

Woody had to fabricate a fault in the sound and ask him politely to do it again, in the hope that it would be less slurred the second time around. It wasn't, he wasn't. So we thanked him politely and watched on as he swayed his way back to the Tribune Présidentielle to catch Floyd Landis parading the yellow jersey.

Now, a few years later, and with Ken Livingstone no longer in power, I was sitting in a bland meeting room with a giant 3D Labour logo pinned to the wall opposite an oil painting of him in his last mayoral incarnation. The man himself was wearing an off-white suit to match his off-white suit in the portrait. He was in the middle of an election campaign and he struck me as looking completely knackered. Before we got started though, he summoned up the energy to lambast the state of journalism, and the state of television generally, after I told him what I did for a living.

'There is a general degradation in the reporting world, and television is a tide of crap, with nothing you want to see.' I nodded my agreement, and smiled apologetically, writing the words 'tide of crap' in my notebook.

He continued. 'Anyway, that's my rant about the decline of your industry. What can I do for you? I don't know what we're going to talk about really. I don't do bicycles.'

'I'm not sure this is going to be of much use in your campaign. I have no idea when the book might get published.' I felt it was best to be honest. I saw his aide look up from his BlackBerry and then glance at his watch. Besides, I was way outside my comfort zone, having no idea how to interview politicians, and felt that the best way to get beyond the spin of an electioneering career politician was to confess that I had no intention really of putting any of the interview into the public domain.

Yet none of this seemed to bother Ken Livingstone. Not even the glaringly obvious reality of the fact that he had granted half an hour of his time to talk to no one in particular on a subject he knew little about, and cared for still less. An hour later, we were still talking, even though our starting point had been inauspicious.

'You're not interested in sport?' I ventured.

'Absolutely completely uninterested.' He smiled that famous wide-mouthed grin back across the table, delighting in his perversity. 'When I was leader of the GLC, I had only ever been to one sporting event. The mayor of Lambeth took me to a test match at the Oval, and I fell asleep.'

He was never that kind of outdoorsy type. He'd never

been bothered. His city of birth wasn't made for it. 'In the 1950s, 60s and 70s London's weather was very much wetter than it now is.' Livingstone recalls a London of his youth that seems to echo with post-war drips from gutters and the stifling swish of wet mackintoshes on buses. It was a black-and-white world, where most people aspired to buying a car. Not a bike.

'It was a thing about status. You wouldn't have a bike. Losers had bikes.'

Yet, despite his bookish reluctance to join the boisterous masses on the games field, Livingstone did, at some undefined point in his Tulse Hill childhood, briefly have access to a pushbike. And he rode it, too.

'My parents wouldn't let me and my sister have a bike because it was too dangerous. So I used to borrow my mate Dave's. I thought I was getting somewhere in demonstrating to my parents that it was safe, and then I ran into the front of a car and staggered home all covered in blood and after that I didn't have a chance. So that was that.'

His flirtation with the bicycle went straight from short-lived to non-existent. These days, he has other ways of keeping fit; he tells me with not inconsiderable pride about how much weight he has lost. 'I've lost a stone and a half as a combination of campaigning against evil incarnate . . .' (Boris Johnson, it seems) '. . . and walking the dog. My doctor almost had an orgasm when I had my annual medical.'

But cycling? No way. 'There are so many Jeremy Clarkson clones who'd just run over me and say it was an accident. "Oooh, was that the mayor? Sorry about that!"' And with that imagined assassination attempt, the *former* mayor of London throws his head back and roars with laughter.

But, he protests too much. Things did change during those years, and, wittingly, or unwittingly, his administration played its part. It's odd. Here I am playing at being a political journalist, full of 'balance' and 'caution' and 'pinches of salt', determined to see through any blatant politicking, and I find myself trying to remind him how well he did. Something tells me I am no Paxman.

'Cycling had dwindled to the absolute minimum you can get, in terms of the number of people cycling and the quality of the experience. It was the all-time low point.' His team are keen to arm me with statistics about GLA budgets and TfL surveys. But frankly, the numbers don't make the hair stand up on the back of your neck, not like the memory of the London Grand Départ does. It is to that subject that I wish to return. Although, Livingstone's recollections of schmoozing the ASO officials from Paris are, perhaps understandably, sometimes a little hazy.

'The old guy who was just giving up and handing over to Prudhomme, who was that?' He is talking about Jean-Marie le Blanc, the legendary director of the Tour, who was just about to retire when Livingstone bought the Grand Départ.

'Jean-Marie le Blanc,' I remind him. His face lights up.

'Yeah, he was great. Working with them was a joy. You had a rule [with the Olympics] that you could only take the IOC members out for one meal during their visit. And so that had to be with the Queen, not down at my favourite Indian or something. But with the Tour officials we went out to a restaurant, we drank too much, we had a good laugh. It was such a pleasure to work with them.'

'You took them to Le Pont de la Tour, didn't you?' I had been told that they had eaten at the same place Tony Blair had chosen to impress Bill Clinton. Bernard Hinault, the five times winner of the Tour de France, had flown in especially for that particular piece of negotiation. 'Do you remember that dinner?'

'Yea-ah.' He looks a little vacant. 'I don't recall . . . it blurs. I think they carried me out at the end of it.'

He goes on to tell me that Boris Johnson had failed to take up the option of a return to London for the Tour de France in 2010 or 2011.

'Why didn't he?' I ask. This is the first time I have heard this.

'Because he's lazy. That's why.'

According to Livingstone, they'd 'shaken hands on it' with the organisation of the Tour. (The next day, in a fit of journalistic diligence, I telephone the Conservative Assembly member Andrew Boff, who has special responsibilities for cycling, and ask him if this is true. He tells me he has no idea, but he will find out, and get back to me. I hear nothing more from him. After a month, I chase him up by email. He never replies. So I guess we'll have to make up our own minds about that.)

I have one more soft question to ask, and, even as I ask it, I think I know what the answer is going to be.

'What is your proudest contribution to cycling in London?'

Ken Livingstone thinks long and hard about this. Then he answers. 'Transparent bike sheds.'

I start scribbling notes.

'We wanted kids to start cycling. So we worked with schools. The real problem is you've got to have somewhere to put the bikes, so we offered schools bike sheds. But there was a real resistance from them because they imagined everyone getting pregnant behind the bike sheds or doing drugs. That's where the teachers all got laid at school, you know? People who are teachers now had their first sexual encounters behind the bike sheds, when they were at school! They weren't having the old-style bike sheds. So we actually built bike sheds that were transparent.'

'Spoiling everybody's fun?'

'Yeah, yeah. That's my favourite cycling story out of the eight years.'

Not the Tour de France, then.

I thanked him, got him to sign a copy of his book for my father-in-law who detests him, and took my leave.

CHAPTER 10

THE MEEK AND THE MIGHTY

I once hosted an event at which I had to interview two bike riders who had completed circumnavigations of the planet Earth. On the face of it, this is fairly remarkable. Or so you might think.

One had ridden all the way round the world simply because he'd wanted to. The other, an environmental activist, had done it with some sort of charitable agenda, which involved raising awareness of solar power or a similar thoughtful endeavour. To my great surprise, and considerable disappointment, I found their stories quite deadening, although I marginally favoured the account of the bloke who just did it because he could. They had traversed vast tracts of the planet alone, on a bike, and yet they had returned to the fold of us mortals with a few holiday snaps and long list of reasonably interesting encounters, rendered somehow dull in the retelling. A snake in Morocco. A terrible toilet in India. Hitting a cow in Texas. Some skirmish with border guards near China, which they had patently obviously survived otherwise they wouldn't have been standing there next to me at a trade fair in Surrey.

Amazingly, these self-appointed adventurers had turned an astonishing achievement, a colossal enterprise, into something you had to follow on a PowerPoint presentation, wondering how many more pages there were to reveal. Perhaps I had misjudged the mood, but the general shuffling in the auditorium suggested that they'd lost their audience by the time they'd crossed into Iran. The mean-spirited green-eyed amateur rider in me railed at their good fortune in having been able to devote a year to such a singular and, yes, pointless, pursuit.

It is with a certain amount of resignation that I read of the charity rides, however noble the cause (and they are often extremely noble). Be it Land's End to John O'Groats, London to Paris or simply Round The World, this is a burgeoning pastime in Great Britain. Cycling seems to have embraced this impulse more widely than other sports. The moral legitimacy of the sponsored act of sweaty endurance, well, who could argue with that? Ever since that somewhat less-than-honest chap Lance Armstrong struck fundraising gold with his Livestrong bracelets, the charities have started to mine the same seam. It clearly yields dividends.

It has become a peculiarly British phenomenon. These islands in particular are home to a bewildering array of causes. Over recent years the proliferation of organised charity-sponsored fundraising rides has ballooned beyond measure. They take out adverts in the broadsheets. They plaster themselves over Tube stations. They loom at you from illuminated bus stop signs. Timelines on Twitter sometimes silt up and grind to a halt with the relentless re-distribution of worthy causes. Just Giving tweets and emailed links to fundraising pages have become the new virtual 'chugging'.

To be, it seems, is to fundraise.

They are all chasing the same money, surely. The marvellously self-delusional, comfortably seated cyclist (for there are many of them) is easy prey. The charity fundraisers have worked out their demographic and established that every office with, say, ten or more workers, will by now, statistically speaking, have at least one cycling nut who would leap at the chance of spending four days riding to Paris to see the final stage of the Tour de France. Then the rest of the office, if only to get the cycling nut off their case, and to avoid having to speak to them about it endlessly in the canteen, will feel obliged to chip in online, probably donating at least fifty pounds each. That's five hundred pounds for the chosen cause without even turning a pedal.

The rider will sweat, and will love every drop of it. It will be a morally unimpeachable one-week pleasure/pain cruise.

Recent trends in celebrity endorsement have upped the ante considerably. It is now virtually unthinkable to launch a charity bike ride without the presence of at least two members of the 2003 World Cup winning rugby team on board, or failing that, a footballer/comedian/TV presenter or two. People are clamouring for a bit of the charity action. From hospices to homelessness, cot death to Alzheimer's. The great crises of western life find expression here, with cancer taking centre stage.

Therefore this conversation would be distinctly unorthodox in 2012: 'I'm thinking of riding to the South of France.'

'Great idea. Who're you doing it for?'

'Me.'

I can't say I knew Ian Meek well, but the last I saw of him was in a pub in Leeds railway station in April 2012.

It was lunchtime, and busy with travellers grabbing a pint and a pie, as well as regulars, who for some reason had chosen this noisy, darkened Wetherspoons to drink themselves wobbly one weekday morning.

I made my way through the crowd towards Ian. Sitting at a high table in the middle of the pub, and joined by his wife Sally Anne, he had changed significantly to look at since we'd last met. He had the same soft smile, the same infectious chuckle. But the scar on his right temple was unavoidably prominent and he now wore two hearing aids. His eyes were sometimes watery and, every now and again, his cheery features would suddenly, visibly, wilt and he would look very tired.

But otherwise he was in good spirits. Just recently, he had seen his psychologist, who had been concerned that Ian had started to brood, to turn in on himself. The doctor had been surprised to see him smiling.

'What's changed?' he'd asked.

'I'm back on my bike,' Ian beamed back at him.

'Is that the only thing?'

'Yes. I'm back on my bike.'

There had been weeks, very recently, when he'd been unable to venture out. As our conversation twisted and turned into life, he recalled those dark days when the doctors had told him (not for the first time) to leave it alone.

Then Ian tells me, to my considerable alarm, that a telephone conversation with me had turned things around. It seems I'd told him over the phone to ignore the doctors and do what he wanted to do, not for a minute expecting him to take my half-baked advice seriously. I had only said it because it sounded like the right thing to say, what I would have wanted to hear in his situation. But, however it came about, and whatever my accidental role in it had been, it seemed to have worked.

'I used to be too frightened to even go and get my hair cut. I wasn't me. I would never have had the confidence to come into a place like this and meet you and buy a drink. But now I'm back to being me, and it's all down to me getting my bike out and riding to my sister-in-law's with my nephew's Easter egg. It's put the biggest smile on my face ever.'

And to prove it, he smiles. Broadly.

'My mum was worried. She said, "Who did you have out with you on the ride?" I said that God was by my side. She said, "Well God ain't going to pull you out of the water is he, when you go straight in the river?"'

He splutters with mirth. It's hard not to join in. And somehow, the Bristol accent of his youth has seeped through into his laughter.

He grew up the son of a carpenter and a nurse in Yate, near Bristol.

'I used to have a Commando with cow horn handlebars on it. I used to go everywhere on that thing. One Christmas, Dad said, do you want a racer? And he got me a Raleigh Winner. It was the most amazing present ever.'

I laugh with Ian at his memory of this, in the particular way that near-strangers (this was only our second meeting) can only do over a shared heritage, in this case the horrifying cliché of a seventies childhood. Although I never had a Commando, the 'bovver boys' in my village all rode them. The saddle was long and, like a motorbike saddle, turned up at the rear. The handlebars were modelled on a Harley Davidson. They had attitude, but as a means of getting you from A to B you might as well have been on a clown's bike from the local circus.

It didn't matter to Ian. He loved it. When he was eighteen, he and a bunch of like-minded mates discovered mountain biking the first time it became popular. They took the train into Bristol with their savings and each came away with a new bike, which they rode all the way home.

His was a Specialized Rock Hopper. I nod as he tells me this, even though I have not the faintest idea what one of those should look like. I get a more accurate picture of how young Ian must have looked rattling through the Forest of Dean on his frequent overnight stays in the woods when he tells me he wore a Toshiba Polka Dot jersey. 'It was horrendous really.' This time, I nod with a little more conviction.

By the age of twenty-two, he'd given up mostly on cycling. More adult stuff had come his way, as it does. Now he had a young family, mouths to feed, responsibilities to discharge. Every day he went to clock on at the Courage brewery in Bristol.

'At first I had a job knocking shives.'

'You did what?' It sounded quaint, skilled and obsolete. It sounded like you'd be expected to Morris Dance all the way to work and all the way back. 'What's knocking shives?'

'Knocking the caps into the casks of beer,' he explains patiently. I wonder briefly if anyone behind the bar at Wetherspoons would have the faintest idea what he was talking about. 'But then I got a better job as a brewer. I was a fermentation operator.'

In 1994, quite suddenly, he was told that he had a brain tumour. At first they told him it was benign. But he knows now that they were simply shielding him from the inevitable.

'It was malignant. They just told me it was benign because there was nothing to get rid of it. I could have all the money in the world and go to America, and they still couldn't do anything to get rid of it. It's just in completely the wrong place. It's too close to my brain. It's too high a risk for them to try and take it all out. I could end up a vegetable. There's nothing that they can do.

'They told me I wasn't allowed to drive any more. So I said, "How am I going to get into work?" It was twelve miles away. I'd have to get the bike out. I hadn't really got a choice. The doctors were saying I shouldn't really be riding a bike with a brain tumour. So I said, "Are you going to come and pick me up then and drive me to work every day?"'

Life went on its course. In the winter, if he was on an early shift, he'd leave the house in the pitch dark at 4.15 a.m. for a 5.30 start. Twelve miles there and twelve miles back. In the summer, when he was feeling more vigorous, he'd throw in an extra twenty miles by following the path all the way to Bath and back.

In 1999 the Courage factory closed and the family moved north when Ian took a job with the John Smith brewery. They settled in Tadcaster, within cycling distance of Ian's other great love, Leeds United and Elland Road.

All the while the tumour bided its time. He would occasionally check in for a 'de-bulking' operation, to shave off the more easily accessible tissue. But over fifteen years he remained fit and well. And he cycled to work every day.

Then, suddenly, in 2009, the doctors had news.

'My brain tumour changed and became terminal. It changed to a Grade 3.' Ian pauses, and momentarily loses his way. 'I'm just trying to think . . .'

His sentence peters out. Sally Anne, who throughout our talk has been holding his hand, steps in to complete his sentence.

'It becomes more aggressive as the grades go up and they struggle to control it as much. And that's when it turns to terminal.'

Ian's smile lights up the table at which we sit. 'So we crack on. We're doing all right, aren't we?'

Ian Meek is a year younger than I am. Wetherspoons is thinning out, the lunchtime crush is subsiding.

The first time I met Ian Meek was in October of 2011, six months or so prior to our meeting in Leeds. Mick Bennett invited me to make a personal appearance at the Cycle Show in Birmingham. Hilariously, this involved some commitment to cutting a ribbon to open the gates and posing in a semi-official capacity. It was one of my first professional engagements where I was obliged simply to turn up and be me. I was deeply flattered and mildly embarrassed. I could only assume that a number of refusals had led to their last-minute booking. No one has ever contradicted that version of events. And, after I arrived too late to cut the ribbon, I wasn't invited back the following year.

Not since I had been dragged, inexplicably, to the East of England Show by some family friends in the mid-1980s had I visited a trade fair. There were certain similarities between the two. Where Britain's premier agricultural show featured the latest tractor technology and seed developments, so the Cycle Show had bikes and power gels. Thousands of people made the trip to the NEC in Birmingham and then paid for the right to stare at bicycles they had no intention of buying, let alone the means to do so. It was like witnessing a great annual migration of ruminant mammals, which, on reaching the lush pastures, opted simply to gaze fondly on them, and not to feed.

Salesman: 'Ever ridden Titanium before?'

Punter: 'Not enough torque in the frame for me.'

Salesman: 'I see. Tried a more aggressive geometry?'

Punter: 'With an oval ring? You're kidding me.'

This is only an approximation of how I imagine a conversation about bikes to go. I tend to tune out after the initial reference to lugs.

I made a brief appearance on the Cycle Show stage alongside esteemed cycling writers like Will Fotheringham and Jeremy Whittle (during which I tended to agree with whatever opinion the last person to talk had expressed), and then I headed for the Condor stand, where I was to sit at a trestle table signing copies of *How I Won The Yellow Jumper*.

I was worried that there would be an all-too-awkward entire absence of people. This had the potential to become my Alan Partridge moment, where he sets up a stand in the middle of Norwich and flogs copies of his autobiography *Bouncing Back* while wearing a market-trader's headset and microphone.

Mercifully, there was enough enthusiasm, or possibly enough disenchantment with the phenomenal prices being asked for pushbikes, to ensure a decent flow of people passing by my little stand. Folks stopped and chatted about all sorts of things: the Tour, Cavendish, Boardman and, more often than not, their own, often quite prestigious racing careers.

I had never met so many amateur stars, so many men and women who had spent a lifetime driving to rainy, secret, windswept time trials up and down the country in the hope of improving on the previous year's 34th place. I marvelled at their industry and the depth of their attachment to this peculiar, lonely sport. I wondered also what it was they sought in talking to me, a self-confessed outsider. Maybe it was the novelty. Perhaps I was like a first-time guest at a tedious family Christmas; some bewildered new partner that a cousin brings along. Such interlopers tend to get set upon by the regulars, all too stultified by the over-familiar nature of their own kind.

I was busily talking to some confused twelve-year-old kid whose dad had pushed him in my direction clutching a book he would never read, when I noticed a tallish, slimish chap standing just to my left, carrying a brace of plastic bags like pheasants from a successful poaching raid.

'I'm planning on riding Land's End to John O'Groats,' the poacher told me. Here we go again.

'Wow,' I said, insincerely. 'That's quite a thing.'

Over the course of what was now becoming quite a long day, this man hadn't been the first person to tell me that he was riding from Land's End to John O'Groats. So, trying not appear as underwhelmed as I felt, I returned my attention to the lad who still looked baffled and still held his dad's book out in the general direction of a complete stranger.

Charity riders. Again! Various different fundraising adventurers had repeatedly accosted me that afternoon. Some had booked flights to Grenoble and were going to tackle Alpe d'Huez in the spring (while raising awareness of prostate cancer). Others were already in full training for the following year's Étape du Tour, in which people get to ride a mountain stage of the actual Tour de France route. So the John O'Groats ride (or LEJOG to give it its full, ghastly acronym) struck me as neither particularly imaginative nor meritorious. I had only a certain reserve of interest in these acts of well-meaning endurance, and it had long since run dry.

But the poacher wasn't put off. 'The thing is,' he said, 'I've got to do it. I want to raise £100,000.'

'That's a lot of money,' I offered. Rather obviously.

'I've got an inoperable brain tumour,' he replied, rather less obviously. 'I haven't got long to live.'

I put down my pen, and looked squarely at the man for the first time.

There was something about his honesty. An openness of approach, a quiet, watchful appreciativeness. Calming company, Ian Meek. Six months later, back in the Leeds pub as I stirred my coffee and listened to him talk, I understood that I had a confession to make.

Irony never translates well on Twitter. That's why people use the little symbol ;-) after their sarcastic barbs. There's a world of difference between saying 'All I want for Christmas is the new One Direction album' and 'All I want for Christmas is the new One Direction album ;-)'. In fact, they are the polar opposite of each other.

And so it was that when I tweeted 'Delighted to announce that I have been chosen to carry the Olympic flame through the Blackwall Tunnel' nobody realised that it was supposed to be a joke. It was barely a joke anyway (although I did like the image of the torch being bravely carried aloft through London's dingiest tunnel. But, I freely admit, it wasn't funny, and what residual humour there was flew straight over most people's heads. Certainly, Ian Meek took it at face value.

The thing was this: Ian had genuinely been chosen to carry the Olympic flame through York. As one of the country's leading fundraisers, he deserved the recognition and was overwhelmingly proud to have been nominated. On reading of what he thought was my selection, and being a sweet, generous soul, he was delighted for me, and replied via Twitter to my announcement: 'Congratulations, Ned. A great honour.'

I had instantly deleted my tweet.

I was horrified at the misunderstanding, and ashamed. I had no idea what to do about it. So when we sat in the pub that day last April, I had to come clean.

'I'm not really carrying the torch, Ian.'

'I did wonder about that. And so did my mum. She kept asking me when you would be doing it.'

Just for a moment he looked wounded. Then he smiled. With the weight of that confession off my shoulders, I could listen with a cleaner conscience to Ian's story.

We had spoken a few times on the phone since our initial meeting at the Cycle Show. I had started to follow his story with interest, and to keep abreast of his plans. Things had been very tough through the winter, but the ambition to set out from Land's End with a team of fundraising riders continued to figure large in his thinking.

'Last year it would have been a good plan for me to ride it. But this year, it's obviously gone wrong. In September I was as well as I've ever been. But in December I was starting to have small seizures.'

They operated again, for the fifth time, on his brain tumour.

'I don't know anyone who's had five operations,' Ian tells me. 'This one's changed a few things. My hearing. My eyesight. I struggle . . .'

'It got to my scan in January, and I went in thinking I'm all right. I'm going all right. The doctor said "How've you been?" I said, "I cycled fifty-four miles on Saturday." She said, "How did it feel?" I said, "It was a bit like the pedals were going round and I was a bit spaced out. But I was all right."'

She'd listened to him. But then she'd cut him short. 'It's bad news.' The cancer was growing very aggressively now.

For a while, Ian was laid low by this newest prognosis and entered a very dark phase. Naturally ebullient, he found himself brooding, depressed. But the planning for the big ride continued. His son Sam, aged just fifteen, was involved too, announcing his intention to join his dad on the ride.

'We talked about my diagnosis. We shed a few tears. And he said, "What about the ride?"'

Then Ian had to tell his son he wouldn't be able to join him. Reality had plans of its own. With Ian's eyesight so restricted (he kept kicking the dog by mistake because he couldn't see it beneath him) and the risk of seizures greatly increased, he reset his targets and limited his ambition to joining the team of riders on one 'stage' only. That day was to be 1 August, Yorkshire Day. That was when they planned to ride from Leeds to Stockton, some sixty-five miles.

'That's the day I am definitely planning to do. I'll do that day, whatever. The only thing that'll stop me is if my bike falls apart, which I'm not planning on. I won't be getting off my bike that day. I don't do getting off.'

'Of course I want to stay alive. But not just existing. I need to keep happy in my head.'

Time spent riding a bike, to Ian, had taken on a different meaning.

'You can sort out everything on your bike, can't you? I don't know if there's anything else I've ever done that's like it. Staying alive's not enough. It doesn't float your boat, as they say.'

We talked about his riding. He tended to go out alone, so as not to be distracted by having to make conversation. Sally Anne worried, but understood what it was that the bike gave her husband: necessary release.

Then, after she had left us alone in the pub to go for a business appointment, Ian looked intently at me.

'I couldn't say this with Sally there. It would have upset her. But if it ends when I'm out on my bike, well, that's not the worst thing. That's not the worst way.'

A little while later I tell Ian that I have to catch my train.

He walks with me for while, through the busy station concourse. We shake hands. And then we head in our different directions.

Over the summer, things changed quite quickly. I was kept informed by some caring folk at the hospice to which he had now been admitted.

On 21 July, the day before Bradley Wiggins was to win the Tour de France, I got a text from Ian.

All around my bedside for 5 tomorrow afternoon to see our man come in in yellow. Had a good day today. Picking up. Ian :)

He saw Wiggins win. But that was the last I heard from him. The next time his number rang, it was a friend who was contacting me instead, to let me know that he was dead.

He had gone at 11.30 in the morning, on 1 August 2012. Yorkshire Day. His team of charity riders had visited him the previous evening on their way from Land's End to John O'Groats. Five days later, four riders completed their journey in his name. They sent me a picture. They were standing in front of the famous road sign at John O'Groats, all of them smiling.

Ian is survived by Sally Anne, and his three children, Keisha, Hannah and Sam.

At the time of writing, the charity that Ian Meek founded has broken his target of £100,000. That money will fund a research student for three years at the Leeds Institute of Molecular Medicine.

And I have had occasion to consider my position.

Sometimes bike riding is wonderfully pointless. But sometimes, as Ian Meek showed me, it is both wonderful and purposeful. There's room on Britain's grey and windy roads for both.

CHAPTER 11

SNIFFING THE SHOE

Simon Mottram was striding now, neatly stepping down a steel industrial-chic staircase, and then walking along a corridor neutrally plastered, and in other places pleasingly displaying the sandblasted yellow warmth of London stock brickwork. Recessed lighting twinkled discreetly in the stairwell, and where windows opened onto the old warehouse space, spring light flooded in, mixing in the air with the smell of coffee and the gentle tapping of Mac keyboards.

This was the house that Simon built, a monument to taste, a love poem to design, a hymn to merino wool. I was entering the heart of cool, with the patron saint of Rapha as my guide.

I had not asked for a guided tour but was enjoying it nonetheless. I drank it all in, amazed at how easily it conformed to my preconception of just how the Rapha offices should look: the rooms full of designers smiling mystically at computer screens, or seated, leafing through a book of photography detailing Neapolitan bathing houses of the 1950s, presumably summoning the necessary inspiration to start to put together Rapha's next bib-short design feature. Simon introduced them all by name as we walked on, and I nodded my hellos, feeling crumpled and ill-fitting in comparison with this svelte squadron of hipsters.

'This is Josh. He's working on toiletries.' He may not have actually said this, and there may not actually be a Josh working at Rapha, nor indeed a separate toiletries department. But you get the idea.

'Hi, Josh.'

'And over there's Sven. He's socks, but not just socks. He does gloves, too.'

'Right. Gloves. That's good.' This conversation about gloves though, was for real.

'What do you normally use?' Simon looked at me, with curiosity and amusement. Josh and Sven looked up from their work and waited on my answer. I was under glove pressure. I glanced down at my bare hands, irritated by the stubbiness of my fingers and the slight traces of dirt under my thumbnails.

'What, me? Oh. I'm not really . . .' Simon looked suddenly sad, or maybe even a little cross. 'I keep losing them.'

'We need to sort you out with some. I must get onto that. Don't let me forget to tell Laura you need gloves before you go.'

We walked on. He elaborated, with some passion, on the theme. 'You should have stuff that is beautiful. You shouldn't have to compromise and wear some shitty polyester that falls apart. You should have the best stuff ever. You're going to die on those climbs.' It sounded like a threat. But he paused mid-stride and smiled sphinx-like at me. 'Why should you wear some shitty, scratchy shorts?'

I had no answer to that. Why indeed.

Needless to say, Simon did forget to mention it to Laura, and I was in no position to remind him that he was going to mention to Laura that she was going to sort me out gloves-wise.

Rapha's clothing is undeniably beautiful. They may be fabulously easy to mock. No, I'll correct that. They *are* fabulously easy to mock: expensive, exclusive, pretentious arrivistes, purporting to be something that they are not. They are designed, say their detractors, for dentists in Surrey. And no one likes dentists from Surrey.

But, boy, can they stitch! I have owned a number of their garments, and, with the possible exception of some rather odd knickerbockers and a duck-egg blue turtleneck jumper, my usual shabbiness has been enhanced utterly by pulling on their merino perfection. Perhaps I will look back on my Rapha years with the same horror with which most people now regard the fad for stone-cladding in the 1980s. But I doubt it.

But here's a good time for a disclaimer: I have been ethically compromised by Rapha down the years. They were the first people ever to have deemed me worthy of receiving free stuff. It just arrived, in a box.

Moreover, since that initial offering of swag, Simon Mottram has kept quite a supply of gear heading in my general direction. And, if truth be told, I have no idea why. There have been no more than two or three occasions over a period of some five years that I have worn any of their clothing in front of the camera in a compliance-baiting act of commercial bravado and naked self-interest. So quite why the parcels full of Rapha clothing continue, sporadically, to appear on my doorstep, I don't know. I can only conclude that perhaps Simon Mottram is a generous man, a nice chap, if you will.

I looked at him, the nattily bearded emperor of all he surveyed, concerned at my glovelessness, and he smiled beatifically back at me. Then it dawned on me: We had a 'relationship', I guess. Perhaps, in some unfathomable way, this was what marketing people meant, when they talked of 'partnerships'. Perhaps I should show more direct interest in the product.

I am not very good at handling situations like this. Once, a major motor manufacturer (all right, Ford) rang me up to discuss building a 'partnership'. This, they went on to tell me after some initial guff about creative relationships with selected characters in the media, would involve giving me a brand-new vehicle.

'Thank you. That'd be very nice,' I told the smooth-sounding man on the other end of a conference call, my mind racing to work out where the catch lay in getting a free car for no good reason. I wondered if I would end up looking like the local pro at a golf club, or a county cricketer, the doors and bonnet to my Ford emblazoned with the name of a local garage. No, I resolved, I would be my own man, not a slave to the corporate machine!

'I'd better be honest with you from the outset. I'm not even remotely interested in cars.'

'Not an issue. Not important.' The voice didn't even break stride. 'We'll put together a proposal for you, and get straight back to you.'

Needless to say, I never heard from them again. The honesty thing hadn't been quite the right tactic after all.

Simon Mottram was rushing on. He wanted very much to show me something he had left on a shelf in Dispatch. We hurried down the steps to the ground floor, past rows of bikes hanging vertically from butchers' hooks. Almost all Rapha's staff commute to work by bike, he told me proudly, and then explained how they had a contractual entitlement to a certain number of days off if they wanted to sign up for a ride or participate in a race. We pushed through into another beautifully restored old warehouse where a further platoon of bright young things were packing up orders for customers all over the world. They looked up as we walked in and smiled at the boss. He returned their smiles. I smiled too, but couldn't quite manage to replicate their insouciance.

'Here it is.' He scurried behind a shelf that groaned with packing cases and reached to the ceiling. Then, from behind the boxes, came a sigh of disappointment. 'Ah. But it's not in the proper packaging. Maybe I shouldn't show you after all.'

'I'd like to see it, Simon,' I said, truthfully. I had no idea what I was asking to see, but judging by Simon's evangelical excitement, I was expecting it to be pretty special.

He poked his head round the side. 'But you won't get the full hit.' A pause. 'Oh, what the hell. But promise not to let on that you've seen this, OK? It's not been launched yet. We've not gone public with this yet.' He vanished again. And then returned with a shoe box. He bore it as you would a newborn, with slow deliberate steps, and deep pride.

In the shoe box, was a shoe.

'Yak.'

'What?'

'Yak skin.' And with that, he carefully parted the paper flaps protecting the shoe from ultra violet light and negative ions, and he buried his nose right up to his eye sockets into the shoe, inhaling deeply, as if snouting for truffles. After a period of time long enough for me to become a little uncomfortable, he came up for air. 'That's the real deal.'

As he re-emerged, I noticed a change. He was in a heightened state. Simon Mottram, the founder of Rapha, had transcended. He had left us all behind.

And at that precise moment, a famous television personality walked into the room. How very Rapha.

I don't know when I first became aware of them, 'The Raphia', my name for the semi-secretive, palpably affluent, metrosexual elite who wear Simon Mottram's stuff. After all, their choice of apparel (not clothing) almost by definition eschews the attention-seeking primary colours of conventional cycling garb.

At first it was an occasional sighting. I'd overtake one of their number on Blackfriars Bridge; as I headed north up Farringdon Road, they'd be swinging right. As they made for their offices in the City, I ploughed on towards King's Cross. Dressed from head to toe in black, they would invariably be sitting astride an achingly cool bike, the kind that is not available for purchase by ordinary folk. At least not at Halfords.

Then there was the Rapha cycling team.

About five years ago I started presenting televised races from the provinces, The Tour Series. These are humble, city-centre circuit races from strictly non-Metropolitan places like Redditch, Woking and Kirkcaldy. Raced over an hour around a tight course, they are full-blooded, honest scraps, which usually end in a bunch sprint. Big crowds cheer the riders on from behind barriers.

British domestic cycling teams fight a constant battle to scrape together enough money to keep going for another season. They rely, at least for the most part, on a headline sponsor and a number of smaller benefactors who demand a little space on their kit. It's a woefully unstable financial model as sponsors come and go, often lasting no more than a season before they wise up to the reality that it's a pricey hobby more than a marketing tool. As a result, the mysterious logos, the exotic and banal nomenclatures, the kaleidoscopic nature of their kits, make up a bewildering and mildly comic homespun patchwork.

It makes for tortured broadcasting.

'So, Matt, do you think that Cycle Premier Metaltek will try to get a man in the break today, or is it a course which suits Motorpoint Marshalls Pasta better?' The longer, and more unlikely sounding the name, the fewer races they'll win, by and large (an equation, incidentally that often holds equally well for the Tour de France, where Team Sky trounced both Radioshack-Nissan-Trek and Omega-Pharma-Quick Step).

But then, and quite distinctly, there's Rapha. They're actually called Rapha-Condor-Sharp, although I always forget the Sharp bit, quite often omitting the Condor middle name as well. It's Rapha that holds sway in the aesthetics of the team. The kit is black (with the merest dashes of preconception-challenging pink). The bikes are black. The cars are black.

Their riders know that they catch the eye in the peloton like no others. As the dark-destroyers of the race stand at the start line, they are aware that all other kits look cobbled-together in comparison; they look like panthers in a room full of rescue cats. This doesn't make them fast, but it makes them look like they're going to be fast, which is, I am certain, a marginal gain.

My experience of bicycle racing in Britain (aside, it should be said, from the Tour of Britain, which is grander by far in scale and purpose) had largely been restricted to these evening 'criteriums' up and down the country; homely, warm, family affairs, attended by crowds of local enthusiasts; middle-aged men dragging reluctant children along after school, programme collectors carrying plastic bags full of their booty looking beadily around for a glimpse of Malcolm Elliott, gaggles of friends from the same cycling club, all dressed in matching Lycra. In other words, the sequence of faces along the hoardings at the side of the race track holds up a mirror to the eclectic constituency of the British cycling scene.

I love these evenings; the bewilderment and resentment they engender among the non-cycling majority of the population amuses me greatly. Barricades go up without warning all along the high street. Traffic comes to a standstill on the outskirt of town. Race headquarters are invariably housed in the town hall. The Victorian marble staircases echo to the clack-clack of cleated shoes, and, for one evening only, busts of local dignitaries and former mayors frown at the passing parade of shaved legs and wrinkle their granite noses at the smell of embrocation.

Outside in the VIP area, the mayor himself, accompanied by his good lady wife, stands shivering under a dripping umbrella, clutching a damp vol au vent and a glass of Chardonnay as the race thunders past every two or three minutes. You can read his mind if you look hard enough. 'Is this really going to get me re-elected?'

It was in this wholesome and distinctly un-Rapha context that Simon Mottram first introduced himself to me. A trim Yorkshireman in his forties with sharp but friendly features, greying hair and something of a smile playing across his face at any given time.

In many ways, this was precisely the environment which so revolted Mottram, the über-aesthete, that he determined to create an alternative vision for the cycling world, if not the world itself. So it was strange to meet him there, in a drizzly car park in semi-deserted Milton Keynes.

Many years later, cosseted by the drifting of quality espresso steam in and around the Rapha office, I listen to the Man in Black tell me how it all began. Or rather, what it was that he was running away from: British cycling, and everything that looked and smelt like it.

'Impenetrable. Totally unaspirational, unengaging, undesirable. I hate it. I never joined a cycling club. I didn't want to go to a scout hut and talk about changing a bottom bracket. That's not my world. I wanted to be on my bike on the Tourmalet, riding in the tyre tracks of the great.

'I'm a Brit who was lucky enough to go to France every holidays. That's where my heart is. Over there. Not drinking tea in a lay-by in a deck chair. I have no interest. British cycling history isn't what I'm about, frankly.'

And then he concludes with, 'I'd rather be in Provence.'

I put it to him that British cycling's got considerable charm, great character, a wonderful, eccentric heart.

He cuts me dead. 'You can romanticise anything.'

But his most withering criticism is not for circuit racing, which, despite its lack of a Tourmalet, is at least racing, but for time-trialling. He loathes time-trialling. And Britain's backward, nerdish, fetishistic love for this discipline.

'Lots of British cycling is still populated by testers (time-triallists). Lots of geeky stuff and winning on your own. It's hard for Rapha to really connect.' I wonder briefly if he uses the word 'Rapha' as the Queen would use the word 'one'.

'We're about looking to the Continent, people in love with the experience of it. Riding in mountains. Riding in groups. Wearing a cap back to front, and maybe sunglasses.'

I remember when Rapha first extended an invitation to me. Would I like to attend something called the Smithfield Nocturne as their guest? It was not the last time that I have gone along with one of Simon Mottram's suggestions without fully understanding what they were.

Except for the fact that it was in Central London, the Nocturne was exactly the same as any other one of these evening bike races: a tight city centre, barriered-off circuit, which the peloton hurtles around for an hour or so. This is essentially all there is to criterium racing. It is borrowed, as is so much of cycling, from the Continental scene, and specifically Belgium and France, where every other little town used to run its own event at some point in the calendar. Historically, and particularly when big stars from the Tour de France have come to the race, the outcome has been pre-determined by payment. Wins would be regularly bought and sold. It was all part of the spectacle, the charade, the fun; so long as it looked good, no one would ask too many questions.

But the British 'crit' scene is different. Aside from the usual skulduggery involving unnecessary pit stops for recovery when phantom mechanical issues suddenly strike with seven laps remaining, these are honestly ridden races. Only last year, I listened to two Dutch riders on the Tour de France talking in reverent tones about the British scene. It was one of those humbling occasions when Dutch people choose to speak English to each other in order to be inclusive.

'You've not heard of the Tour series?'

'Never.'

'They're amazing. They're like actual races.'

'How do you mean?'

'You know, an actual race. A real race.'

'Oh!' They both looked at me, as if demanding an explanation for such a quaint practice.

'I don't know.' I threw my hands up.

Smithfield's is the old meat market right next to Barts Hospital on the fringes of the City of London. It is a wonderland of ornate Victorian steel, wood and glass, which is ringed these days by gastro pubs and eateries for the chattering classes. At night, lit up for the occasion, and thronged with doctors from Barts, lawyers from the chambers and bankers from the Square Mile, it bristled with wealth and grooming. There were no kagouls here, no plastic bag clutching, bearded cyclo-fans. No one had ridden down to the race with trouser clips. This was the sleek, dark heart of Rapha.

And at its core the Rapha VIP area, into which I untidily spilt my presence. Simon Mottram greeted me warmly and pointed me in the right direction for a free glass of wine and an organic sausage. He looked in his element.

'The Nocturne. That came out of our heads,' he later tells me. 'We didn't have to do that. We've never made any money out of it. We lost loads of money on it. We could have just done a day at Hillingdon – that's what anyone else would have done.' Rapha, though, are not 'anyone else'.

In the VIP area, the uniform was the thing: black jeans with discreetly expensive and minutely reflective trim, slim-fitting merino wool, old-fashioned-looking racing jerseys, either cream, or black, but with traces of colour in cunning little places, and caps; black, white with rainbow stripes, or discreetly tweed in nature with a black strip woven into the fabric bearing the embroidered name (black on black): Rapha. Pink T-shirts with black lettering. Black T-shirts with white lettering. Rapha.

Mottram's appropriation of the word Rapha is a curiosity in itself. In the 1960s there was an iconic French cycling

team called St Raphaël, sponsored by a sickly sweet eponymous aperitif. It was the team of Jacques Anquetil, the first
French five-time winner of the Tour de France. But their
second team often raced simply under the shortened name,
Rapha.

Mottram hit upon the word 'Rapha' in 2004, and needed
to buy it. 'It sounds brilliant. It sounds European, Mediterranean,
which is, I think, what the sport is. It sounds aspirational, a
bit luxurious. So I bought the trademark.'

He cut a curious, and legally tenuous, deal for the right
to use the name with Raphaël Géminiani, the former team
manager (his first name a strange coincidence). It kept
him awake at night, worried that Géminiani would renege
on their arrangement and come hunting him down.
Géminiani had a reputation for wanting to have people
hunted down. But eventually the name belonged to Simon
Mottram.

And within a short space of time it was being worn en
masse, outside a meat market, for post-work drinks and a bit
of a bike race in the middle of London.

'Whether you work in advertising or the City or technology,
if you've got the right sort of mentality, if you're that sort of
person who likes the stories and the richness and the design
and can afford it, you'll be a Rapha customer.'

It was overwhelmingly homogenous. The aesthetic extended
way further than just the clothes. It seemed there was no one
there with nothing to say for themselves. I was introduced to
a documentary filmmaker, a corporate lawyer and a museum
curator. I made small talk with the CEO of a Soho advertising
agency. Being uninteresting, unengaging, unglamorous was
off-limits. I struggled for things to contribute. After enough
time had elapsed for me to decently be seen to take my leave,
I necked my wine and fled, without even waiting to find out
who had won.

It was at around about this time that I started to hear the rumours that James Murdoch was a Rapha fan. Things were getting serious indeed.

Back at Rapha HQ, with a glass of water and a fresh espresso at his side, Simon Mottram was getting a bit exercised.

'When people actually meet people from Rapha, they realise that we're not wankers. We're just like them. We like riding. But we also quite like talking about it and telling stories about it.'

Once a month, he tells me, he allows himself to dive into the shark-infested waters of the Internet and scour the forums for messageboard threads about Rapha's latest initiative. They have their haters. And by Rapha, what they really mean is Simon Mottram, since his thumbprint is on everything they do and everything they sell. It's not always much fun reading what is being said.

'I have no problem with them. But they continue to have a huge problem with us. The more charitable among them admit they don't understand why it's working. The less charitable think that we are some kind of marketing construct, that's raping their heritage. Rapha aren't stealing the sport. We're just doing it rather well.'

'Do you get stung by them?'

'Yes, I do. I do.' He stops to think about it, as if trying the statement for size before committing to the following sentence, knowing for sure that I would find it irresistible. That I'd have to print it.

'Frankly I think I'm doing more for the sport, doing what I'm doing, than pretty much anyone else.'

Wow.

I'm enjoying this. Sitting behind his desk in his airy office, surrounded by items of heritage and beauty, shoes, books, posters, bottles of St Raphaël aperitif, and tubs of moisturiser, it's surprisingly fun to experience quite how passionate his love for the brand is. But still, it's a bold claim, especially when set alongside the monolithic marketing drive of Team Sky and the individual successes of the British cyclists. Rapha, I can't help thinking, sponsor a few minor teams, stage a few events and sell kit (including 'chamois cream', which, in case you're not aware, is an antiseptic ointment for your bum. Rapha's is 'Inspired by the flora of Mont Ventoux').

Now he's talking about his ambitions to sponsor a Tour de France team. 'We're on the outside. If we were right in the heart, imagine what we could do?'

What indeed? I have no idea what he means really, but it sounds very exciting. Or at least it's exciting to witness how exciting it is for Simon Mottram to imagine it.

Then the penny drops. I wonder if he's about to sponsor Team Sky. I had heard rumours that Sky was thinking of dropping Adidas. I am putting two and two together. I sit up on the couch, take a sip of espresso, and mentally sharpen my pencil. A question has formed of its own volition. Hell, this was exciting stuff. This was pure investigative journalism. I was onto something and I wasn't going to let it slip out of range.

'Is James Murdoch one of your devotees?'

'Yes. James Murdoch is a customer.'

Ha! I think to myself. I very nearly say it out loud, which would have appeared amateur and not at all sleuth-like.

'Did you have talks with Sky?'

He pauses. Choosing his words carefully. I've got him now. 'I know Brailsford.'

'Was it ever mooted? Did you talk about it ever?'

'We're friends. You know. We talk.'

Ha!

'I want the sport to be the most popular sport in the world. I think it should be because it's the greatest sport in the world.'

*   *   *

Is Simon Mottram a madman? The thought crosses my mind that I may be in the presence of a megalomaniac empire builder who will stop at nothing before he's got the whole world dressed in minimalist retro snug-fitting soft and durable sweat-wicking fabrics. I consider making a run for it, before he presses a button under his desk and I drop into the Rapha crocodile pit in the basement, and have to fight my way out armed only with a micro-pump and a tub of bottom cream.

But instead, I just left. And I didn't see him again until a succession of chance encounters threw the Rapha story back into my life.

The first of these occurred at the Adidas headquarters at the Olympic Park. I say, at the Olympic Park, but what I really mean is Westfield Shopping Centre. I was just on my way out from hosting a press conference with David Rudisha, the winner of the gold medal in the 800 metres the night before. But as the lift doors opened, Dave Brailsford and Shane Sutton emerged. Sutton shook my hand briefly and headed straight into the inner Adidas sanctum. Brailsford collapsed on a couch in the lobby, and muttered something profane about Sutton dragging him from pillar to post. I sat down next to him.

He was more relaxed than I had ever known him. The track events had finished a few days previously and he was contemplating heading home for a day before flying to Spain for the start of the Vuelta. After all, as he told me, he still had his suitcase from the start of the Tour de France in the athletes' village. It had been that sort of a summer.

He started, unprompted, to talk about the future of Team Sky, the improbability, or possibly even the inadvisability, of retaining the services of Mark Cavendish, as well as telling me off the record all the riders he'd already signed for the following season. And in the middle of it all, I stopped and wondered what he was doing there, anyway? Then I went out on a limb.

'Aren't you finished with Adidas?'

'Yup.'

'It's Rapha, isn't it?'

'Yup'.

Ha!

The next day, I was filming an item about commuting in London by bike. We passed by the new Rapha Club just off Brewer Street in Piccadilly Circus. As I stood on the pavement outside with the film crew, Simon Mottram suddenly appeared in front of me.

He gave me a brief guided Tour of his brand-new café/ clothes shop. He told me how they'd celebrated its opening by throwing a party for the riders after the Olympic Road Race. Mark Cavendish, understandably, hadn't shown up. But David Millar had, and by all accounts took full advantage of the free refreshments. Until early in the morning. Someone had a picture of Millar sprawled across the bonnet of a car with a bottle of claret in each hand.

Then I congratulated Simon on the impending deal.

'When's the announcement?'

'What announcement?' He grinned impishly.

'OK, then. If you had anything to announce, what day might you choose to announce it?'

'I would have thought that the first of September might be a good day for such an announcement, if such an announcement were planned.'

'Excellent. Will there be a party?'

'Yes. Here.'

'Good. Can I come?'

'I don't know what you're talking about, Ned.'

So Rapha and Mottram have reached the top. The brand so beloved of London's chattering elite, so embraced by moneyed Scandinavia and Euro-culture-hungry Japan and

North America, has muscled its way into the big league.

It is a curious echo of that sponsorship deal between a sugary alcoholic drink and an ex-cyclist from Clermont-Ferrand: forty years later, the name Rapha (shorn of its fuller version) will once again be worn on the roads of the Tour de France. But to get there it had to go via London. And it took this man from Sheffield to make the match.

And for Mottram's project itself, it marks something of a crossroads. His desire to grow the brand has to be cross-referenced against the appeal of its exclusivity. In a way, its not dissimilar to the growth of cycling in this country overall. The more the secret's out among the wider population, the more alienated the cognoscenti will feel. They yearn already for the days when nobody understood them.

Mottram, for once, is in tune with those British cycling fans who feel that something has been ripped from them by the relentless march on ever-greater popularity, their otherness.

'I think of my Dad. He hated things that everyone else liked. He liked to be his own man. I liked being the only cyclist in the office. I liked being weird and different. So part of me doesn't like the fact that it's become everybody's favourite sport. And yet, I'm all about making it everybody's favourite sport.'

He bites his lip and looks pensive. But it's not without great satisfaction that he says, 'It's a classic dilemma.'

And, as I write the last sentence of this chapter, I am left wondering whether another box containing an item of Rapha couture will ever come my way again. And if it does, what then?

Should I wear it?

CHAPTER 12

TWO TOMMY GODWINS

I was about to find out that the history of cycling on these shores boasts not one, but two Tommy Godwins. They were both remarkable, in their own ways.

There are few more upstanding names. In fact, if I were called upon to design a name for a British cyclist of yesteryear, I would choose Godwin (subliminal references to deity and victory), and offset it simply with Tommy (subliminal references to pinball wizardry).

The first Tommy Godwin, born in 1912, had a job as a young boy delivering groceries by bike. One day he rode, and won, a twenty-five-mile time trial on his delivery bike, having carefully dismantled the parcel tray from the front. Getting rid of that, I reckoned, must have been the earliest recorded marginal gain in British cycling history.

The second Tommy Godwin was born eight years later, in 1920. He too got a job as delivery boy for a chain of grocers. It seemed, at the time, the natural career path. He rode this heavy contraption up and down steep hills, laden with groceries. It made him strong.

Two greengrocer's boys, then. Two legendary riders. Two Tommies.

How British is that?

I just wish I'd known beforehand. But I didn't. And so, with unspeakable predictability, I brought about a moment of considerable embarrassment during an email exchange with Tommy Godwin's daughter.

One day in May 2012 I had spent a few sunny hours in the company of 'Tommy Godwin 2', the gentleman who had been born second, in 1920. Several weeks later I tried to get in touch with him again: there were a few lines of enquiry that I wanted to follow up, and a number of biographical details I needed to check. Like a fool, at the time of our meeting, I had quite forgotten to get a phone number for him, so I was reliant on others to help me get in contact. Someone had very helpfully given me an email address for the daughter of Tommy Godwin, a lady called Barbara Ford. So I duly wrote to her.

Hi Barbara,

I do hope you are well. I had the great honour of meeting your dad at Herne Hill a month or two ago. We had a long and fascinating chat about all sorts of different things.

I wanted, as a result, to get hold of his book. Do you know how I could go about it?

I hope he is well. Please pass on my regards.

Best wishes,
Ned Boulting.

A little while later, I received a reply.

Hello and thank you for the email,

Sadly my father Tommy Godwin the World Mileage Endurance Record Holder died in 1975. He is still very sadly missed by us all.

You obviously met the 'other Tommy Godwin'.

However if you would care to know more about our Tommy Godwin just input 'Tommy Godwin 1912' into any search engine and be prepared to be blown away!

Regards Barbara Ford (née Godwin and very proud)

I had just informed a total stranger that I had spent an afternoon chatting to her dead father. I sent a fulsome apology by return, and then did just as she suggested, and I looked up her dad.

'Tommy Godwin 1' was indeed something of a phenomenon.

The record he set in 1939 was so extraordinary that the people at the *Guinness Book of Records* (yes, it still exists) are refusing to ratify any more attempts to break it. Their reasoning is that it is 'too dangerous'. That makes it harder than Felix Baumgartner's 2012 jump from space, which, I think we can all agree, fell into the category of 'highly risky'. Besides, it seems to be a remarkably difficult record to verify. Indeed, when a rider called Ken Webb appeared to have broken it in the 1970s, the verification of the distances he rode was brought into question, and his achievement fell (perhaps unfairly) into disrepute. So Godwin's septuagenarian record still stands, to this day.

The lunatic, bloody-mindedness of the man!

He rode, in one calendar year, 75,065 miles: more than two hundred miles every day. Even as I type it, I find Tommy Godwin 1's powers of endurance hard to comprehend. In pictures he appears brutishly strong, bent over quaint handle-bars, which gave their name to the voguish moustaches of the era, not that Godwin had any need for such fripperies as facial hair. The only accessory he sported was a milometer that he had fixed to his bike, which seemed to have been ripped from the cockpit of a Hawker Hurricane. His trademark pose is 'knackered', his head on one side, open-mouthed as he gulps in British air and metabolises it.

The record itself had been set and broken repeatedly since its inauguration in 1910. In the same way that in France

L'Auto newspaper had established a bicycle dash around the country in order to boost its flagging circulation figures (a race that still exists, it's called the Tour de France), so its British cousin *Cycling* established what it called the 'Century Competition'. The winner of this prize would be the rider with the 'greatest number of complete 100-mile rides in 1911'.

The French idea, I'll confess, has enjoyed a little more durability in the public imagination, but the 'Century' was big news for a while.

A Frenchman (wouldn't you just know it) claimed first prize. Marcel Planes, who ensured that his 'checking card' was signed every day by a local official (to prove that he'd ridden as far as he claimed), pedalled for a verified 34,366 miles in a year. That record stood for twenty-one years, presumably while everyone else admired its utter pointlessness from a comfortable distance. Besides, the First World War served as a pretty considerable distraction, and by the 1920s everyone had discovered jazz and cocktails, both of which seemed much more fun than riding a hundred miles every day on a cast-iron bike.

Then, in 1932, the competition reignited. The magnificently named Arthur Humbles spent a year riding out of North London as far as he could along the Great North Road, and then turning round and heading back home for his tea. After twelve months of this, he'd clocked 36,007 miles. He had set a new record.

Other holders came and went. And not all of them were British. Not by a long way.

In 1933, a Tasmanian called 'Ossie' Nicholson took unfair advantage of Australia's better-than-it-ought-to-be sunshine quotient to set a new standard of 43,966 miles.

Three years later, on 6 January 1936, a one-armed, teetotal vegetarian named Walter Greaves set off from Bradford on a specially adapted bike (he had a single brake lever for both wheels, and a twist grip gear changer all on the same side of the handlebars). When he finally came to rest, on New Year's Eve, outside Bradford Town Hall, he'd amassed 45,383 miles. To this day, he remains the only one armed, teetotaller from Yorkshire to have held the record. But, interestingly, not the only vegetarian.

In 1937, Ossie set out to reclaim his record. At exactly the same time an English resident, a Frenchman of Scottish descent (I am not making these people up) named René Menzies launched his campaign. Ossie prevailed, riding a staggering 62,657 miles, beating Menzies by just 1,096 miles. Intriguingly, although scarcely of any relevance, Menzies, who had been decorated for valour in the First World War, went on to become Charles de Gaulle's chauffeur during the next war, a bizarre biographical detail which, by now, probably won't surprise you.

Then, our hero, Tommy Godwin, admiring Ossie's record from his home in the Potteries, decided he would win it back for King and Country. So, he duly set off in freezing conditions

on New Year's Day 1939 from outside his sponsor's bike shop in Middlesex. It was reported that so many people turned out to see him off that the police thought there was a riot and called for back up.

He averaged more than two hundred miles a day, through an appalling winter, and even overcame the minor inconvenience of the outbreak of war in September. The introduction of rationing affected his vast dairy-based intake (Tommy, like Walter, was a vegetarian), and the blackout meant he could no longer use his lights to ride in the darkness. He had to wait for a full moon, and clear skies.

He did it, though. 75,065 miles. Then he carried on, just for fun. By Whitsun he had ridden the fastest ever 100,000 miles. It took 499 days, on each of which he averaged more than two hundred miles.

Eventually, he did settle down to the rest of his life. He was called up to service, but by now wasn't any good to the army. All those days in the saddle had changed him for ever. His heels wouldn't touch the ground, and his hands remained slightly curled. So he served out the war for the RAF and started a family.

That was when Barbara was born. She was the lady I'd emailed, erroneously claiming to have spoken to her dead father.

I get back in touch with her, and ask her what she recalls of her dad. Incredibly, she grew up with no idea of what he had achieved.

'The most amazing thing about him was he never boasted about his world records,' Barbara, who is nearly seventy years old herself, writes to me. 'I was sixteen years old before I knew. It was my headmaster who asked if my dad was the famous cyclist. I said I didn't think so, though he had a bike and he belonged to a cycling club. When I got home that afternoon I asked Dad if he was famous, his reply was "Who's told you that rubbish!"

'He was the most wonderful man, a fabulous dad and a devoted husband. I do know without a doubt why he was such an achiever, some say he wasn't "wired" like other athletes, and I think that is true.

'Dad gave everything away, trophies, cups, medals, anything to make someone else happy.

'I wish you could have known him.'

Tommy Godwin died, seemingly as do so many cyclists, having returned from a ride with friends. He was just sixty-three.

Some dedicated soul, in a noble effort to preserve his place in the public imagination, has set up a twitter feed to commemorate his achievement. Each day, they tweet his mileage. The astonishing totals read like the mad wall scratchings of a man in solitary confinement. Here, at random are four days in the summer:

18 July: Tommy Godwin rode 333 miles today in 1939
19 July: Tommy Godwin rode 308 miles today in 1939
20 July: Tommy Godwin rode 348 miles today in 1939
21 July: Tommy Godwin rode 235 miles today in 1939
And then this:
22 July: Tommy Godwin rode 255 miles today in 1939

On exactly that same day, 22 July 1939 and probably not very far away, the other Tommy Godwin won his first race, on a track in the Midlands.

'I was eighteen,' he tells me. And, though 'Tommy 2' is now ninety-one when he tells me this, I can scarcely believe he was born just two years after the end of the First World War. He is so strikingly well, so rudely healthy, that it's almost a bit unsettling. Has the man lied about his age? Or has he been locked away in some cryonic chamber? What's his secret?

'On 22 July 1939, I won my first ever prize in open competition. I was handed a note inviting me to take part in the Olympic trials.'

Tommy Godwin beams with pride, his manicured fingers play over the polished surface of a wooden box that sits gently on his immaculately creased trousers. We are sitting side by side in the stands at the Herne Hill Velodrome, as a procession of young riders takes to the track. We have time on our hands, as the afternoon drifts on; the racing is over-running somewhat. And so Tommy talks freely and warmly about a lifetime spent in pursuit of speed on a bike, a life whose pinnacle was reached at the very place we've met.

He is a remarkable man, a living connection with the London Olympic Games of 1948. But it isn't his longevity that makes this Tommy Godwin every bit as extraordinary as the other Tommy Godwin. It's simply being a Tommy Godwin that does that.

Where else but Herne Hill would have been so fitted to the moment, to the man? The location, and the man, were perfectly aligned.

A date in my calendar had been fixed for months. It was the Inter-Schools Championship Day at Herne Hill. An enthusiastic, extremely well spoken, young teacher from nearby Dulwich College (a palace of Victorian brick and expensively honed values) had asked me, and Tommy Godwin, to attend. I liked the idea of schoolkids using the track. I was reminded of stories I'd heard from a number of London riders, who'd told me how their first experience of cycling had come when their schools had taken them down to ride at Herne Hill. Most of South London's secondary schools would have sent kids to the track. It had been a treasured local resource, before it slipped into anonymity and decline, only recently to be re-animated a little.

It was a perfect early summer's day. I rode down to the track, this time on my own. Again, I locked my bike to the railings and made my way towards the stands.

It wasn't quite the meeting I had thought it would be. Handed a programme, I glanced down the list of competing schools. Far from being drawn from the velodrome's natural constituency of comprehensives, they were all private schools and from as far afield as Bedford. That was where I had been educated, where my dad had been a teacher; my old school had sent a team down to London! I caught on a breeze the particular strains of self-confident boys' voices that had once been so familiar to me. My childhood seemed a very foreign place.

There, sitting in the stands, was Tommy Godwin. He was unmistakable.

A small collection of men and women clustered disciple-like on the rows beneath him, so they sat at his knee level, their heads inclined towards him and angled slightly to catch his every word. Tommy sat in their midst, occasionally gesticulating. He looked twenty years younger than he actually was, his hair smashingly parted and fulsomely silver, his glasses framing eyes of steely blue. He wore a blazer, a club tie, a pair of English brogues and some mathematically pressed slacks. He was holding court. Even from a distance, as I approached, and took my seat to listen, I could tell he was on a roll.

'I was a good all rounder. I could rough it up. I could sprint. I could ride pursuits, team pursuits, kilometres, time trials . . .' Suddenly he was interrupted.

'Go on, Tommy!' a passer-by yelled at him, clenching his fists and smiling.

'Oi! I'm talking about you!' Tommy fired back, with a dash of a Brummie accent like a drop of Worcestershire sauce. The passer-by laughed back, clapped loudly, and walked on. Tommy beamed delightedly. And then, seamlessly, he carried on with the point he was making, the point to which he often returns, the touchstone of his ethos.

'You must have respect for people. You must behave your-selves. You gotta have ambition and determination. You've got to be prepared to make sacrifices. Listen to your elder people who've got the experience, because you might think you know it all, but the people who've been through the sport can tell you where you're making the mistakes, and you must listen and you must get the work ethic into your mind. You will only get out of life what you put into it.' He does not draw breath.

On he goes. 'The work ethic is absolutely the essential thing in any walk of life. If your kid's going to be a musician or a doctor, they've still got to work hard in everything they do. You've got to be dedicated and be prepared to make sacrifices.

'And I do live this life. I live it absolutely to the minute.'

He rapped his fingers on the wooden box, and resettled his glasses on his nose.

'Amen!' we all wanted to shout, cultishly. At that moment, we, his disciples, would have gladly packed our bags and followed Tommy to wherever he wanted to lead us: to a lake-side in the Caucasus, a mountain top in Kenya, a hide-out in Wyoming. Or, perhaps more realistically, to Herne Hill, where we had come as pilgrims. We would sit up straight. We were the Godwinites.

'Look at those two, buggering around, now.' Tommy suddenly broke the spell, and drew our collective attention to two schoolboys whose sprint had just started. They were playing at being Chris Hoy and Grégory Baugé, standing virtually motionless on their pedals, the one in front of the other, looking each other in the eye.

This thrilled Tommy. 'Isn't that bloody marvellous. Oh! Priceless. They've been watching too much of that on the telly. Go on lads!' he hollered at them, and sat back chuckling to watch the race unfold.

No two riders are the same, just as no two Tommy Godwins are the same.

Though outwardly the epitome of the English gentleman, he had actually been born in Bridgeport, Connecticut. His father Charles, originally from Birmingham, had sought a better life in New England (Old England had simply delivered a murderous regime of breaking pig-iron for smelting; a job he'd started at the age of thirteen).

In America in the 1920s, things were hard, but wholesome. Schooling was in fact pretty good, and young Tommy grew up sledding, skiing, boxing and even golfing. Charles was seized by the notion that his oldest son should be a sportsman. Stumbling back drunk from a party one night he woke up his son and made him promise he'd compete in the Olympics one day. Young Tommy agreed to the request, presumably so he could roll over and go to sleep again.

In truth, inseparable though they were, Tommy and his dad were very different characters. Charles was a bit of a rogue. He hung out with the odd gangster. He set up a moonshine operation during the years of prohibition, roping his kids into the illegal distilling trade and getting them to deliver the whisky to his Italian friends in exchange for their equally illicit wine.

Certainly he was no angel. Yet, in everything that Tommy recalls, his approval is sought. Through him, and throughout his life, Tommy looked for affirmation.

'My father was a very disciplined man. He laid down a strict code of listening to him. Do what he says. "Don't do as I do, do as I say." He was a drinker, a smoker and a gambler. But I had to be the gentleman. I had to behave myself, respect people, show my appreciation to other people. "Civility is cheap," he said.'

But the Depression put paid to their American dream. It was time to return. Tommy recalls in his autobiography, *It Wasn't That Easy*, the moment at which his dad knew it was over.

'During 1932 my father, rightly or wrongly, made a decision after seeing some children searching for food in a garbage can while on his way to work one morning. His decision was, that, as a patriotic Englishman who refused to swear an oath against the King to obtain American citizenship, he would return to England, the place of his birth, and infant nurture.'

On the track, a bell rings to indicate the final lap of a sprint. One boy is a hundred metres ahead of his rival, who comes panting past us in the home straight, quite hopelessly beaten. We all watch on. Tommy shouts a few words of encouragement at the kid who's been vanquished, and then mutters a much more honest assessment of the boy's potential under his breath. 'He's not got much, that lad. Sad to say.'

Herne Hill is still playing out these little dramas. For Tommy Godwin, they are viscerally real. As he remembers racing, the words trip and tumble, overlap and catch up with one another. He can't get them out fast enough. The emotion is far, far ahead of its expression. Every now and again, and very suddenly, he will start to cry, recovering with a smile just as quickly. Such a torrent of memory and regret is exhausting to witness. It must be much harder still to be feeling it.

'Oh dear. I'm living it too much . . . Yes . . . I'm living it too much. I'm going through it all again. My life. Oh dear. Oh dear.'

After all, we are right where the ley lines intersect, right at the scene of his greatest moment. It happened at Herne Hill.

In 1948 he picked up an Olympic bronze medal in the Team Pursuit and another on his own in the 1,000m time trial, the 'Kilo'.

That race went off at 9.30 at night in horrendous, blustery conditions. Dusk had fallen prematurely. There was no lighting at the track, only the yellowish spill from lamps in the pavilion and other official buildings showed the way. He reckons he lost over a second on the home straight when the wind got up and pushed him backwards. This is what track riders call a 'Hard Straight'. But he got that medal he had dreamt of.

Winning the Team Pursuit bronze was also a considerable achievement for the decidedly ramshackle British team. They were, according to Godwin, just 'buggering about'. From start to finish, they were riding with hope and desire, guts and pluck. Science didn't enter into it.

'It was all strictly amateur. You rode for watches and clocks and things like that. You worked forty-eight hours a week on whatever job – I was working on concrete floors, climbing ladders, working in polishing shops, working with all the dust around me, or the next day in a breaking shop with all the fumes. It was all no good for bike riding.'

He breaks off to applaud another winner, coasting around on his lap of honour. 'He's done well, him. Looks all right on a bike, too. Good lad.'

Then, in a flash, without skipping a beat, he's spun back the clock again.

'There was no real training. There was no understanding between ourselves. There was no anything, you know.'

But they were up against seriously well-prepared French and Italian specialists. That lack of preparation, that lack of serious-ness was poison to the meticulous-minded Godwin. After retiring four years later, he went into coaching. He was deter-mined to try and change British cyclists' dilettante attitudes towards training. But it didn't stop there. Long before Brailsford's marginal gains, Godwin was leaving no stone unturned.

'The most comfortable chair? A straight-back dining chair. You slip the small of your back in it. You sit upright, and you never feel tired. And when you eat, you must chew for a count of twelve and you must get your food down to a pulp. Thirty-six times. I chew my food very well, before I put it into my system so my system doesn't have to work that hard to digest it.'

I put it to Tommy that he has aged considerably better than the old pavilion behind us. He glances over his shoulder at it, crumbled, flaking, and unloved, and then he launches into a passionate sermon. He invokes the rhythm and the vernacular of a charismatic preacher, measuring his words with increasing conviction and unshakable faith, and it starts very simply.

'Even of a morning, a glass of hot water first thing. One glass of hot water to clean the system out.' He looks at me acutely. I can see that he doubts the healthiness of my regime, and I feel a little uncomfortable. But now, he's warming to his subject.

'Bran flakes and muesli. A bowl of fresh fruit at the start of every week, with apples, oranges, kiwi fruit, grapes and a cut banana. Then I have three rounds of wholemeal bread, two with either pâté or cheese or a boiled egg. And one with honey on.'

He goes up a gear, as we head towards the lunch and then the evening meal.

'Even now, as a ninety-one-year-old man I still cook sea bass, salmon. If I do a meat meal like pork, I do apple sauce, sage and onion stuffing. I do spinach, carrots and potatoes. I do three vegetables for a main meal.'

Diet, and its consequences, became a feature of his coaching career. 'One rider had an iron deficiency. We put him on a diet of Japanese dried fish and Guinness.'

He was, in many ways, ahead of his time. He coached the British National team at the 1964 Tokyo Olympics, and he set up a training camp in the sunshine and mountains of Mallorca for the British squad; an island base still used by British Cycling's Olympians and by Team Sky and Bradley Wiggins himself. He started the first track course at Lilleshall, where he did a deal with local greengrocers to ensure the kids had a proper diet.

'I had friends in the fruit market that used to provide an apple, an orange, a banana every morning. I got the Milk Marketing Board to buy us a pint of milk a day. I got Horlicks to supply us. They wanted chips and egg butties and all this sort of thing. I said you're having what I'm telling you.'

He enjoyed successes as a coach, too. He trained Hugh Porter to repeated national titles. He trained Graham Webb to the British Hour record. He trained Mick Bennett, who also went on to win two bronze medals at the Olympics.

Listening to him recall his innovations, and even allowing for a margin of exaggeration, I am struck by his attention to detail. It seems to me that his work fitted the template that has made the current generation of British coaches the envy of the world.

And yet, thinking back, I do not recall his presence at that British Cycling gala dinner that first sparked my interest. I ask him if he was there. He tells me he had not been invited. I have touched a nerve.

'And you know, I've never once been invited along to Manchester, under the present scheme. With all the work I've put in. I've never been asked to see a training session. I feel very bitter almost with British Cycling. They've never had the decency to say, Tommy would you like to come and spend a few days?'

I find myself wondering if there is a reason for this. I can see, mixed into the chivalry and the charisma, a wilfulness in Tommy Godwin. But whatever the reason, it is uncomfortable, neglectful even, that the sport that gave him his purpose, and to which he dedicated so much of his life, now has so little room for him. Instead he sits here, on a plastic seat, talking to me about it all instead, talking to a virtual stranger.

'You would have loved the science of it all now, wouldn't you?' I put to him.

'Oh, I would have loved it.' He looks up and away, across the track. It seems like he's imagining an alternative version of the past.

'So, in a way, do you think you were born into the wrong generation?'

I have barely got my question out, when he interrupts loudly, and almost angrily.

'Yes. Yes. Exactly. That's exactly how . . . you're the first person to ever realise that. You've greatly complimented me by saying that. And I thank you.'

And, with that, he bursts into tears. Which wasn't what I had intended.

During the course of that long afternoon, and before Tommy and I are finally called upon to walk down to the middle of the track and make our speeches, we are regularly interrupted. People want to see the medals.

Every time he is asked, Tommy Godwin delights in opening the little wooden box to reveal them, dark brown and serious, nestling in the kind of green baize normally found on snooker tables. They are fine medals, but they are shaped by their age; unelaborated, gloomily tarnished, smallish. If you saw them in the window of a charity shop, propped up against a *Shoot!* annual, a teapot and a defunct ZX Spectrum, you would think nothing much of them. Like the man, so the medals. Unassuming.

'I'm very strict with the control of my life. I've never had any envies or jealousies for anyone. I live a very modest life.'

We shake hands. I think about him all the way home.

Not long later, as the London Olympic Games approach, I hear that he has become very ill. His daughter, Kay (and this time it *is* his daughter), emails me.

Sadly, Dad is not at all well at the moment – he has been diagnosed with cancer, so that has come as a great

*shock to us all given that he has been so remarkable in
the lead up to the Olympics. We hope he will attend the
opening ceremony tomorrow and an evening of track
cycling next week and then we can take life a little
more gently.*

I tune in for the opening ceremony. Sure enough, right
towards the end, just as the torches are being passed to the
children to light the flame, I catch a glimpse of Tommy, beaming.
The director has framed the shot on Steve Redgrave and Kelly
Holmes, but there, just in the edge of the picture, is Tommy
Godwin. A few days later, he was trackside to see Great Britain
take home the gold medal in his discipline, the Team Pursuit.

He was in his rightful place. Right in the thick of things.
He'd made it.

Tommy Godwin passed away on 3 November 2012, two
days short of his ninety-second birthday.

These two Tommies represent, in some ways, opposite
extremes. The fact that neither man appears in British
Cycling's Hall of Fame is surely a remarkable omission, given
what they both achieved in their separate ways. The one,
humble to the point of denial, dedicated to the lonely pursuit
of records on frozen roads, day after day. The other, quicksilver,
forthright, almost a bit natty, his heart shaped by the contours
and the speed of the track and the application of science.

The two men never met, as far as anyone can tell. I wonder
how they would have got on. Perhaps they might have had
little in common. They might have had scant regard for each
other's achievements. They might have rubbed each other up
the wrong way, Tommy 1 could easily have found Tommy 2's
volubility and propensity for emotion, a problem. Tommy 2
might have been dismissive of Tommy 1. Or they might have
been soulmates. Who knows.

For now I prefer to close my eyes to the unpredictable and fractious reality of human relationships, choosing instead to read their stories as you might a favourite childhood adventure.

Their stories have both been published. *Unsurpassed* tells the story of the World Endurance Record holder, and *It Wasn't That Easy* recounts the life of the Olympic medallist.

The subtitles are subtly different:

The Tommy Godwin Story, and *The Story of Tommy Godwin*.

CHAPTER 13

THE LONGWICK TEN

I was standing in the corridor of a well-appointed West London basement flat, staring at a picture of a naked man pleasuring a lady. I was surprised at how easy it was, in the course of researching a book about cycling, to end up leafing through a copy of *The Joy of Sex* with a management consultant.

Avril Millar was telling me about a book she wanted to write called *The Joy of Work*. It would be, she enthused, a user-friendly manual that would help people to re-engage with their work, an antidote to growing alienation, a balm for the schism she saw in people's lives between the family and the workplace. She was surprisingly passionate about it.

So that's how it came to pass that she and I were looking through those iconic pencil drawings from the original naughty 1970s manual, wondering what the copyright restrictions might be on using the same beardy man to illustrate *The Joy of Work*.

I have no doubt that, one day, this book will get published because Avril Millar is a force of nature. In fact, the home page of her website (avrilmillar.com) boasts just that turn of phrase, credited to George Bernard Shaw: 'Be a force of nature, instead of a feverish, selfish little clod of ailments and grievances complaining that the world will not devote itself to making you happy.'

She is just sixty, and has a long and varied career to her name as a very successful CEO of significant businesses, and latterly as someone whose advice is sought at the highest levels in the City. She is a deep thinker, with considerable verbal energy, firmly held beliefs and a broad vocabulary.

She is also the mother of the British cyclist David Millar.

She'd rung me up one July when she'd heard of a terrible crash on the Tour de France in which her son had been caught up. Could I tell her that he was all right? I promised to find out. Her voice had been edged with fear. She was his mum.

I put down my coffee. Through a window at head height, I occasionally caught a glimpse of a pair of heels or a booted ankle walking past at street level. It was one of those London basement rooms that you look down on as you pass: quiet, warm places.

Cocooned in such comfort, she tells me about their shared past, David's and hers. She begins to recall how she experienced, as a total outsider, her son's complete (and completely traumatic) immersion in the British cycling scene. Her account, it struck me, might help in my roundabout quest to discover the values at the heart of the country's changing relationship with cycling. As soon as she started to talk, I knew that she had spent half a lifetime amused, appalled, delighted and despairing of the hidden world that she had opened up so casually to her son.

It had all started with a simple phone call to the High Wycombe Cycling Club. This was, in itself, already an act of mild desperation. After her divorce from David's father Gordon, the summer holidays were characterised by a child-swap arrangement. Her daughter, Fran (of whom, more, later), would fly to Hong Kong to be with her dad for a few weeks. And David, in his early teens, would return to England to be with Avril. As the long weeks dragged by, sometimes she found herself at a loss. She didn't know what to do with him. Perhaps, she thought, cycling might offer a welcome distraction. And that led her to trying to find a club for him to join.

The voice on the other end of the line explained to Mrs Millar what to do. 'The best thing is just to turn up on a Tuesday night. It's the Longwick Ten.'

That's exactly how Avril remembers the instructions. She laughs.

Her softish Scottish accent is peppered with a surprising number of profanities. Maybe it's just me being naïve, but I'm always a little shocked to hear people's mums talking like this.

'When people are in cycling, they say things like that. And you're left thinking, "What the fuck is that?"'

After my experiences with Ron Keeble and others, I know just what she means. 'I totally agree with you. If it's not the Longwick Ten, it's the Pocklington Challenge.' (I had been to an extraordinarily long prize-giving dinner at a cycling club in Yorkshire. The Pocklington Challenge was still embedded in my memory.)

She laughs again. 'Tossers!'

But that's far from being her final word on the subject. 'So there's this place called Longwick. But is that the start? Or the end of it? And what is a time trial? And how does the whole thing work?'

Back then she went along, though, making sure to leave work early enough to get David to the start line in time.

He, too, had no idea what he was about to experience. Sitting on his saddle at the start, his bike held by a volunteer, he turned round, as the seconds counted down and confessed to the man, 'I don't know what to do.'

'Just go as fast as you can for as long as you can.' And with that, a young David Millar was pushed off into an exhilarating, uncertain future, one which even now continues to throw up twists and turns and high drama. That day, needless to say, he broke the course record.

They settled into a routine. Avril would buy all the newspapers on her way to the time trial and sit ensconced in the car, while her son 'did what he had to do'. It was almost as if she were complicit, encouraging her son to indulge in some hidden, filthy practice.

At first she didn't know what to make of the cheery enthusiasts and volunteers who kept the High Wycombe Cycling
Club ticking over. She'd remembered driving past them before,
years ago, with a seven-year-old David in the back of the car.
They'd lodged in her memory; or at least the sight of a group
of men and women standing around in a lay-by in wellington
boots and kagouls, carrying clipboards or holding bikes. At
the time, she had genuinely wondered who on earth they were
and what they thought they were doing. Was it a protest? A
hunt? Were they ramblers? Should she report them?

It was only in 1994, when she drove her seventeen-year-old
son to the same lay-by for the start of the Archers junior road
race, that she realised what that first sighting had been about.

And now she too, unconsciously, has started to play their
game. She has started to assume I know what she is talking
about.

She says, casually, 'He won the Archers that year.'

'The Archers'. I make a mental note to look it up.

She is on a roll now. Nostalgia, once it gets uncorked, is
hard to squeeze back into the bottle. Very soon, Avril Millar
had been totally won over by this disparate band of cycling
folk, with whom ostensibly she had nothing in common.

'There was a very strong preponderance of people who had
ridden their bikes for years. And their fathers before them
had ridden their bikes. And bike riding was in their DNA. It's
what they did. The concept of getting up on a Sunday morning
and going to ride forty miles just seemed so utterly normal to
them and it seemed so utterly bonkers to me. There were
people there who were steeped in it. And then there was us.
Not a clue. But it was great fun.'

It was a welcoming, homely, non-judgemental world that
must have seemed a very far cry from the sharpness and
clamour of her life in business. It was a form of therapy, not
least for David, for whom it lent a structure to his trips back

to visit his mum. But she, too, could see the purifying, whole-some delight in the sport.

'It had the nature of going to a working men's club. The sense of it felt like that. Many years ago there used to be all these reading rooms up and down the country especially for miners, so that people could educate themselves outside their working lives. That's what these things felt like. It felt like they were saying *this is good for the soul.*'

But David was crossing a boundary already. He had moved quickly through all the gears at his disposal, and wanted more. His legs spun too fast for British roads. It's an innocent arc that I was, by now, beginning to see replicated in the biographies of so many British riders. You start because it's fun. You get good. Then you win races. You discover there are more and more races, most of them overseas. And then, and only then, does it dawn on you that this could be a career. So, you start to turn your back on your peers. But the truth is you've already left them behind.

He was enrolled in the 'Southern Centre of Excellence', which he details in his book *Racing Through The Dark.*

'In my mind's eye,' writes Millar, 'I imagined a smart building with a lab and a gym, white-coated technicians, a bank of cutting-edge technology and pages of data and test results. It was actually Ian Goodhew's living room.'

'It was hysterically funny. That is how it was.' Avril remembers the ramshackle trips to race in Belgium, squashed into the backs of cars. These brushes with the Continental scene were the loosening of the admittedly slight grip that British cycling held over David Millar. His soul had been hijacked, for better or worse, by the lure of the Continent.

Later on that day, after I have left West London and Avril Millar behind me, I sit shivering in my car, watching my youngest daughter playing football on a godforsaken patch of ragged astro turf. The rain is pelting against the windscreen.

I am put in mind of what Avril has told me about her evenings at Longwick, huddled in the warmth of her car, occasionally looking up from behind her newspapers to see if her boy had started yet.

While her words are fresh in my memory, I dial David Millar's number. He picks up the phone in an Italian hotel room. In the background I can hear his Canadian teammate Ryder Hesjedal laughing at pictures from a 1997 edition of *Procycling* that the pair of them have been leafing through.

'We're cycling fans too, Ned,' David tells me.

I tell him that I have spent the day interviewing his mother, a fact he takes in his stride. I am not certain that I would want journalists interviewing my mother about my childhood. In fact, I'll rephrase that. I am *certain* that I *wouldn't* want journalists interviewing my mother about my childhood. It speaks volumes, I conclude, about their trust for one another that he is not remotely fazed by my disclosure.

I wonder how he remembers it all, as I squint through the raindrops at my daughter's team conceding yet another goal, and turning, shoulders slumped, back to the centre circle. How did he remember those early inductions into the secret world of the cycling clubs?

'It was quirky. That sense of being an outsider. I was young enough not to care. I just wanted to race. I signed a clipboard on a lay-by and paid fifty pence. That was brilliant.

'I had nothing in common with the people at High Wycombe Cycling Club. Neither age, upbringing, nor education. And yet we all shared a common eccentricity. We loved cycling. We shouldn't shy away from using the word eccentricity.

'When I went to race in Belgium I instantly fell in love with it. I thought, this sport is actually part of the national identity here. Whole towns used to shut down for a junior race. That's when I was awoken to the fact that the grass was greener, and that it really was oddball and small time in the UK.

'Once I got to eighteen, and I realised I wanted to be a pro, that's when I thought I have to get out of here now. There was a massive gulf. It was much bigger than the English Channel.'

I turned the ignition key once and flicked the wipers. My windscreen cleaned itself of the blotchy rain to reveal a clutch of kids listening, knock-kneed with cold, to some point their teacher was making, presumably about defending.

David Millar's words chimed with what Avril had told me earlier that afternoon. His mother understood. She saw something in the boys' eyes, when they returned from these forays overseas. Ravaged, but radiant.

'They'd come back shadows of their former selves, but fired up to the hilt, because they had been there, and they had smelt it. They had smelt their future.'

Avril helped him realise that future. She bought him a car, and packed him off to Picardie.

'He drove off in a battered Ford Escort, not a word of French, we gave him some money and he drove off to VC St. Quentin.'

She thinks about it for a while. 'It's almost biblical in its immensity. That would never happen now. You'd be horror-struck.'

But he had to go. 'Frankly, what did Britain have to offer? He'd fucking hated it.'

I remind David Millar of the year when we first met. It was that infamous Tour of 2003. It was the Tour that, for me, produced my 'yellow jumper' moment, but was packed with intense memories, too, none richer than when he was declared the winner of the final time trial.

I had interviewed him on live television, I remember the occasion clearly. Of course I did not know at the time what has subsequently become clear. He was doped. Or, as his mother puts it, 'He was well and truly in the midst of his own horror story then.'

If truth be told, Millar had been a bit tricky to deal with all the way round France that summer. He was the only British rider on the race, and we had pursued him with the weight of a nation. It wasn't that he was evasive, but we weren't half persistent.

'A quick word for ITV, Dave.'

'Just one line for TV back home, David, please.'

He had done his duty by us, but had made it clear that our Britishness was of no great heft.

Had he loathed the association with his 'homeland'? A decade later, I can ask him outright.

'I was French. At that time, it meant nothing to me. I had separated myself so far from it all.'

And a year later, he was busted.

It's worth noting that not everyone buys into Millar's tale of redemption. He himself freely uses the term 'Marmite rider' to describe his status in the eyes of the cycling public.

There are those who wonder if the whole truth has really emerged. There are those who wonder if any of it would have come out if he hadn't been caught in such flagrant circumstances. There are those who would rather he had never been allowed to ride again.

There are also riders, British riders, who did not dope, and find it hard to wipe his slate clean. One British pro told me that in 2004 Jaguar had promised him a free car. Given that he was surviving on the minimum UCI wage, a new set of wheels would have been a significant bonus, unaffordable any other way. But they'd also promised one to David Millar, and when news of his disgrace reached Jaguar's marketing people they got cold feet, and ordered the withdrawal not only of Millar's car, but of all the cars they'd promised to British cyclists.

This hurt. Why, asked this rider, should he have to bear the consequences for someone else's dishonesty?

These are not easy questions to answer. Millar has spent a long time facing them, and will continue to do so for as long as he has a public profile in the sport.

I was speaking at a dinner in the winter, talking about his 2003 Prologue, and my memories of the drama of my first ever day reporting on the Tour de France. David Millar sat to my right, as I spoke, and quite suddenly interrupted me, mid-sentence.

'I was doping, Ned.'

It rather took the wind out of my sails.

David Millar moved back to Britain. That much was inevitable.

In his autobiography, he outlines the about-face that this involved. 'I had always sworn I'd never return to live permanently in Britain, yet now it was my port in the storm and I was thankful for that.'

Avril Millar, with a glance at a photo of her children, recalls how close he now was, but how distant her returning son had become.

'He cleaved very tightly to his sister. Fran was the person to whom he turned. She had a flat round the corner from here, and he went and lived there. But he was drunk for that first year. I barely saw him. He was ashamed and embarrassed and upset. He was just a mess.'

Fran Millar is, in her own way, a significant player in the British cycling scene. With her erstwhile business partner James Pope, they founded a business called Face Partnership some ten years ago, when Fran was still in her early twenties. Alongside PR and agency work for riders, they also established a series of bike races, both on the track and the road that have proved highly successful. Fran went on to work for British Cycling and subsequently Team Sky as head of PR. Over recent years, her influence has grown within the organisation. She now has a job description that encompasses pretty much everything: logistics, PR, admin, budgets and riders' contracts.

The last time I had any significant dealings with Fran was in Chartres on the 2012 Tour de France. Bradley Wiggins had just clinched the overall win. It was the moment of history to which the race had been building for a month.

We were at their Campanile hotel, waiting around to film Dave Brailsford raising a glass to his team, when suddenly Fran received an email from ASO, the Tour organisation, reminding her that the next day tradition dictated that the winning team should hand out champagne to all the other teams on the race. This would be done as the convoy of support vehicles trundled along the roads towards Paris. Champagne flutes would be passed from car to car, all courtesy of the winning team.

But nineteen bottles! Fran had none. Other teams might have come prepared. But no British team had ever won, so therefore no British team had ever had to deal with this eventuality. It was late. It was Saturday night. All the shops were shut.

I offered to help. Fran handed me a Team Sky credit card, whispered the PIN number to me, and I set off in the car to beg, borrow and buy at exorbitant prices, all the bottles of bubbly I could find in Chartres. It was a very cycling moment, somewhere between grandiose and two-bit.

I got them, though. And the Tour had its fizz the next day.

Fran Millar is right at the heart of an organisation to which her brother will always be denied access. Team Sky's recruitment policy specifically excludes him on the grounds of his doping ban. But there it is. It's a curious situation for both of them. It's curious all round, according to Avril.

'I know that the people he would have loved to be working with and riding with are the people sitting on the inside of Team Sky. When he gets to ride with them [Team GB] at the Worlds, he loves it. He just loves it.'

And then her voice is edged with the toughness she must at times have called upon as she tried to refocus her errant son. This is where she sounds like a force of nature.

'But he can't and so that's that.'

Millar's affection for the British was rekindled during his rehabilitation. It became apparent that he was dealing with people whose duty it was to pass sentence (British Cycling were charged with the implementation of his two-year ban), but not necessarily to judge; the French had done that bit for them. There was an avuncular innocence about the panel that had been assembled to hear his case, as if they were dealing with a particularly nasty murder in a charming Cotswold village: this kind of thing just didn't happen to chaps like us.

The voice on the other end of the line grows a little indistinct. It might be the connection to Italy from my South London car park. Or it might be that even now these things don't tell themselves easily.

He's remembering that confession. 'Sitting in that hearing explaining to them that this was where I'd been. It had been eight years. I'd gone as a kid and come back as a broken world champion. And that was because I'd been out of their hands.

'The UK became a refuge. I discovered that there was so much right that was going on over here, compared to what was going on over there.'

Perhaps, I suggest, at the core of what was right, was the abiding amateur heart of the British scene?

'That's what we mustn't lose as we become these corporate sportsmen. As we become mega-money-orientated and success driven, we might forget about the purity of it all.'

And then, in a sentence, it sounds like he hits a nail right on the head.

'We shouldn't lie to ourselves about where we've come from and what we're going to become.'

Is he talking about himself? Or is he bemoaning the inev-itability of change? On reflection, I am no longer sure which nail it is that he has just hit.

The football match is coming to an end, and soon I will be nursing a frozen child back to warmth in the car. But before I hang up, we have a brief chat about his book cover. I tell him how, when out riding with Gary Kemp, I met the excellent Nadav Kander, who it transpires is godfather to David's baby Archie. He tells me how much his wife Nicole thinks that Kander's photo perfectly captures him.

I opt not to tell him what I really think.

'He came back. That's the only way I can describe it. He came back. My David came back.'

David Millar's mum and I are heading towards what she describes as being a 'deep and meaningful'. She and her son often stay up until deep into the night, talking stuff through.

'Geography is nothing. Places are not your home. People are your home.'

That's true, I agree. But, I put to her, there is still a value in the shared identity, which spreads beyond the intimate confines of the nearest and dearest, the identity that is defined by a sense of place.

Actually, where cycling is concerned, it is defined, literally, by geography; by A roads and hill climbs and lanes and dual carriageways, by westerlies and sunshine and showers.

'Yes,' she agrees. 'There's always a significant lay-by some-where, where people will congregate.'

What, we both wonder, will become of those homely cycling clubs in the Great Leap Forward?

Seen through the refracted experience of the Millar family, what appeared, twenty years ago, to be impenetrable, arcane and musty, suddenly seems gloriously soulful.

Avril Millar, being exceptionally good with words, expresses it very neatly.

'I think there was a time when we were truly blessed. There is something really wonderful about that. People would do it come hail, rain or shine, for no glory and no prizes, because they absolutely loved it. The sheer, visceral joy. What I think I saw, and I hope it still exists, is a complete love in the turning of your feet. In the pedals. On your bike. On Sunday. On a club run.' She pauses, and resettles her glasses on her nose.

'I don't think that's gone.'

She points at the three bikes that clutter up her hallway. After years of resistance to cycling, she too has found her will broken. She has started to ride.

'I would love to turn up one Tuesday night, at Longwick, with David, and do the ten mile time trial. That's on my tick list of things I have to do before I die. I will do the "Longwick Ten". With David.'

That would close a chapter.

CHAPTER 14

BECKETT OF THE BEC

I have never been a member of a club, unless you count the Young Ornithologists, briefly, in 1979. They gave me a badge and a copy of the *Observer Book of Birds*, but there was no annual dinner, and no transparent, democratic process for electing the club secretary.

More recently, I was made honorary president of a Putney-based cycling club. Flattered, I have since proceeded to attend not a single one of their society functions, for which I am honestly sorry. It's just that I am not well suited to this world in which the bottom bracket is king: the cycling club.

You might have seen members of Britain's many strangely named cycling clubs (often known as 'wheelers') riding on the roads, in pairs, their kits matching like the neatly pressed clothing of identical twin children dressed by the same proud mother. Or perhaps you'll swerve out into the middle of the road to avoid wiping out a cluster of them, stretched out along the gutter of some unprepossessing hill on a Sunday morning, their differing ages and physiques as quaintly dysmorphic as their Lycra is joyously absurd. Huffing and puffing into the winter air. How do you get drawn into their fold? And is it a happy world, once you're there?

'I'm in David Millar's VCRC club. Do you know about that?' Gary Kemp had asked me, lowering his voice to a whisper that I could barely make out over the howling and grind of coffee machines. 'It's slightly Masonic.' I nodded conspiratorially.

The VCRC. What could that possibly stand for? As soon as I'd got home from meeting Kemp, I had googled it.

The Internet contained a disappointing lack of information. In fact, all it presented me with was a list of organisations to which David Millar, for all his breadth of reading, surely had no affiliation.

The Vasculitis Clinical Research Consortium. The Virtual Catalogue of Roman Coins. Or the Vietnamese Christian Resource Centre. I guessed it was none of them. Then I stumbled across the merest trace of it.

Someone had posted on their personal blog, an account of spotting David Millar riding in Richmond park one day. They had noticed that his jersey bore the name Velo Club Rocacorba. What could that mean? they wondered.

Now we were getting somewhere. The initials matched. The location fitted, Rocacorba being a few miles outside Girona in northern Spain, where David Millar and Nicole now live. And a strange twitter ID then confirmed that I had tracked them down. The profile @velorocacorba followed five people, had tweeted three times and was followed in turn by absolutely no one. The profile read: 'Velo Club Rocacorba. President – David Millar.' I clicked on 'Follow' and got the message 'Pending'. It seemed I had to be approved first.

I even emailed him about it. 'David. What is the VCRC?' No reply.

How fitting that David Millar should somehow be involved in a mysterious, elite-sounding institution that counted Gary Kemp among its number, and left no trace of its existence in the outside world.

After all, membership of a club with bizarre rules and hidden rituals has always been a part of his life. He's a British cyclist.

It surprised me not one bit to learn that we had another mutual connection. Cycling's small world seemed to shrink further with each acquaintance I made. So there was nothing unusual in the fact that the last time I saw David Millar was not in Paris or Biarritz, but Croydon.

You see, we had both been invited to lunch by the same man, Garry Beckett.

The Bec Cycling Club (originally from Tooting Bec) is one of many dozens like it up and down the country. Garry Beckett (the 'Bec' at the beginning of his name is merely a happy coincidence, like Arsène at Arsenal) is some sort of ill-defined honorary figurehead, or, as he himself sees it, the club drunkard. The Bec was established in the 1920s to 'increase sociability among cyclists'. Garry Beckett is still working hard at that bit.

This was not the first time I had been invited to the Bec Cycling Club's annual lunch. On my first visit in 2010, I was even the guest of honour. It took place in the top room of a mock-Tudor pub called Le Chateau. It was the afternoon that I had first been introduced to Maurice Burton. Germain, his son, had collected the key prize of the day, the youngest-ever winner of the 'Bec Hill Climb'. There were many prizes; a trestle table, covered in a tablecloth, groaned with silverware waiting to be handed out.

Few of the guests, apart from Garry, had a clue who I was, which meant my hilarious anecdotes about life on the Tour de France fell rather flat. But to my relief and surprise, it didn't matter much, because almost everyone in the room was so plastered they barely knew who they were themselves.

Sitting cheerfully around four or five round tables, the thirty or so guests, with associated toddlers charging about the room, tucked into a heart-warming Sunday lunch, that was loosely modelled on school dinners. It was served from under domed stainless steel lids. After the lager, which we had guzzled on arrival, came the white wine, and after the white, the red. Then the 'cross toasting' began.

Garry kicked it off. He banged the handle of his knife loudly on the table. Then he stood up.

'I would like to take wine with anyone who has not finished taking wine.' At which point, anyone who wanted to carry on drinking had to stand up, and drink. The penalty for a dishonest reply was, I guess, drinking.

Thump thump! Another gentleman stood up.

'I would like to take wine with the ladies of the Bec and their guests.' The three or four ladies, including Kath, who I had dragged along, had to stand. They took wine, except for Kath, who doesn't drink. Sheepishly, she just sipped an apple juice. I pretended I didn't know her.

'I would like to take wine with anyone who hasn't yet stood up to take wine, or indeed anyone who has been asked to stand up and take wine.' We all stood up and took wine.

'I would like to take wine . . .'

Thump . . .

'. . . take wine . . .'

Etc . . .

Weeks later, when I had found my way back from Croydon, and located my phone and wallet, I rang up Garry. Those fleeting, snapshot memories (all that survived the declaration of chemical war I had pronounced on my synapses) of the Bec and its membership had fired my interest. If anyone could claim to incarnate the unpretentious soul of the typical British cycling club, then it was probably the Toastmaster General Garry Beckett.

When he's not the life and soul of the Bec, Garry Beckett is a soigneur (or 'swanny', as he insists) for Team Garmin, with a special attachment to David Millar. A swanny's duties are manifold, covering everything from massage to message running. In the early season, Garry will spend whole days on a motorbike, with Millar riding on his back wheel, trundling

up and down the hills around Girona. That makes him, in other words, right on the inside, where he has been for most of his life.

Every summer I see Garry on the Tour de France, driving a minibus full of wide-eyed, big-mouthed corporate VIPs. This, seemingly, is another one of the occasional responsibilities of the twenty-first-century swanny. I struggle to think of a man less suited to the job of indulging the precious whims of a bunch of middle-management types from Ann Arbor, Michigan.

But here he was, one day in 2012, in the searing heat of Luchon, culturally as far away from South London as it is possible to travel and yet still be in the neighbouring country. The elegant spa town in the Pyrenees was putting on a show. The bars and restaurants of the Allée d'Etigny were coining in the money from Europe's itinerant cycling flock.

I was just on my way back from unloading a disproportionate amount of euros at a town-centre mini-branch of Casino Supermarché, stocking up on appalling snacks for the long transfer that awaited us at the end of the day, when the voice of Beckett called my name.

'Wotcha, Ned.'

Dressed from head to toe in Garmin's largely black uniform, he was gloomily traipsing back to the restaurant where he'd taken a group of American VIPs for lunch. One of them had left their iPhone, or wallet, or wife, there.

His language, when describing this particular individual and their general carelessness, was choice. Choice, of course, is the wrong word to use here. It was filthy.

In 1956, a year before Garry Beckett came cussing and kicking into the world, an institution known as the 'Bec Hill Climb' was born.

Every year since then, when the leaves start to fall, you may witness a peculiar pilgrimage to a junction just off the B2024, some way below Croydon on the map. Riders and spectators too, of all ages and builds, on tandems, on mountain bikes and often simply in cars, head south from London into the North Downs to celebrate a festival of unutterable pain under some cheerful bunting strung between trees, where kindly volunteers sell milky tea in Styrofoam cups for 50p.

On 14 October 2012, I paid the race a visit.

That Sunday was blessed with perfect autumnal weather, the sort of bright, breezy day that you see featured in heartwarming adverts for soup or double glazing. The kind of weather for children in scarves and primary-coloured wellington boots, scuffing their happy way through mountainous piles of crisp dry leaves. It looked picture-perfect, but it was keeping its horrors hidden. The Bec Hill Climb had towered over my diary for many weeks, growing taller, darker and more imposing with each passing day, until, like a dentist appointment, I could no longer escape it, and stood gazing up at its terrifying edifice. The day had dawned.

I had been severally warned that what I was about to undertake was the most nauseating thing you could do in cycling. But I had not taken these warnings seriously and, as a result, I was on my way to take part in, to *race* no less, a hill climb.

There is an amusing Wikipedia entry relating to hill climbs, which has clearly been written by an American cyclist, as it refers to events in San Francisco and Hawaii. But it is also quick to reference the thriving British scene, which is pre-eminent:

> *In Great Britain there is an end of season tradition of cycling clubs promoting hill climb time trials in October, for small cash prizes. The hills tend to be relatively short, usually taking between three and five minutes to complete, and the races attract many spectators, including locals not otherwise interested in cycling, who come to watch the pain in the faces of the competitors.*

It was, you will understand, the final sentence that caught my eye. Wanting, though simultaneously fearing, to know more, I picked up a copy of *Cycling Weekly*. There was a preview of the race.

'The atmosphere is always superb. The final metres will be lined three deep with screaming supporters driving you to the finish, just at the moment that your legs are pleading for mercy. You'll be doing well not to topple over, let alone race.'

Had I chosen the correct option when answering, 'OK, then' to Garry Beckett's harmless sounding question? He'd simply asked me if I fancied riding 'the Bec'.

But Garry, whose race it is, just happens to be the kind of guy you end up saying 'Yes' to. Even when all of you means to say 'No.'

*   *   *

I first met Garry at the Tour Series evening bike races. He used to hang around the pit lanes; a lugubrious presence, tall, and long-striding, he was attached to various teams, helping out. He'd drive cars, change wheels, fill bottles, shout encouragement. And swear. Garry loves to swear, investing his F-words with a fullness and a texture that make them rich and admirable.

Publically, he describes himself as a 'big-nosed, baggy-eyed cycling nut'.

Privately, he describes himself as a 'big-nosed, baggy-eyed, bald geezer who likes a drink'.

I have also heard him described as London cycling royalty, spoken of in terms of awe, but also with genuine affection and occasional wild amusement. He is a warm-hearted and foulmouthed chap, who I am now lucky enough to count as a friend.

I am not the only one. He has many friends.

Bradley Wiggins and he, for example, go back years. They first met when Garry was a constant presence at the Herne Hill Velodrome, and Wiggins, pre-sideburns and celebrity, was 'just' a prodigiously talented teenager from Kilburn. Garry has a collection of photographs of him and a young Bradley Wiggins that publishers will have been scrapping over as 2012 produced a sudden welter of Wiggomania-related literature, all needing to fill their colour plates.

They maintained their close relationship as Garry went on to work as a swanny in the GB Cycling set up. And when Wiggins signed his big money contract with Sky, he took Garry out for a posh dinner and offered him a job. So for a while in 2010 he was Bradley Wiggins's personal batman.

For various reasons that appointment didn't last a huge amount of time. But Garry's never really stuck at anything for terribly long, except for the Bec Hill Climb.

For all the time he spends on the road, swearing at foreigners (and as I write this he is currently boarding a flight to Japan, swearing at someone), he is never happier than when he comes home.

One day I pinned him down, in between international race obligations with Team Garmin, and we arranged to meet up in town.

London Bridge, the scruffy old station, cheek by jowl with the absurdly refined Borough Market, had been the spot where we'd agreed to meet. Garry was coming up from his South London suburb, and I, too, from mine. Our two railway lines would converge there, and so it seemed convenient.

Wafts of fragrance hung in the air of the newly gentrified quarter. Flavours competed for attention. Chorizo buns were being prepared right in front of me, the sausages griddled to perfection, and slapped in a sourdough bap with a fistful of rocket and a drizzle of lemon juice and olive oil. Beyond that stall, and into the sizzling heart of the market, I made out cheese stands, charcuteries, game butchers, fishmongers, bakers, wine merchants, and, yes, greengrocers. Crawling all over this foodies' carcass were the middle-classes, picking at their endives, sniffing at quiches, pinching a nectarine. Journalists from the nearby *Financial Times*, barristers from the inner-London courts, bankers from over the river. Tourists, clutching damp maps, gazing on in delighted mystification at this cacophonous arrangement, mentally converting from pounds to dollars, pounds to yen, pounds to euros. Three euros for a cucumber! Borough Market, a point of reference for London's health or wealth. A barometer for its aspirations. Where, if you please, was the recession?

I stood in line for my chorizo bap, fingering my £4.95 in my left hand. Unwittingly, I touched the peak of my bright pink Plowman Craven cycling cap. It was in homage to a now defunct and largely unsuccessful domestic cycling team.

They'd given it to me as a present and promptly gone bust. I'd hoped the two events weren't linked. Subliminally drawn towards it, I had chosen its neon pink shape to place on my head as I left the house.

'I know that fucking hat.' Garry, also smitten by the smell of frying chorizo and the obvious lure of the sponsor's day-glo colours, had ended up in the same queue, and was right behind me. His gruff South London voice, at least two octaves lower than is audible to most humans, was unmistakable.

It began with his dad and it returned, often, to that same touchstone.

The Good Friday Meeting at the Herne Hill Velodrome was a part of Garry Beckett's life. His father had been a towering figure at the track, a well-known judge and commissaire. On the day of the venerable old meeting in 2005, just after the racing finished, Ron Beckett, who had been there all day, collapsed very suddenly and died.

Ron Beckett had been a telephone engineer, back in the days when there was real engineering to be done in order to make and receive a phone call. He was also a considerable, prodigious bike rider, and in his son's words a 'right skinny bastard', the result of a pauper's diet, Garry suggests. Perhaps that's why most of his peers knew him as 'Porky'. Brits are funny like that.

For Ron, like with so many others of his post-war generation, car ownership came later. He used to go everywhere by bike, neatly integrating his working life and his passionate hobby. Sometimes, during the holidays or when childcare arrangements had broken down, young Garry would go to work with him.

'I can remember going to a big Taylor Woodrow's [the builders'] yard somewhere out near Heathrow, and going into the exchange room, with all these machines going *clack clack*

clack. A massive room. These things used to fascinate me. He'd be wiring them up, and I used to pull them all back and watch them click round. I didn't know that I was actually dialling a number.'

But it was cycling, not telephones, that his dad lived for. Ron's weekends, and often his evenings, were spent chasing round and round flat left-handed circuits in pursuit of prizes.

'His big thing was grass-track racing. My mum's still got a drawer at home full of old left-hand pedals that were all bent from cornering at grass-track races. That's where you could make your money.'

In the 1960s this particular branch of the sport was very popular. It didn't require a velodrome, for starters, just a field, some whitewash for the lanes and a few hay bales. It goes without saying that it was strictly amateur. Although 'strictly' was an elastic term.

'You were only allowed to win a certain amount of money, which wasn't very much, before you were considered a pro. So at grass-track meetings they'd win all manner of products to get round that rule. It was a way for him to more than double his weekly salary.'

Keen that his son develop a passion for the sport, Ron introduced Garry at an early age to the very particular world of bicycle polo. This is an eccentric sport, which involves a lot of trying to stay still on a bike. There are few things more quixotic than this. It's like trying to walk to work on a step-ladder, a bit daft.

Nonetheless, it is a sport with a surprisingly long history and, once upon a time, considerable status beyond the vague hipster modish appeal that its reborn version now enjoys in the achingly cool East End of London. It used to be, if not mainstream, then fairly common. Bicycle polo exhibition games were often staged before kick-off at football grounds, to give the crowd something to laugh at, I can only imagine.

It even put in a guest appearance at the London Olympics of 1908. But then again, those games were quirky to say the least, and were mostly obsessed with firearms: 'Army Gun' and 'Running Deer', also featured in that particular Olympic line-up.

'I was a skinny little ten-year-old, and all the other boys were fifteen or sixteen. Like in football when you'd line up in the playground to get picked – I was the last one. And I was always stuck in goal. I was useless. I didn't enjoy that. It was always fucking cold. Wet. And when I did get onto the pitch I got knocked off in the air all the time.'

He stuck at it though. 'Eventually I loved it, and I became good at it. When you know you're better than the others, you start floating along.'

It wasn't long before, in the reasonably small gene pool of the bicycle polo world, he achieved the highest imaginable honour. 'I was the England captain for eight years, which sounds very grand, but in a sport where there aren't many people playing . . .'

I interrupted. 'You were the England captain, Garry?'

This revelation seriously impressed me. Perhaps more so than it should have done. In fact, so amazed was I to find out that Garry captained his country that I failed to follow it up with the obvious question: who on earth did England play at bicycle polo?

The Beckett family, it seemed to me, had quite deliberately gone out of their way to find, and then excel at, cycling's most abstruse manifestations.

Grass-track cycling and bicycle polo were, in their different ways and to my uneducated ears, as far removed from the grandiosity of the great bike races of the world as it was possible to get, and still maintain that you were part of the same genus. I chanced my arm with Garry. 'Was there something a bit weird about you?'

'Absolutely. A bit of a weirdo.'

'Is that how your mates saw you?'

'Oh, yeah, yeah, yeah.' Garry didn't seem to mind me calling him a weirdo, which I found a bit weird. 'Perhaps there's something inside each and every cyclist that celebrates their inner weirdness.'

He carried on. 'I went to a funeral last week for a guy in his seventies. I never saw him not on a bike. This guy never owned a car. Well, two hundred people turned up on bikes. And you've got to say, some of the guys who turned up, well, fuck me! They probably hadn't changed their bikes since the late fifties. Or their clothes. There was a lot of the old knit-your-own-shorts brigade, with beards with sparrows' nests hanging out of them. That's the type of person that cyclists used to be perceived as.'

But their shared family passion for sweating (or, in the case of bicycle polo, not sweating) on a bike went deeper than that. Or rather, further.

Like Garry, Ron, the popular, no-nonsense figure at the track, was also a high-ranking member of the Bec Cycling Club.

For many years the club had lacked a flagship event, the signature race that it now boasts. The rival Catford Cycling Club, also from South London, had a longer history, and a notable hill climb which to this day claims to be the 'oldest continuing cycle race in the world', although it was not held during the war years, which knocks a bit of a hole in that claim.

Either way, the Catford Hill Climb was first held in 1886. And it was very prestigious. So the Bec needed a hill. And Ron Beckett went off looking for one.

'My mum and dad, my uncle and my aunt went out searching for a hill on their tandems for a few weekends, and they came across that one.' It was White Lane, a 700-yard climb from the B269 to the B2024 out of Titsey in Kent. The road is single track, very steep near the top, and shrouded in a dense canopy of wild woodland.

'They tested it on their tandems and said "This'll do." And that was it.'

For thirty years, as Garry was doing all his growing up, the whole family would administrate the hill climb every October. Some of his earliest memories are of standing in the pelting rain, or the bitter cold, or both, with a clipboard or a sign. They'd marshal the roads, set up the finish line, help with the time keeping, and generally make sure it all went off as smoothly as it could.

Ron eventually handed over the reins to his son in 1987. It proved to be a memorable autumn, not a bad year to pass the buck, as it happens. Perhaps he'd been fixing the phones at the Met Office and had overheard someone talking about what was brewing up over the Atlantic, and heading for Britain.

'That was the year of the Great Fall, two days before my first one. A load of fucking trees come down.' The first hill climb Garry took charge of coincided with the Great Storm, which turned nearby Sevenoaks into Oneoak, and wreaked almighty damage on the woodland around White Lane. It took hours of hard work to clear the road of the debris, but the race went ahead.

By coincidence, and almost at the same time, the stock market crashed, which also left Garry with some tidying up to do. Three years previously, Garry had changed jobs and had moved into a brave new world. After a spell working for Harrods in their warehouse, he had decided to send a CV, rather speculatively, to a firm in the City that was looking to hire foreign exchange traders. This was the time of unfettered growth in the Square Mile, and there was a voguish and defining move away from the privately educated Oxbridge graduate towards the more streetwise local recruit. Garry, with his natural charm and sharp tongue, would probably impress, but, he still had to cobble together a convincing CV.

Garry recalls how he squeezed every ounce of relevance from a thinly populated list of achievements. Under the section 'Other Qualifications', he listed his captaincy of the England bicycle polo team. Not perhaps the first thing you would demand for the role of Forex trader. But maybe they saw something in his ability to stand still and not fall off.

'Stating that on my interview papers got me a job in the City.' I look at him incredulously. 'Seriously. I put captain of the England bicycle polo team. The guy stood up in front of all the other people and said, "This is Garry. He's going to be joining us. Because anyone who has captain of the England bicycle polo team on their CV has got to be given a chance."'

For years he sat at a desk in the noisy trading room of Tullet and Tokyo Forex, juggling telephones, fielding calls from across the globe and effecting huge trades on international markets. His desk, he recalls, had a semi-circular section cut out of it to accommodate the expanding girths of the traders. Presumably, the bigger the semi-circle, the older the trader, the fatter the bonus, and the closer the heart attack. Their professional life expectancy was limited to about thirty-five years old. By forty they were toast.

Garry thrived in this world, conducting his intercontinental symphony; the master of a clutch of telephones, connected to the eighties equivalents of those whirring and clicking exchanges that his dad had used to maintain, often trying to lead two conversations simultaneously, one phone on either ear, men in suits in Hong Kong and New York hanging on his every bid. He was, for a while, prodigiously good at it.

But, what he didn't know was that his right ear was failing him. He was going progressively deaf. The first signs were easy to ignore but, step by step, he started to miss trades. Vital bits of key information, prices shouted down the wires and through crackling receivers slipped through the net. No one needs a deaf trader.

In 1993, although he was still a young man, he was pensioned off on medical grounds. His foray into the City was done. It was a tumultuous time in his life, and it ushered in an era of slapstick comedy. The payout he received was generous, and Garry was followed for years by private detectives from the medical insurance company, convinced that he was committing a fraud. They'd wait in cars outside his house, and if he went anywhere, they'd follow. Garry became expert at throwing them off his scent.

But with a life of high finance already behind him, and many good years still to come, he renewed his childhood passion. Back to the bikes.

'I was a debauched, drunken bum. Great years. But hell did they take their toll.'

I took my leave of him, pushing through Borough Market to get back to the station. I crossed Borough High Street, and re-entered some sort of normality.

At London Bridge I glanced across at the dense mass of banks and investment houses, their lights twinkling in the dusk, their impenetrable business thundering silently on. Right here is where a little of the City's wealth spills over like a tidal surge and splashes the South London Thames shores. That's kind of what it did to Garry, in real life.

My start time for the hill climb was now frighteningly close.

'Whenever I'm up there, I still see the old man. With his Eric Morecambe glasses, with his Bec top on, with his loud-hailer. It's special.'

We were at the top of the hill, gently free-wheeling down to the start. It was race day. Garry had decided, on his fifty-fifth birthday, to try and race the hill climb for the very first time. He had passed a childhood, swiftly followed by an adulthood, of watching on and recording times, but never participating. Today this would come to an end.

Cleverly, I got him talking about his beautiful steel frame bike so that I didn't have to contribute anything to the conversation. I no longer cared if he was as scared as me. I'd make him do all the talking, so I could wallow in my fear.

It was not only the fact of the race. It was the setting, too. It had attracted a ghoulish host of onlookers, some of whom I knew very well. What was I doing here, flesh and beating blood?

Maurice Burton had brought half his team down to watch (I would be racing in their vivid yellow colours), including his son Germain, who had won the last two Bec Hill Climbs. Germain was still recovering from a chest infection that he picked up after riding for Great Britain at the Junior World Championships, so he would not be defending his title. Instead, they were hoping that I didn't dishonour the 'De Ver' brand by finishing stone last.

There was some talk that this might indeed happen. Maurice had looked particularly unsure when he saw me before I went off to warm up. Germain had also exuded scepticism.

Ron Keeble, never one to knowingly relax an amateur cyclist, had been on my case for weeks, offering to look my bike over to check I'd got small enough gears. He'd even offered to drive me down to the hill 'any time I want' so that I could put in some training efforts. I had found a range of excuses not to, opting instead to bury my head in the sand.

He grabbed me on the day, just as I was turning to head down to the start.

'There's a tree, covered in ivy, right in front of you as you start. Head for that, and it'll take you onto the right side of the road for the climb. The gradient's not so bad there.' He looked me up and down, full of visible paternal concern, mixed with violent paternal fury. 'You'll be all right,' he said. He might as well have been pushing me over the edge of Tower Bridge by booting me up the arse.

Alan Peiper, who rode the Tour de France five times and who had shared that bizarre accommodation in Ghent along with Maurice Burton and Jan 'The Papers', would be racing. So would a clutch of very decent domestic elite riders, a host of keen and experienced amateurs and the reigning National Hill Climb Champion, the curiously Scandinavian-sounding

Gunnar Gronlund, who had smashed his way up a certain Long Hill in Buxton quicker than anyone else to gain the title and red, white and blue bands.

And last, but by no means least, there was a frighteningly outspoken, no-nonsense rider called Tony Gibb, one of the undisputed hard men of the British track and criterium scene, and a man who had competed in dozens of races which I had televised. He was the MC for the day, with microphone, and loudspeaker. In a strange reversal of the norm, he would be commentating on my effort.

All around me, men and women in perfectly fitting kit with specially adapted handlebars had been getting bikes out of the back of liveried estate cars, and had started to warm up on 'rollers'. My warm up had consisted of a brief ride up and down a bit of the B2024 and a cup of tea. Kath, I remembered, had very kindly offered to provide some soup from a Thermos that would fortify me for my effort. Knowing what I now know about the hill climb, I am very glad that I didn't accept. Soup and hill climbs wouldn't work well together.

And suddenly I was at the bottom of the White Lane. I had the number '30' pinned to my back. Number '27' had just started his race. I understood the intractable, fateful grind of time. I felt crushed by the weight of the inevitable.

By the time that '28' and '29' had both disappeared from view, my mouth had gone completely dry. I made my way forward to the start position.

'Number Thirty. Ned Boulting.' A race official unsmilingly noted my number, made a few tick marks on a clipboard, and pointed with his pencil at a digital clock that was counting down from sixty seconds. We were already at twenty-four seconds.

The friendly chap who was holding my bike upright seemed concerned. 'Are you all right?'

'Well I am now. But I'm not going to be very soon,' I hazarded a guess.

I looked away from the clock as it entered the final ten seconds. Ahead of me, I could see Ron Keeble's ivy-covered tree. I blinked, and when I refocused, I could swear it had moved back a few yards, as if playing some devious reverse-flow vegetation-variant of Grandmother's Footsteps.

'Fucking tree.' I said that. I didn't just think it.

Three. Two. One.

I stepped hard on my pedals. Well, as hard as I could. And I set off up the hill.

Within about thirty seconds, I knew that I had made a grave mistake. No crowd had gathered on the lower slopes of the hill, and I was alone with the awkward grunting and febrile moans that already, involuntarily, escaped my lips. I had gone off way too fast. I knew I would. I was a hopeless amateur, and that's what hopeless amateurs do.

But once locked into my ludicrous effort, I understood that I had no other option than to plough on to the best of my ability. I understood, too, that I had nothing left to give, even though I had barely started climbing.

This, then, was perhaps the merest, most fleeting glimpse into the world of 'suffering' of which cyclists talk. This is the greatest virtue a rider can possess. Forget speed, stamina, acceleration, bravery and brains. It is the ability to endure agony that defines them. Mark Cavendish once told me that it's like someone pulling out your fingernails very, very slowly. Not shouting 'Stop!' is the thing you have to learn. The loser shouts 'Stop!'

After those opening thirty seconds, and as my breathing went from laboured to grotesquely rasping, my body was trying to transition. The exercise had ceased to be 'anaerobic' (i.e. the kind of effort a one-hundred-metre runner puts in), but it was too early and too extreme for it to be called 'aerobic' (the graduated, smooth effort of the endurance athlete). So this was why cyclists feared hill climbs so intensely! Like the 800 metres in athletics, it is essentially a sprint over a far, far greater period of time than anyone can reasonably be expected to sprint. It confuses the system. It messes with everything. In short, the body has nothing to feed on, and nowhere to turn for succour.

And so, as the road suddenly bore steeply upwards, and I entered the unreal world of the second half of the Bec Hill Climb, I was assailed, not by the furies, but by the clichés. The head spun, my eyes popped, my tongue glued to the roof of my mouth, my legs burnt. And my vision, as if conforming to some sort of cartoonish aesthetics, blurred at the edges, eventually narrowing to a small saucer-sized circle of clarity, which veered wildly left to right, and then right to left as I swung the bike, in agony, from side to side. I tried to change down a gear, and heard a crunching sound as I screwed it up. My pedals jarred as they missed a beat.

'Shit!' I commentated, although by now, my mouth had lost the ability to articulate a hard 'T' sound. So it came out more as 'Shish!' Which is a chicken kebab, I thought to myself. And, filled with the oddly relevant mental image of skewered meat, on I went.

I could hear voices shouting encouragement. I began to feel sick. I glimpsed my name, in chalk, on the road. I very nearly was sick. I felt the road steepen even more as it neared the finish line. I moved beyond sickness into pure horror.

But miraculously, it stopped. As all things do eventually stop, relent, or end in death, this one too had passed. I had walked out of the dentist's room. I had left the examination hall. I had landed on Free Parking. I had crossed the line, and coasted through a melee of other riders and concerned friends and family towards the main road. I couldn't figure out how to stop.

I just wanted to fall asleep on my handlebars.

And that, once I had finally ground to a halt, was pretty much exactly what happened.

I did eventually wake up.

As my eyes opened again, I lifted my head, still connected by a useless neck to my shoulders, both slumped against the frame of my bike.

I looked towards a bright sky, towards a figure occluding the glaring, low sun. The silhouette reached out a hand to me, and placed it gently on my back. He smiled beatifically, his single earring glinting at me, a halo of light caught in his silvering hair.

Then, with a euphoric rush, I suddenly knew who it was. Sean Yates, the former Yellow Jersey of the Tour de France, was offering his congratulations.

'Good ride,' he said, trying not to laugh. 'Well done.' Those were the very words he used. I've framed them in my head.

'Cheers, Yatesy!' I slobbered. I would absolutely not have

called him Yatesy, had I not been in a state of delirium. Clearly, I now thought I had crossed a Rubicon, and that I, too, belonged. But 'Yatesy'? Unforgivable.

When I think about that encounter, I wonder if I dreamt it. Sean Yates had guided Bradley Wiggins all the way around France, cajoling, imploring, praising, exhorting his charge to ever-greater efforts. But the clock was ticking down fast on his own career. A couple of weeks after this odd exchange on the top of a hill in Kent he left his job at Team Sky.

The last rider he called home might well have been me. I am certain that this was not what he would have wanted.

For the record, this is how it ended:

The winner, with an extraordinary ride, set a new course best. Jack Pullar conquered the White Lane in 1'42".

Alan Peiper, riding as if his Tour de France depended on it, bust his guts to finish it in 2'34". And he beat me by four seconds, which I find entirely reasonable.

My time of 2'38" prompted Ron Keeble to text me later:

Give me a ring, when you have stopped bleeding from the arse. If you'd kept your head upright, you could have gone faster. Well done, though. Proud of you.

And Garry? Garry Beckett made it up the hill a long time after me. This is no boast. There were good enough reasons for it: folklore has it that he stopped for a cigarette on the way up. Eventually he rolled over his own finish line in a record-setting slowest ever time in the history of the Bec of nine minutes and thirty-five seconds.

We all sang 'Happy Birthday'. He had a face like thunder.

Unobserved by the wider world, this scene has been repeating itself for half a century. A not-particularly impressive hill, ridden by somebody-and-nobody cyclists, a race of great unimportance, honour in small measure, celebrated with devotion and cream teas.

Men like Garry Beckett, and before him, Ron Beckett, ensure the perpetuity of these exclusive traditions, the church fetes of the cycling world. 'Come! Chance your arm at the coconut shy!' 'Bob for apples!' Or: 'Ride the hill climb if you dare!' The last rider up the hill is cheered as throatily by the Thermos wielding, trouser-clip wearing community as the first.

This race is why God made bunting. This race is what makes Garry Beckett. Men and women like him will never let go of their clipboards. They are as dependable as the onset of autumn, as unselfish as the warming, soft October sun casting mottled shadows down onto rutted tarmac.

Herne Hill was blustery and not particularly warm, the last day I went there. It was also empty, its tilted bowl open to the slate sky, not one bike cutting across its grey skin. I was there with a handful of colleagues to film an interview for a documentary on Bradley Wiggins, just six weeks before he would go on to win in Paris.

We had chosen the location, and invited Garry to join us, to talk on camera about his memories of a young Wiggins. He had brought with him, after an afternoon spent digging through old boxes in the attic, a wonderful photograph of a bicycle polo team, Garry in the middle, and the future Tour de France winner an awkward, gangly presence at the side, his features half hidden by a mop of unruly hair.

Garry arrived early for the interview, while our cameraman was still busily filming other bits and pieces. A very fine drizzle, whipped in by sudden winds, dampened the air and clung to our jackets and bobble hats, forming a fine mist. I could see him taking in the old place, gazing at it, as if looking at it properly for the first time. And because he was looking, I looked at it too with fresh eyes.

The old pavilion, earmarked for demolition, crouched down behind the ugly temporary stands, the series of Portakabins and containers behind that, which served as changing areas and storage rooms, and then the long, elegant sweep of the track, away towards the woods and the back straight, then bending homewards again, parallel now with the gravel track running in from Burbage Road. Then there was the open expanse inside the track, grassy and exposed, the wind picking at a crisp packet. It stuttered its way towards the finish line, and then snagged on the foot of a table with a Formica top, left carelessly trackside after the last meeting had come, raced and left.

I searched the velodrome for meaning. For me, its story was theoretical, I was simply trying to Photoshop together faded images and paste them into the here and now. I was trying to place people in this landscape, to imagine voices of men I never knew, nor saw race. Herne Hill, in its splendid isolation and cellular decay, was a symbol for something else, a cipher, a code by which to read another culture. I didn't get it.

I had not grown up here. This was not my playground, and the sport I had grown to love had not fully taken hold of my heart. It merely dressed me, and informed my outward choices from time to time.

But to those who can hear them, places like this talk. Garry, perhaps even tipping his good ear towards its voices, was listening to his childhood, and before that even. This was where his parents, Hazel and Ron, had courted. And this is where, for Ron, it had ended.

'I've not been back since Dad died.' He smiled at me, a quick wistful smile. 'Not once.'

I gave the track one last glance, then thanked him for his time, and wished him all the best. Then I took my leave, for the time being, of Garry. And, in doing so, I took my leave of the world to which I had fleetingly been introduced, Beckett's world.

It's a rather noble, if sweary, place to be.

CHAPTER 15

DEVON IS A PLACE ON EARTH

Some rides take much longer than two minutes and thirty-eight seconds.

Somewhere in a gloomily lit hotel near Minehead, one mid-September morning, four men sat in a sullen circle. Our dour quartet was not only in the early stages of a middle-aged decline but, more pressingly, a cooked breakfast.

Some of us knew each other well. Others had met for the first time over the course of the nervy evening before, where we had swapped prognostics and indulged in industrial-scale expectation management. 'I'll just be pleased if I don't die.' Now each one of us was lost in thought, cutting through pasty sausages and chasing slimy, bruised mushrooms round a plate.

Our minds were already riding out on the road, getting wet and cold and wondering frantically what malformed impulse had dragged us to this creaking establishment in this part of the world on this particular morning.

Our helmets, next to each place setting, rocked gently as we sawed at our food, their foam innards exposed and naked. The scraping of butter on toast at times was the only sound, save for the comings and goings of a surly waiter. He left us in no doubt how much he resented being called into action before dawn on a Sunday morning by noisily refilling the bowl of limp, translucent grapefruit slices, and then sighing showily at the sight of the orange juice carafe, whose levels had sunk, again. We sipped guiltily from our glasses, and squinted out of the window.

It was still dark enough for the one sodium lamp outside the old inn to burn brightly against a background of ink-blue rain clouds. A beastly sky had started to drip heavily against the ancient glass of the window, blown in by sideways gusts. I watched John lining up his home-made energy bars, and wrapping each one carefully in cling film. In fact, we all watched him, envious of his evident preparedness.

We could delay no longer. One by one, and wordlessly, we collected our bikes, zipped up our various jackets to the chin and stepped out into the rain.

Not one of us had undertaken this lightly. Each had carefully apportioned the time needed (three whole days) for this indulgent jaunt. Gone were the days, by about twenty years, when a trip like this could be an act of spontaneity, the simple impulse to hitchhike to Dublin, or cadge a lift from Munich to Marseille. Nowadays going away like this required Internet research, seeking out and reserving bed and breakfasts, quid pro quo negotiations with family members for favours granted and liberties taken, intricate logistics and loads of carbon fibre.

Jauntily, my two travel mates on the way down to the West Country had estimated that the three bikes on our roof rack were collectively worth about £24,000. This, unfathomably, was the truth. My car, the same hopeless vehicle I had driven for a decade, was worth about 2 per cent of that at best.

You will, by now, have heard of the Middle-Aged Man In Lycra, I have no doubt.

By God, if we weren't MAMILs, I would like to know was.

Pointlessness and cycling are closely related. In Britain they are first cousins, maybe even siblings.

There is a man who crosses Blackheath most days on a mountain bike without using his hands, wearing a mask, and with a dog leashed to the handlebars. His arms flail wildly at his sides, as he wobbles his way across the common. He is very slow, and very odd and seems to have cornered the market in pointlessness.

Or perhaps he's discovered something that's eluded the rest of the sport, like the man I gave a lift to who lived on an island in the middle of a Scottish loch. The lesson that particular middle-aged Briton taught me is this: that actions that appear hugely pointless may well have some serious point visible only to the actor.

This wiry, shy hitchhiker, who climbed into my car at Brent Cross, had developed, over many years of solitary training, a new way of running that he was convinced would one day allow someone to complete a marathon in less than one hour. This 'new running' was based on a genetic throwback to earlier species of human. It involved swinging your arms in synch with your legs, rather than in opposition. I listened with as straight a face as I could as he told me his tale. It transpired that, after many months of letter writing and badgering, he'd been invited down to Channel Five's headquarters in Battersea to demonstrate his discovery to a potential documentary maker. The meeting had not gone well. My hitchhiker had felt humiliated when the filmmaker had asked him to run up and down a busy London street to demonstrate his craft.

'I froze,' he told me, as we continued our drive north. 'I just couldn't do it. I felt as if he were laughing at me.'

I let him out at Knutsford, where I was turning off the motorway. I hope he got home.

At least he felt imbued with purpose. What do I think I am achieving when I am out on my bike? Training? Travelling? Developing new, hitherto undiscovered ways of pedalling? None of those, really. I am just turning the pedals increasingly slowly.

I am always on the lookout for uncompromisingly selfish trips with like-minded friends. These rides exist for no reason other than to feel twelve years old again on descents (and fifty years old on the climbs). I treasure these rides, and I like the feeling of having achieved something and nothing in particular; the vacuous, fulfilling charm of the stretched calf and aching hamstring; that sense of having passed through the length of a bit of the world. Trees, towns, clouds, puddles.

There have been all sorts of poorly orchestrated excuses for daft bike rides down the years. I have crow-barred them into my everyday life. Once I suggested that the whole family go to Hastings and stay in a crappy bed and breakfast. I invited neighbours with kids to join us (only those with carbon bikes were eligible, i.e., John from the other side of the hill). We ate a simple meal of battered carbohydrates with appalling vegetables in the evening, a dinner that will be remembered mainly for one of his kids vomiting all over my laptop while watching a Disney DVD at the table. This served us all right for being the sort of parents who allow that kind of thing.

But the next day, my masterplan of cycling hubris came to fruition as John and I indulged in the futility of riding back to London, through rolling Sussex, up and down the cheekily sapping Kent climbs over the M25 and home. It was good, if exhausting, and, on balance, it had been worth picking the drying semi-digested peas out of the keyboard of a MacBook Pro.

My job helps, due to the large amount of unpredictable travel. Even when I am working on a big football match at Wembley, I will arrange for someone in a car to carry my suit to the stadium, and I will ride the eighteen miles there. After the match, having interviewed the winning and losing players and manager (which, in football, for some reason necessitates the wearing of a suit), I will leave the players' tunnel, change back into Lycra in the toilets by the service entrance, scrunch up my carefully pressed clothing, stuff it into a rucksack, and then cycle home.

I've stuck the bike on the roof of the car whenever the opportunity has presented itself, via work commitments, to go and explore another bit of the country. A day filming with Plymouth Argyle meant forty miles of agony on Devon's roller-coaster topography. The Grand Slam of Darts at the famous Wolverhampton Civic was an opportunity for my good friend Steve to guide me along the lanes of Staffordshire on a freezing November morning. Liverpool versus Benfica in the Champions League prompted sixty unplanned wintry miles around the Wirral Peninsula, until my antiquated Tom-Tom lost power and I ended up getting thoroughly lost somewhere near Runcorn.

All these miles have been memorably pointless, as self-centred as a long shower when everyone's queuing to use the bathroom, and as uninspiring in the retelling, too. These, for me, are my rides. This is what the whole cycling thing is about.

And epic? You can keep your epic.

The rain was hammering down, now.

We rode as quickly as we could to the start of the 115-mile 'sportive' ride in Minehead, trying to warm up. The early-morning rain stung, and it was hard to keep your eyes fully open to the spray. Against our better judgement, we formed an impromptu and very poorly executed 'paceline', each rider trying to shelter behind the wheel of the bike in front. One of our number, wearing many hundreds of pounds' worth of cycling clothing, some of it Rapha, and sitting atop a celeste green Bianchi road bike, touched his brakes as he battered along a stretch of dual carriageway. Thus it was that Joad Raymond, one of the country's leading experts on the works of John Milton, found himself skidding on a painted white line at the side of the road. He slammed into the tarmac, ripping open a hole in his badger-skin cycling shorts, and beneath that, his buttocks. (I may have embroidered the badger-skin detail. But the buttocks, I stand by.)

We all stopped, and did our best to help him onto his feet. We looked at his bike as the rain continued to rattle on our helmets. It seemed to be OK, but Joad wasn't. After gingerly accompanying us to the start, he rode back to his car, and abandoned the venture. He'd trained hard for the event, and had evidently been keen to explore how he shaped up against the rest of our delusional little group. We all commiserated with him, but were secretly delighted it wasn't us. Later on that day, Joad would find deep bruising appearing like ink on blotting paper all across his torso.

The rest of our number then lined up in the half-light on the seafront at Minehead and, with nerves on edge, eyes on stalks and shivering from the cold and wet, we set off as a group to climb onto Exmoor and to head for an unimaginably distant finish line on the south coast.

We, being MAMILs, had mistaken this for fun.

Fun, real fun, comes for free. It is part of the package we are born with, an inbuilt DNA reflex that lasts a lifetime but morphs into many forms. At first, fun is simply gurgling with newborn pleasure at the sight of a light fitting on the ceiling. With the advent of walking and running, however, fun gains in scope and sophistication. Fun, for at least a decade, is mainly based around three things: getting muddy, doing damage to stuff which has cost your parents' money and torturing indigenous British wildlife.

But gradually, with puberty and beyond, things take a more sinister turn. Fun is no longer as charmingly innocent and as one-dimensional as the naïve impulse to smash to pieces your best friend David's expensively assembled toy car collection with the lead weight from a grandfather clock. (He joined in, by the way, it wasn't just me. And anyway some of them were already dented before.)

As soon as we are legally able to vote, a darkly assertive, masochistic drive begins to take hold. Ingesting six pints of premium lager and a kebab made inedible by the application of at least an inch of chilli sauce may well be a profoundly rewarding pastime, but it is not necessarily the answer to man's quest for existential authenticity. Yet, this is the mystifying path British youth willingly treads, a wobbly route back from the pub spattered with undignified bouts of sickness and impromptu trips to non-existent urinals. It is, technically, 'fun'. But it requires stamina, strength, money and determination to turn dizziness, nausea and bankruptcy into amusement.

By the time the beer and kebabs penetrate at a cellular level the firm, muscular flesh of male youth, turning it incrementally to a sad flab hanging over the belt, the fun-seeker is staring, with ghastly inevitability, at the cold heart of his fortieth birthday.

Now, and only now, for the MAMIL it begins. The horror has hit home. The presence of a dependant or two often amplifies the angst, suggesting, quite accurately, that a generation has been reared that is ready, and cold-bloodedly willing, to take the place of the one that went before.

The problem for the British MAMIL (is there an equivalent overseas?) is that he doesn't feel forty, and has, periodically, to check his own birth certificate to be sure. If the baby boomers who went before us were prematurely aged by wearing suits and having stable careers and affordable mortgages, then the generation to which this current army of MAMILs belongs is just the opposite: stubbornly immature. Their fortieth year, rather than being meticulously planned for, comes up from behind and mugs them, like the best man might assault the groom on a stag night.

In their panic, they have to get away. Literally. For some, this involves having an affair. For many, it involves facial hair or flowery, fitted shirts. For others, huge numbers of British others, it involves bicycles. 'Fun' has been reinvented again. Now it must be worked at. 'Fun' can only co-exist with 'pain'.

Sacrifice and reward is the Brailsford mantra: not something you need to tell a MAMIL.

A perfect day out for the afflicted seems often to involve a degree of misery on wet, cold roads, attempting rides of ill-advised length, where the only quantifiable joy is stopping.

Which brings us back onto a drizzle-whipped, blustery Exmoor.

Ten miles into the ride, after the initial enthusiastic bubble of conversation had popped, we had started our first 'climb' of the day.

Climbs in Britain are often short, but they make up for this by being brutally steep. This, I was once told by a professional rider, was because road builders on these shores have tended to favour the direct route over an obstacle, rather than the gradient-sparing, circuitous alternative of the switchback, beloved of sophisticated Continentals. I can't help feeling a bit let down by our nation's road builders on this one. I can't even really blame the Romans, since I gather they were fairly active on the Continent for a while, too. It's just something we have to live with over here.

Mercifully, this climb was neither short nor steep. It was longish, and shallowish. Satisfyingly, there was enough of a gradient for sweat to saturate the foamy compound that sat between my bike helmet and my head, and then run down my temples. This was an important accessory. Without sweat, the MAMIL feels no sense of achievement.

It was a leisurely enough ascent for me to maintain a respectable speed, or, at least, the illusion of a respectable speed (cycling always feels fast when there is no one faster than you for comparison). I was able to keep the bike moving steadily and more-or-less straight. It is when you start to climb at less than walking pace, on gradients of 20 per cent, that you begin to wonder what, quintessentially, is the point of the bicycle.

Beyond a certain gradient, it becomes impossible to push the cranks any longer, the back wheel spins around without purchase, and, well, you fall off. At this point a bicycle is an encumbrance, something of great beauty that is no longer fit for purpose, like trying to use a clarinet as a makeshift funnel for decanting yoghurt.

Our little group, which, minus the unfortunate Joad, had set out together, began to splinter. People climb at very different speeds. I was surprised and horrified to discover that, while I was very far from being the best, I was also quite some distance from being the worst. In fact I quickly established, to my growing disappointment, that riding uphill was something I wasn't shockingly bad at. I should rephrase that: something I felt I could do marginally better than dreadfully.

This was not necessarily good news. Nobody actually likes climbing. It is gruelling and it is masochistic. The thought that it was my 'strong suit' depressed me greatly. I would now have to make an unpleasant experience still more unpleasant by trying really hard at it. Just to show everyone (including myself) how almost-not-too-bad I was.

Flanked by a couple of other riders I had never met before, I crested the top of the hill. In fact, in common with lots of quixotic British 'climbs', the uphill bit just kind of petered out, indeterminately. There was no summit to speak of, no defining crest. There was no vista, just more trees and a road leading off into an unremarkable and curvaceous middle distance. The pressure eased in my legs, and I stopped pedalling. And that was where it all went wrong.

In an instant my rear wheel froze solid. My bike, in a violent attempt to throw me over the bars, settled instead for the equally painful, much more effective and significantly less glamorous tactic of ramming my genitalia firmly against the stem. The freewheel mechanism had suddenly locked up, stopping my back wheel as certainly as if you'd stuffed a poker in the spokes. I came to a juddering, lopsided, leg-splayed, almost-upright halt. One leg grounded, the other still clipped into a bike which was suddenly, violently crippled.

This was a problem. We had a hundred miles still to ride, and we were in the middle of Exmoor. I tried my phone. There was a bit of signal, but no obvious number to ring. I wondered vaguely if my dad wouldn't mind driving out to pick me up. But then I remembered he lived in Scotland.

Bikes, or at least bits of bikes, are profoundly boring.

Yes, I have owned bikes in which I have invested inexplicable emotion. But I have done this in the same way that a racehorse owner will turn up occasionally at the stables to admire his thoroughbreds, and then let someone else muck them out and fine tune them for race day. I have no idea how they work, and, frankly, I couldn't care less.

There is a whole grammar to be absorbed and observed by cycling enthusiasts. Often it relates to gear ratios. 53 x 24. 48 x 36. Or, let's try another: 36 x 22. I would wager that not one of these actually exists. Already there will be people clicking their tongues disdainfully at my wilful ignorance. Let them click.

But I do know that, despite their commonplace functionality, and semi-antique design (how much have they changed, really, in sixty years?), they contain a mystifyingly high number of working parts. Thousands, perhaps.

I know this, because when help finally arrived, my bike's back wheel was opened up and laid bare in all its miniature glory.

When I first came to a juddering halt, there were almost a dozen soulmates who stopped with me. But after a two-hour wait for assistance in the sporadic rain, their number had dwindled to three or four, and, eventually, none. In the end it was just Andy, the mechanic, and me.

By the time he finally found the offending pin, or whatever the minute component was that had prevented my wheel from turning, I had turned almost entirely blue with the chill. He removed it with the precision of a surgeon, and sent me off again, with the warning that 'at any given moment it might lock up again. Maybe on a descent.' He advised me to 'go easy'. I looked at him aghast.

I was quite alone. I pushed on, aware that I had a hundred miles of undulating road still ahead, and that I was older than forty.

I rode for another ten or fifteen miles on my own. It was awful, lonely stuff. The route followed a river that bent round again, headed north and dropped off Exmoor. I hit the coast in a little town, and there I found a group of about half-a-dozen guys who had decided to wait for me. Most of them had been complete strangers before that morning. I was so touched I nearly wept. Instead I just wiped my nose and shook them one by one with my snotty-gloved hand.

I have made friends on a bike. That day, running up and down the contours of a county whose topography simply doesn't know how to unwind and relax, I forged a few friendships with a couple of blokes. I still ride with them every now and then, when we get the chance. When I started to cycle, in my mid-thirties, it was decidedly not my intention to meet new people. In fact, I was fairly sure I'd met enough people in my life already. But I was wrong. Cycling's proved me wrong.

This is not to make any exceptional claims on behalf of this sport. Any team activity bonds people together. But there's an understanding for, and a patience with, the strengths and weaknesses of others that I have found, at times, moving. The courtesy of giving someone a tow by letting them slipstream behind you when they are struggling is as rewarding for the donor as it is for the recipient. Everyone, too, must climb at their own pace, safe in the knowledge that if the ride splits up into pieces on a hill, the first to get to the top will wait for the pack to re-form.

People share: expertise, kit, flapjacks, water. And people share themselves.

There are those whom I have known for years, but with whom I thought I had nothing in common, who have become close confidants. I had a colleague who was a shy man in his mid-forties. He was undergoing a rather ghastly divorce and had been forced out of the family home. In order to remain close to his children, he rented a one-bedroom flat near to their school, and cycling became his surrogate emotional life. He joined a club, and rode thirty or forty miles most days when he could. He told me once, with a glint of mad love in his eye, how he had drilled two substantial hooks above the fireplace in his tiny living room. That was where, nightly, after he had washed and dried it, he would hang his bike.

'Sometimes, a whole evening will pass, Ned. And I'll not have moved from my armchair. I'll just have been staring at it.'

I must have been staring at him, since he added, meekly, 'I love that bike, Ned.'

Far from scoffing at the absurdity of his obsession, I find myself nodding at him, with him. I understand his devotion to the bike, even if I cannot share in his deification, the bond built up between aluminium and deluded fool. Those hours spent gazing down and seeing in minute detail the stem, the bar tape, the brake levers. The gentle ticking of the chain and swish of rubber on tarmac is a fertile bed for reflection. Something appreciative, open and calming comes with each pedal turn. Mile by mile, often unwittingly, a fraction more of a rider's nature is revealed. The rhythm of the road sets the rhythm in the head, loosening with each turn. This is not a race, and nor should it be. This is a ride.

And so, Steve and Jim, Rob and Luke, Simon, John and the rest of the apostles, have become very particular types of friend. I see them seldom, if truth be told, but when I do, then time passes easily. Like in a pleasant dream, when the ride is over, I have no recollection of the dialogue. Only certain images, specific sensations endure in the memory.

That's how I explain that over the course of two or three hours of plugging on, up and down hills, in the company of this band of virtual strangers, only a few moments have lodged with any clarity. Once we got stuck behind a muck-spreader, and inhaled cow-shit for twenty minutes. And another time I dropped off the front of our proud but rather feeble line of riders who had been sheltering behind to avoid the worst of a headwind. I had been determinedly setting the pace for what felt like half an hour, but in reality was probably only five minutes, and as I pulled away, exhausted and free-wheeling back, I felt a hand gently at my back, and the grizzly West Midlands voice of a wiry bloke called Andy saying, 'You're strong, boy, you are.'

At that moment, I felt like a world champion. Because Andy from Dudley reckoned I wasn't bad.

At a feed station after eighty-five miles, the worst of this interminable ride was surely done.

At least that's what I thought, as I hobbled through a village hall that had been requisitioned for the occasion, hungrily scooping up cakes as I went. It was only shortly after I had eaten my third slice of Victoria sponge that my bowels registered their presence for the first time that day.

Extreme amounts of cycling seem to have a curious effect on your natural rhythms. The body, in its concern that you might end up running out of food and water, tends to absorb more of it, and lets far less simply go to waste. Basically, what I'm saying is, you can go for hours without going. The year I ran the London Marathon, I drank fourteen pouches of Lucozade, followed fairly swiftly by two cans of Grolsch, before I even slightly felt the urge. It was most curious.

But now, and with an unanticipated urgency, I knew I had to act. I headed for the toilet, which, given that we were almost the last riders on the sportive (my mechanical incident had slowed us down by two hours) had already been used by several thousand MAMILs, not all of whom had fully signed up to the universal toilet principle enshrined in British common law of leaving the place in the same state in which you would like to find it. It was a mess, but, as I locked the door behind me, I couldn't have cared less. Only then did I encounter a sudden, unforeseen problem.

This ride was a new experience for me in more ways than one. It wasn't just the distance involved, it was also the clothing I had chosen. Because, for the first time in my life, and for reasons I still cannot understand, I was wearing bib shorts. I continue to wear them to this day, but have failed to grasp what it is I think I am achieving by doing so, other than conforming with the aspirant world of the MAMIL.

These strange devices, for those of you who may be unaware, combine the absurdity of the padded Lycra short and its over-engineered seat with the grotesque aesthetics of the mankini. The male human form, sporting only a pair of bib shorts, is risible. There is no other way to describe it.

In addition, as I was about to discover, there was another entirely undesirable side effect of bib-short wearing. A pee is manageable without the need to undress entirely. Evidence for this technique's application in the pro-peloton is abundantly clear if you watch any race live on the TV, though these are the bits of footage which have usually been tidied up in time for the more family-friendly highlights shows.

Anything more than a humble pee, though, requires the weary cyclist to undress almost entirely. You get the picture.

The problem was though, that I couldn't. The hours of riding had left me with a pair of virtually useless shoulders, just about the last body part I imagined would become impaired by sitting on a bicycle. It must have been the transferred strain of bracing myself against the handlebars, but for whatever reason, I had lost most of the mobility in my upper arms. I couldn't lift them above chest height. As if weighted down with dumbbells, they simply wouldn't rise to the occasion, which meant that I couldn't reach the shoulder straps of my mankini. I started to panic, picking at the material with my teeth, trying to yank the straps off with increasingly desperate sideways jerks of the head. It was all in vain. I was stuck, in a toilet in Devon, in bib shorts.

Already I knew that this was going to be a test of a friendship. I retrieved my phone, and dialled a number. I listened to it ringing in on the other side of the toilet door.

'Matt?' I ventured, timidly. 'I'm in the bog.'

Cycling is a very bonding experience. Often in unexpected ways.

We pushed on for home.

'I think I would like to get out and ride my bike for a bit now.' Matt Rendell's dry one-liner wasn't particularly witty, but it hit the spot. Already tired to the point of wanting to weep, I cried with laughter. There was only the absurd, quivering impulse to remount, and get to this cursed, arbitrary finishing line.

Our legs were hollow, useless and British. Our humour, it now seemed, was just the same.

So, to our own surprise, we set off again. It seemed such a small distance, given how far we felt we had ridden, but the final thirty miles just wouldn't give up and leave us alone. They took us down to the south coast of Devon, and into Sidmouth. There we hit the sea front, and a howling headwind, which led us neatly to the foot of Peak Hill.

There had been much talk of Peak Hill all day and for most of the weeks and months before that, as our group of intrepid middle-aged fools swapped their worries and advice in a series of increasingly panicked emails. It had assumed an awful status in our minds, it would prove our undoing, would provoke our collapse. Peak Hill. Approach, all, with awe and fear beating in your heart.

The climb began.

As the tarmac reared up, so too did the tension. I could feel an artery above my ears begin to swell with blood and thump quite alarmingly. I was taken back in an instant to an image of my old history teacher, who had an appallingly active 'head-vein', which throbbed more and more visibly the deeper he delved into the background politics of the American Civil War. Perhaps cycling would have helped him too. Lost in such thoughts, my legs turned over and on I climbed.

For all of four minutes. At which point it was all over. I mean, it was unutterably unpleasant, obviously, but it stopped quite abruptly. It is amazing how everything passes, given time.

With Peak Hill conquered, a silver dagger planted squarely through its black heart, we then hurried for home, or rather Teignmouth. And I say 'hurried', but perhaps 'held on for grim death' would be slightly more accurate.

At one point, I heard, above the roar of a main road, one of my co-sufferer's bike computers emitting a beep, which denoted the passing of a mile. Steve turned to me, with a smile, and congratulated me on having just ridden a hundred miles.

'Your first century, Ned. Well done.'

There was no ceremony, no daubing my forehead with the entrails of a magpie, nor tying me to a stake dressed in a bridal gown, but I felt uncommonly proud of my achievement and, for the first time since our shaky start in the Somerset gloom, 'one of them'.

And eventually, it was done. By the time we crossed the line, beaming, covered in crusty layers of perspiration and snot, our party had been whittled back down to just four. Almost nobody was there to watch us, four abreast, nor were any of the casual onlookers even vaguely interested in the immensity of our mission, and the glorious poetry of its execution.

It is often the way with greatness, that it goes unappreciated in its own backyard.

I wish I wasn't a MAMIL. There is almost nothing about the species, seen from the outside and, indeed, observed from the inside, which isn't at best laughable, and at worst, ghastly. And when compared with the more exotic leisure rider from the Continent, whose numbers feature many more women, considerably more pensioners and a large cohort of terrifyingly able children, the narrow demographics of the British MAMIL are depressingly slight.

But this is what I am. No use pretending otherwise.

That evening a clutch of us, including the heroic, battered Joad who'd put his bike in the boot of his Saab, and driven all the way to the finish to be with us, sat in a truly disgusting pub in Torbay and ate the worst fish and chips we have ever been served. Fortunately the beer was just as bad, so at least there were no discrepancies.

It tasted bloody brilliant.

The next day, with £24,000 of bikes back on the top of a car worth less than £500, we drove home again. Our dander was up.

CHAPTER 16

THE LORDS OF LIFE

Irritatingly, on my way out of an NCP car park in Liverpool, I ripped off my roof rack, bruised my bike and bent all four doors to my car.

Seen from any one of a dozen CCTV cameras pointed down at my stationary vehicle, the accident must have seemed comically avoidable. There was no clear and present danger; just a Renault Scenic with a man behind the wheel trying to exit an otherwise deserted car park one Friday morning.

I had wound down the window, pulled the car park ticket from between my teeth, and slotted it into the machine. As the ticket was ingested, and the barrier prepared to rise, a moment of time elapsed that was short enough to have passed by inconsequentially, but long enough, surely, for me to have understood the impossible physics of the manoeuvre I was about to execute.

It was like this. I had a bike on a roof rack. Ahead of me was an exit barrier with restricted headroom, clearly marked with the words 'Restricted' and 'Headroom'. The barrier went up, I slipped the clutch and drove forward. It was, in short, a bit bloody stupid.

The sound was visceral. A crack, followed by a boom, which faded into a teeth-clenching ripping, metallic howl as the clips that held the roof rack to the car heaved free of their homes, bending the metal of all four car doors as they did so. A twang.

Then a tiny slice of silence, as I sat in my car in horror, eyes raised roofwards.

Next came a comedic clatter, like the cartoon dustbin lid that continues to spin long after the collision. But that wasn't quite it. The bike falling over was the last noise, slapping sideways onto what remained of the roof rack. This produced a cacophony of clattering spokes and chains and pedals all resonating their own distress like an orchestra (whose members all hate each other) warming up in order to perform a particularly unpleasant contemporary symphony.

I sat still, my hands on the wheel. I wore Wallace's grin from *The Wrong Trousers,* with the ticket held once again between my teeth.

Then the barrier came down, blocking my exit.

It was a good job that the man I was about to visit had a refined sense of slapstick.

Tony Hewson was the winner of the 1955 Tour of Britain, a veteran of the 1959 Tour de France, and the author of two fine books on his experiences. As one of British cycling's pioneering road racers, he had traversed the Continent in a retired ambulance that doubled up as a makeshift mobile home to three aspiring cyclists. Bits falling off and the regular heart-stopping mechanicals were a fact of life for him and his band of unlikely comrades, They were known as 'Les Nomades du Vélo Anglais', which he used as the subtitle for his excellent memoirs *In Pursuit of Stardom.* Tony's writing is full of encounters with chaste French ladies in the confined space of the ambulance, bumping heads and tripping over tables. His life on the road was like a monochrome episode of *Terry and June,* but set in July, and in France. He had a career like a particularly awkward-to-unfold deckchair.

And yet, when it came to owning up to my moment of mechanical chaos, I still hadn't quite the courage to admit my folly to him. An hour after the incident, and en route to visit him, I was still adjusting myself mentally to the havoc I had inflicted on my self-esteem and my possessions. I was going to be a bit late, too, which I hated.

I dialled his number and waited till he picked up his phone. 'Hi Tony.'

'Is that you, Ned?'

'It is. Listen, Tony, I may be a bit late.'

I was standing in a windy, drizzle-flecked car park outside Birkenhead, while a man in a Halfords boiler suit wrenched at the mangled remains of a roof rack with a crow bar. He stopped and, dropping the tool down temporarily to his side, actually scratched his head in the way that you might imagine someone acting a perplexed mechanic in a second-rate drama would do.

'I've had a problem with my car. They're just having a quick look at it.'

I did not dare confess that the damage I had done had started with a serious injury to a bicycle. I had learned after a few years of exposure to cyclists, that harming bikes, as well as neglecting them by failing to clean them and allowing them to rust, was sacrilegious. The bike, in whatever form, was an object of reverence. Like the idol of any cult, the bicycle inspires great passions, peculiar sensibilities and blind devotion. Turning up to an appointment with an ex-pro sporting a mangled racer I'd casually driven into a height restrictor would be like attending an Alcoholics Anonymous meeting with a can of Diamond White.

Tony, now seventy-nine years old, once told me about a dream he'd had. In fact, it had become a recurring dream, and was starting to cause him some distress.

'This is the nightmare.' He looked intently at me. 'I lose my bike. Right?' There was a pause while he let this horrifying notion sink in. 'I lose my bike' he repeated, with added gravitas.

The dream over recent years had taken various forms and guises, but recently had settled down to this scenario. It takes place on a hill on the outskirts of what he calls a 'large town'. I imagine it to be Sheffield, his birthplace.

'I am standing outside what I think is a fish and chip shop, but it turns out to be a sort of refuge for the homeless. Outside, there's a little congregation of young lads. I've got my bike with me. It's my latest bike, my Trek. It's leaning against me. I haven't got my hand on it. I'm looking in this shop because I want to buy some fish and chips or something. And when I look back, the bike's gone. It's disappeared.'

In his dream panic sets in. He turns to the boys hanging around, and asks them where it is. They look blankly at him. 'Did you even have a bike?' they ask.

'Then I look up this long hill, and there's a guy running away as fast as he can. But he hasn't got a bike with him. *That's the illogic of it.*

'Standing at the side of me is a policeman on a motorbike. So I appeal to him. "Look, I've lost my bike. I think that guy might have it, running up the road." The copper's got no time for me. He says, "What are you doing riding a bike at your age?"

'When I wake up in the morning after this dream, with the sunlight streaming in through the windows, sometimes I have to stop, and I have to think, "I'm here. I'm not there." And the bike is in the garage. I know it's safe.

'The bike, of course is a symbol. It's a symbol for loss of youth and vigour and all the crap that comes with old age. It's loss, basically.'

That was what bikes meant to Tony Hewson.

Pressing the phone to my ear in that desolate Halfords car park, I did not want my host to think that I had so casually mangled his youth and vigour. Lee from Halfords had disposed of the wrecked roof rack by now. And I had taken off the bike's wheels and squeezed it into the boot. No one could see it. It would be my guilty secret.

'I'll be with you at lunchtime, I hope.'

Tony didn't seem too put out that I would be late.

I drove the rest of journey with my mind elsewhere, still slightly buzzing from the morning's absurd messiness. I stopped to refuel near Chester and spent an extraordinary amount of time in a terrifyingly neglected toilet, scrubbing my hands like an oily, male, Lady Macbeth.

But as Cheshire yielded to Shropshire, and I turned to head along the A49 towards the Welsh Marches, a calmness took hold of me again. It's an unreal landscape, long plains and valleys populated by hills that can only be described as hillocky, perfectly naked and green, as if drawn by primary school children. As I passed the little town of Church Stretton, I glanced to my right. A road led up the side of the hill, straight up its flank, making no allowance for the crazy gradient. Again, a child's drawing, almost dream-like in its simplicity of purpose.

'Up!' It said.

And just past Craven Arms, which is a town not a pub, my traumatised car came to rest outside the lovely secluded house of one of British cycling's great thinkers. I rang Tony Hewson's front door bell, with one more downwards glance at my fingernails, checking them for oil.

'Do you think this table is solid?'

I glance the length of the pleasant wooden dining table in the Hewsons' airy, modern extension. Everything about it looks solid. In fact everything about the room, and their house, the Golden Placket, looks solid. Kate and Tony Hewson have retired to a patch of English soil so perfect, with its terraced garden and sweeping views to the west across acres of Shropshire farmland, that it fills the soul with just that: solidity.

It's not only metaphysical. The food is solid, too. Kate has made lunch. Or rather, Kate has 'put on a spread'. Home-made bread, English cheeses, a light salad, and thick slices of salty, succulent ham. It is all just exactly right to perk up this miserable October Friday, already prematurely darkening. The man to my side (Kate has left the house, leaving us alone) hasn't stopped talking, energetically, amusingly, fluently, while I haven't stopped eating, also fluently. He claims he can't do both at the same time. 'I'm a bit like that famous American president who couldn't walk and chew gum. I know that if I start eating, I can't talk and eat.'

And now we are talking about particle physics.

'Do you think it's solid?' He wraps his knuckles on the wood, and looks playfully at me.

'I don't know,' I say, knowing that the correct answer is clearly *no* but not wishing to spike his big revelation. 'Yes, it must be solid.'

'No. No.' He's thrilled I've got it wrong. 'It's full of empty space. In fact you could roll up all the solid matter in the whole of the human race into one little ball.' He cups his hand, and we both stare at seven billion bodies, scrunched

up and sitting in the slightly tremulous hand of the winner
of the 1955 Tour of Britain.

'There's great mystery. The universe; it's spellbinding.'

Tony Hewson looks at me from his seat at the table a
couple of feet away. He is slim, upright, with a full head of
white hair, parted to the side as it was in those black-and-
white photos of his racing days. His eyes search you out. He
looks directly at you, and he talks as he thinks: in the moment.

Although I have heard these arguments about the nature
of matter rehearsed over dinner tables many times before, I
find myself listening to Tony Hewson's retelling of them as if
I were listening for the very first time. He has that effect.
When he stopped racing, he became a teacher. He must have
been a very good one.

The first time I ever saw him was at that gala dinner in 2010,
to celebrate fifty years of British cycling, the one where it all
began. After the food had come and gone, whisked onto plates
and then whisked away, we were all left with coffee and a
small foil-wrapped chocolate leaning against the hot cups and
gently melting onto the saucer. It was time for the speeches.

The evening's proceedings had been hosted by a Sky News
presenter, who I understood was heavily into cycling, having
discovered it, like so many of us, fairly recently. Dermot
Murnaghan made his way to the lectern at the high altar on
the far side of the hall from where I was sitting. The lights
dimmed in the auditorium, and a hush descended. Murnaghan
introduced the event as if he were coming back from a break
and rounding up the news headlines. He was slick, imperi-
ously slick. Before long, he was inviting selected guests to
stand up at their seats in the hall. Tony Hewson was the first
man to be called upon.

A spotlight swooped onto him. A microphone appeared.
Seated behind him, but directly in line with the beam of the

spotlight, I could make out his form only in silhouette: white hair against the darkness of the hall. He started to speak.

In measured Yorkshire tones, he started to tell the hall about the 1959 Tour de France, which he had ridden as an independent (a kind of semi-professional) in an 'International Team' alongside three other Brits: Jock Andrews, Vic Sutton and the great Brian Robinson. His words were crafted to reflect their age, his wit was sharp, his pride never too far from the surface, with a humility that ran deeper still. All these gifts were rolled together as he recounted the horrors and the honour of being in a race against the greats of the day: Anquetil and Gaul, Robic and Bobet. That hall in Manchester fell quiet. He had turned it black and white, in an instant, with his words.

But, the spell, once cast, was easily broken.

Five minutes into his account of the race, it became apparent that Tony Hewson had gone off message. He had clearly not been briefed as to what it was the organisers required. Indeed, he had been hideously misinformed. Worried-looking officials, conscious of the ten other guests still expected to talk and of the fifty names still to be inducted into the Hall of Fame before the evening was out, appeared at his side, pointedly looking at their watches.

Murnaghan was fidgeting. They were all looking for a way to silence the talker.

But Tony sailed happily on. His eyes on the notes, and occasionally looking up towards the blinding light shining down on him, he would have been quite unaware that they were preparing to drop the guillotine.

'And so we came to Stage Four, two hundred and thirty kilometres from Roubaix to Rouen . . .'

'Tony! Hello? Tony!' Murnaghan virtually shouted at him from the lectern.

Tony stopped, and looked up, surprised at the interruption.

'Are you going to tell us about *every* stage of the 1959 Tour, Tony?'

Caught in the glare, he looked around the hall, as if taking it in for the first time. His audience, most of whom now avoided his gaze, started suddenly to unwrap their miniature chocolates or to fiddle with their cufflinks. And without another word, mid-sentence, mid-story, mid-Tour, he sat down.

There was a ripple of sympathetic applause. Murnaghan moved on.

'I suppose this book you are writing is called *The Great Eccentrics of British Cycling*.'

Back in the Golden Placket, Tony has rumbled me, it seems.

'No. Not at all.' The fact that my editor and I were still fighting over differing titles for the book was no longer in the back of my mind. 'But maybe, something a bit like that.' And, briefly, I wondered if I shouldn't suggest exactly that as a book title.

To my profound surprise, Tony Hewson picks up a copy of my previous book. The bookmark suggests it's half-read.

'I always get a bit embarrassed when real riders read that book,' I tell him, truthfully. It wasn't intended for them, but for those on the outside.

He starts to quote some of my writing back at me, which is hugely discomforting, and although it is very well intentioned and he is being very flattering, I find myself eager to move the discussion on. I ask him if he remembers that evening in Manchester and his speech being cut short.

'It was an ambush!' Tony is fond of military phraseology. 'I started getting all this barracking from Dermot Murnaghan. He doesn't really know anything about cycling, I don't think. And I was thinking "I've got to finish the story."'

That, I tell him, is exactly why I am now sitting at his table, listening to him, and all the while stuffing his excellent ham into my mouth. It's time for him to finish it.

Tony Hewson is passionate about the story, not just his but the national story of cycling in Britain, and its associated backwardness. He has a Continental spirit, and wistfully imagines an alternative life spent in France, rather than 'at the coal face' of a Kent Comprehensive, where he taught English for twenty-five years after retiring from racing. He's a self-confessed Francophile, and his attention has always drifted over the choppy waters of the English Channel.

For him, a moment of great significance in the early, backwards, evolution of the sport in this country occurred on 21 July 1894, when a rider called F.T. Bidlake, in the company of two other cyclists, overtook a horse and carriage while nearing the finish line of a handicap race. The horse reared and the three cyclists fell. Though no one was injured, the lady in the carriage complained to the police. The issue gathered traction nationally, and within three years the National Cyclists' Union (a forerunner of British Cycling) had voluntarily banned racing on the road.

That was the moment that British cycling, forced underground, embraced the time-trial culture that still, to this day, defines it. It was to be a path of separate development, involving semi-clandestine, early-morning starts on half-deserted roads, or else hammering in isolation up and down dual carriageways, the only roads wide enough peaceably to accommodate both car and bike. The Testers (as time triallists are sometimes known) held sway, unopposed, for the next half-century.

The British Isles, in cycling terms, had become the Galapagos Islands. Its indigenous species were evolving into something unique and endangered, oblivious to, or obdurately resisting, influences from overseas.

It took a war to change all that, and a visionary called Percy Stallard. Arrogant, intransigent, irascible and stubborn, Stallard saw it as a divine crusade to bring the light of road racing to these gloomy, fog-bound islands. Having spent time overseas before the war, and ridden at a high level in Continental racing, he was determined to establish a similar scene back home. After all, according to Hewson, wherever he went overseas, cycling folk would always ask him the same question: 'You're the only blooming country in Europe that doesn't have road racing. What's wrong with you? What's wrong with you?'

In 1942, as the nation's police service and Home Office were preoccupied with the war effort, he gathered together a band of like-minded comrades. The first meeting of the British League of Racing Cyclists was held at the foot of the Long Mynd Hill in Church Stretton.

'That's just round the corner, isn't it, Tony? I think I drove past it coming here.' It was that road I'd spotted on my way to his house. Inadvertently, or perhaps by Hewson's design, I had been sent on a journey right through the cradle of the sport in Great Britain.

'That's right, you can see it from the main road,' he carries on, warming to his theme.

Shortly after that meeting at Church Stretton, came the pivotal moment: 'Llangollen to Wolverhampton, in 1942. That was the very first road race in this country. By the end of the war, road racing was established. There were those in the Home Office who resisted it still, but it was too late. They couldn't ban it. It wasn't British to go around banning things.'

Civil war within the curiously pugnacious and intolerant cycling community duly broke out and continued largely unchecked for twenty years and beyond when the various factions were brought under one roof, and what we now understand to be British Cycling was established. The time triallists, still fearing a public and police-led backlash to the perceived anarchy of the road racers (or 'the superfluous excrescence', as they were once described in *Cycling* magazine), were forced finally to accommodate their bitter foes, when the Road Traffic Act of 1960 enshrined the legality of the mass start bicycle race. It was time to move on.

Tony Hewson had brought me up to speed, at least on his version of events.

I am left with a feeling, given all the allusions to in-fighting, feuding, resignations, ultimatums and petty agendas, that should I consult any of the riders whose careers span back as far as Tony's does, that I will get as many different versions of the truth as there are men and women to do the telling. But for now, at this table in the very middle of Britain, a few miles from Church Stretton, this one appears cogent, plausible and exciting.

And all the time Percy Stallard's figure looms large in the conversation.

'He was our Churchill. He fought the war for us. He was prickly and arrogant. He fell out with almost everyone. He kept resigning and rejoining. He was the right man to fight the war, but the wrong man for the peace. He was a very, very difficult guy.'

As Tony Hewson tells me this, there is a tightening of the neck muscles, a clouding of the expression, and a slight reddening of his features. Even after all these years, a man who he never met, and who had simply been a talented and dogmatic sports administrator, can inspire passionate loyalty, and command such unexpectedly strong feelings. And then, as Tony finally takes a pause to drink slowly from his tea, which must surely now be cold, I understand why.

'That's where the heart of cycling resides. Road racing matters. It carries the whole culture of cycling with it. And it's shaped me.'

His racing years, dogged by accident and illness, were an education in the most literal sense. To Hewson, raised as a Catholic, and imbued with post-war grammar school virtues,

his years in France, trying to make it as a pro, were a libera-
tion, both physically and spiritually. He took a typewriter with
him, visited the local library in the village that they finally
settled down in, and started to fall in love with the written
word. When he wasn't out on his bike, he was tapping away
on the keys.

'Everything I wrote was sub-Hemingway. I had all my heroes
dying very dramatically in the arms of their lovers. It was
absolute tosh. But at the time, I knew no better. It was the
plots and the stories and the drama of Hemingway.'

I doubt very much that it was tosh. The 1959 Tour ended
for him on Stage 7 when, already the last rider in the General
Classification, he was told to wait for a teammate. He later
abandoned, climbed into the broom wagon and dropped out
of the race. It is a capitulation that is perfectly recounted in
Hewson's memoirs *In Pursuit of Stardom*.

> *Next morning I watch the Tour departing for Bordeaux.*
> *It's like that bad dream where the train you want to*
> *catch leaves you on the platform, paralysed, its tail-lights*
> *disappearing. What do I feel? Stultified, superfluous, like*
> *a lump of dough trimmed off a pie and tossed aside.*

When, in his late twenties, the realities of earning a living
finally forced him to retire from racing and take up a profession, he tried at first to get into acting, completing a three-year
course at Bretton Hall, an institution that would later become
famous for producing some of the most radical influences on
the contemporary British Theatre in the late twentieth century.
From there, he went on to complete an English degree at
Leeds University. Already a free-thinker, an 'outsider' in his
own words, he became radicalised.

'Britain was changing at a hell of a rate. It had been a very
stuffy, sort of black-and-white country to be in. You had all

the rebel movements at the time. I was a bit of a lefty. Some of the people I knew were Trots.'

Tony roars with laughter at this recollection. And by 'roars' with laughter, I mean just that. I almost jump in my chair as he bellows his amusement across the table at me. 'They used to go around at night painting the walls with Fuck The System!'

He attended political debates. Though he had much to say on many issues, he was normally too shy to speak. Indeed, he once found himself sounding off to a bemused stranger in the urinals of a public meeting room.

'I went to have a pee, and said to this bloke that I thought the public schools had been an absolute disaster for the country. He said, "I wish you'd stood up and said that outside." And I looked across at him. It was Jack Straw.'

And then, surprisingly, in reference to the former Labour Home Secretary, he quotes from D.H. Lawrence's *The Snake*. 'I lost my chance with one of the Lords of Life.' Again, the Hewson laugh, but a chuckle this time, not a bellow. It seems a strange way to describe Jack Straw.

Then I put it to him that this, being the mid-sixties, must have also meant long hair.

Indeed so. For a while he taught English at a school in Yorkshire, at which he had made himself unpopular by refusing to make the children pray at assembly ('Oh the hypocrisy!'). So, when he asked the head teacher for a reference so that he could apply for a new job elsewhere, he got what his long hair and generally subversive attitude deserved.

'He gave me a bloody awful reference,' Tony recalls. An exhaustive list of his shortcomings and general flaws ended in the damning conclusion: 'This is a man who wears a beard.'

He got the job, though. And for the next twenty years he taught English and drama in a comprehensive school outside Maidstone in Kent.

'It was a grave mistake to go into teaching. Teachers' pay was piss poor. And it was such a grind. I thought, I came out of the working class, so I should give something back to the working class.'

He shakes his head with real sadness. Then he slips inadvertently into an impression of Donald Sinden. 'Ohhh! It was a great, great mistake!'

He hated it, retired at fifty-five, and then, together with Kate, ran an antique furniture business, which suited him much better. And now here they both are in Shropshire.

Two days after I visited Tony Hewson, and in a curious subversion of everything he stood for in cycling terms, he rode a competitive time trial: the Johnny Helms Memorial 2up TT – the Grand Prix des Gentlemen.

I could not imagine a more fittingly named race for him to enter in his eightieth year. The Grand Prix des Gentlemen bit speaks for itself, fusing as it does the bipolar nature of Tony Hewson's anglo-continentalism.

But the fact that the race was named after Johnny Helms was somehow just as perfect.

Helms, up until his death in 2009, had contributed cartoons for *Cycling* magazine. Like his predecessor Frank Patterson, who produced wonderfully affectionate sketches of cycling through rural England, Helms's work constituted a body of drawings solely dedicated to cycling, a colossal visual library for the devotee. Quite correctly, given the artist's longevity, dedication and sheer volume of output, they inspire great nostalgia and affection in the cycling community.

But they are singularly unfunny, spectacularly so.

They are simple, almost childlike drawings, often featuring dogs, and with jokes which are so straightforward that they are regularly barely more than slightly mundane observations. Look for the layers of meaning all you like, they aren't there.

I am certain that this is a shortcoming in me, and not vice versa. Perhaps the Helms cartoons represent a world to which I, with my Johnny-come-lately ways, will forever be prevented access. But, to me, his cartoons stand as a totem for the unchanging, modest ambition of British cycling over many, many years.

Either way, I enjoyed the fact that Tony Hewson would be turning out to honour his name. Both men had ridden the waves of British cycling, through their lowest ebbs to this unexpected tidal surge of success. Both men had interpreted, wholly differently, their respective worlds and left a record for posterity.

Now that Hewson's health has finally prevented him from fell running or marathons, he has rediscovered the joy of riding a bike. His carbon-fibre Trek, the one that nightly gets stolen from his dream-like grasp outside that ghostly chip shop, lives in the garage alongside the skinny steel frame of the bike on which he rode the Tour de France. And although he 'bitterly regrets' buying the Trek, because it is 'ugly, ugly, ugly', this is no nostalgist. He has a keen eye firmly fixed on the present. All July he was glued to the television coverage of the Tour de France.

'I can still read a cycle race, you know. I can read what's going on, why some guys are working and other guys are not working. That smell. The sound of the wheels whirring in your ears. A clinking-clanking of the chains hitting the chain stays.

'Just wonderful', he concludes.

But what's become of the political firebrand, of the old Trot, of the non-conformist? What does he think of the new wave of cyclist pounding up and down the roads on their absurdly expensive bikes? What does he think about the democratisation of cycling in reverse? Doesn't the class warrior in him object to the rape of a working man's sport? And what about Sky, for heaven's sake?

I have goaded him enough. I sit back, and let him answer.

'Oh, I think that's wonderful. Wonderful. Wonderful. Wonderful.'

He pours some more tea.

'I'm such a hypocrite. I sent my daughter to Chetham's, because of her talent for the piano. We ended up sending our own daughter to a private school! If I'd stuck to my principles, we'd have said no, no, no, no.'

He takes a long, thoughtful sip. 'But we change, you know. As life goes on, it teaches us to change.'

For Hewson, the adventure in British cycling has spanned his lifetime. What began in 1942, when he was just nine years old, has not yet reached its endgame.

'What has happened is the best thing that could ever have happened to cycling in this country. It's what we used to dream of in the 1950s. Percy Stallard. It was his dream that one day there'd be a winner of the Tour de France from these shores. We've had to wait seventy years for that.'

Last September, when the 2012 Tour of Britain started a stage in Welshpool just a few miles up the road, Tony Hewson was asked along as a guest of honour. He had taken the leader's jersey in the Welsh stage of the Tour of Britain in 1955. And here he now was, invited back to the race and after a fifty-seven-year absence, to greet the riders as they signed on.

He was greatly looking forward to meeting Bradley Wiggins.

'I was hoping against hope that I'd bump into him. But the message came through that he wasn't going to ride.' Wiggins had succumbed to a stomach bug, it seemed, and abandoned overnight. Tony Hewson, who had driven down to the start in the hope of shaking him by the hand, and meeting the man who finished what he, among others, had begun, was left high and dry.

'So again, I lost my chance with one of the Lords Of Life.' And this time there is no chuckle.

It was only now, leaving the Golden Placket after a promise to return and a heartfelt handshake, that I realise how my understanding of what it is to be a British cyclist has been framed and formed by those who have, one way or another, done it differently. Perhaps I had skirted the real issue, shied away from the truth that, for many, the club run, the time trial, the lay-by and annual dinner among friends was enough, more than enough. For many, it began and ended here.

But not for everyone.

I had, instinctively, been drawn to men like Tony Hewson, like Maurice Burton, like Graham Webb, like Mick Bennett, men who had spoken to me about yearning for elsewhere, for something else. Ian Meek, too. And David Millar. The act of escape, of getting away, implied a destination elsewhere, a trip into the other. The bikes ridden by these men, and by all of us who share the same desires, have a will of their own. They could steer themselves.

Maybe Rapha were onto something after all.

I drove back down to London, listening all the way to the whistling of the wind blowing across the tiny gaps that my roof rack had ripped open. My bike sat dismantled and wounded in the boot. I was keen to get it mended, and get it out on the road. After all, that's what a bike is for.

FORETHOUGHT

Belgium. The blank canvas, the barren landscape. Belgium, just over the water. Belgium, the insurmountable obstacle, flattened to the sky, threatened by the sea.

I travelled there for work. The start of the 2012 Tour de France was in Liège. It was to be the tenth Tour that I would cover for ITV, if you include the first few during which I floundered about like a salmon in a bear pit.

A decade then, all in all, spent moving through the gears of the great race; from Armstrong's dope-fuelled jihad, through the more-or-less chaotic aftershock of those tainted years and into a vaguely brighter, probably cleaner, certainly more human future.

But some immutable things, through these turbulent years had remained constant: our difference and our deference; our otherness. We, charged with the duty of bringing the race back home to Britain, were never under any illusion as to our minor place in the grand scheme of things. Despite Mark Cavendish's serial heroics in his very particular skill, despite Bradley Wiggins's exceptional ride in 2009, when he somehow finished fourth (third if you discount Lance Armstrong), we never really troubled the scorers. We lived off scraps, scavenging at the margins of a race that belonged to someone else, somewhere else.

Even when Team Sky appeared to trumpet their preposterous ambitions across the water at a laughingly sceptical Continent, things fell predictably, Britishly, flat. Wiggins flopped in 2010 and crashed in 2011. And that had been that.

Plus ça change, the more things change, the more they stay the same.

Until, that is, the summer of 2012 came along, when Britain grabbed France by the throat, turned it upside down and emptied its pockets.

Liège. The eve of the Tour.

The doors open, and into the glare walk Mark Cavendish, Bradley Wiggins, Chris Froome and the six other members of Team Sky. The sight that greets them exceeds their expectations. All of them are experienced media campaigners, all of them have been the subject of press conferences, but the scale of interest here, the number of camera crews, reporters and photographers, is unlike anything they've seen before. Suddenly, and in the case of Bradley Wiggins specifically, they realise the reality of the burden they will have to bear round France for the next three weeks. They are the favourites to win the Tour de France. Wiggins is the favourite. This is the scrutiny their effort will invite, day after day.

'Jesus Christ.' Wiggins's appears to be temporarily wrong-footed, but is still, refreshingly, unable to refrain from swearing in public. That much, too, is expected of him.

Nothing much emerges from the press conference. There is a tiredness in the responses to simplistic questions that is entirely understandable. How else can you answer, 'Do you feel confident that you can win the Tour de France?' other than with the obvious, cautionary, 'I feel confident in my own ability, but we'll have to see how the race unfolds.'

Wiggins understands he is being bland, but can do nothing about it. We are in the neutralised zone, the roll-out to the race itself. There is no evidence one way or another yet. Only hope and nerves.

Outside, once the ludicrous formalities of the pre-race press conference are finally put to one side, there is a brief semi-regal walkabout from Bradley Wiggins. He slouches across the car park, saving energy with every lazy stride, towards where a cluster of important people has gathered by the team bus.

On his way over there, he is stopped by a member of the public, with whom he poses for a picture. That done, he politely declines to shake the outstretched hand, for fear of picking up last-minute infections. By the time he reaches the cluster of VIPs, he has mysteriously abandoned such principles of hygiene, and warmly shakes the hands of Fausto Pinarello, who owns the eponymous bike brand. So it seems that not all bacteria are equal.

As we drive away from their hotel, and back to ours over the Dutch border in Maastricht, I ask Chris Boardman what he makes of Wiggins's frame of mind, which is not always easy to read, but which can have a huge impact on his performance.

'I'd have said he's just very happy,' is Chris's assessment of the man he mentored through the early years of his career. 'Why wouldn't he be? He's ridden the year to perfection, and he knows he can win the Tour de France. That's not a bad place to be.'

'I guess so.' I try to get inside that observation, to imagine how that must feel. I give up, and watch the windscreen wipers flicking the Belgian rain from in front of us. I note that this was where Wiggins was born.

Belgium. Not Britain.

Somewhere else.

ACKNOWLEDGEMENTS

Many people gave up a great deal of time to help me tell this story, not least the ladies and gentlemen who feature heavily within. So thank you Chris Boardman, Mick Bennett, Garry Beckett, Avril Millar, Ian and Sally Anne Meek, Tony Hewson, Ron Keeble, Graham Webb, John Herety, Maurice Burton, David Millar, Simon Mottram, Gary Kemp, Brian Smith, Germain Burton, Ken Livingstone, Nadav Kander, Bob Elms, Tommy Godwin, Joe Clovis and Jim Robertson. Also to Dan Gordon, Brian Robinson, Phil Griffiths, Barry Hoban, Barbara Ford, Kay Jones, Matt Stephens and Kristian House for providing me with considerable help in my research.

Thanks to the welcoming people at British Cycling who sent me an invitation to their gala dinner back in 2010 and set me off on this path.

To all my fellow Real Pelotoneers, in whose company I completed the 115 miles of the Tour Ride, and whose better knowledge and companionship kept me going, thank you. In particular, thanks to my good friends Joad Raymond, Luke McLaughlin, John Beech, Matt Rendell, Adam Tranter, Chris Alfred, Jim Clayton and 'Skipper' Steve Trice. Simon Taylor, who attacked me on my local hill, sneaks in here, too, along with his hand-painted steel frame Graham Weigh bike. I also owe a debt to Ian Cleverly of the beautiful *Rouleur* magazine, to Gavin Brown from *Metro* and to Lionel Birnie from the *Cycling Anthology* for keeping my writing arm in practice. To those riders, and ex-riders, alongside whom I have learned about the domestic cycling scene, I am very grateful. They have had great patience. So, thanks Maggie Backstedt, Paul Manning, Yanto Barker, Ben Swift, Andy Tennant, Ed Clancy, Lizzie Armitstead, Dean and Russell Downing, Julian Wynne,

Alex Dowser, Dan Lloyd, Roger Hammond, Tony Gibb, James McCallum, Tom Southam, Rob Hayles and Graham Jones. Hats off to those who make sure that the Tour of Britain and the Tour Series get on the telly, in particular to Mark Sharman and Niall Sloane at ITV, as well as Sharon Fuller, Rohan Browning, Glenn Street and Mat Pennell (amongst many others) at Century TV. The staff at the Caird Library in Greenwich let me use their space, despite the fact that I was blatantly not interested in maritime history. Simon Bromley was kind enough to let me use the picture he took of me struggling up the Bec Hill Climb.

I should acknowledge Mark Cavendish and Bradley Wiggins, who provided me, and you, and all of us with the absurdly improbable sight of a British Yellow Jersey leading out a British world champion on the Champs-Elysées. They've played a not insignificant part in all this. As has everyone at Yellow Jersey Press, in particular Justine Taylor, Kris Potter, Fiona Murphy, Frances Jessop, Myra Jones and the excellent editor Matt Phillips, who has now become a dad to young Maggie, and, although he does not yet know it, is hurtling towards his own mid-life crisis. Thanks too to Mark Stanton if he can bring himself to read past the title to get this far.

Thanks to my magnificent and largely indifferent children, Suzi and Edie. And thanks to Kath, who has shown only limited and occasional interest in this book. Which is no bad thing, because she probably won't like what I've written about her. Those three people are, once again, my full stop.

LIST OF ILLUSTRATIONS